Photographs by Ole Brask

jazz
people

Text by Dan Morgenstern

Foreword by Dizzy Gillespie

Introduction by James Jones

DA CAPO PRESS • NEW YORK

To all musicians

Library of Congress Cataloging in Publication Data

Brask, Ole.
  Jazz people / photographs by Ole Brask; text by Dan Morgenstern; foreword by Dizzy Gillespie; introduction by James Jones.—1st Da Capo Press
ed.
    p.   c.
  Originally published: New York: H. Abrams, 1976.
  ISBN 0-306-80527-8
  1. Jazz musicians—Portraits. I. Morgenstern, Dan. II. Title.
ML87.B65 1993   93-24751
781.65′65′092′2—dc20   CIP
                                                        MN

First Da Capo Press edition 1993

This Da Capo Press paperback edition of *Jazz People* is an unabriged
republication of the edition first published in 1976. It is reprinted
by arrangement with Harry N. Abrams, Inc., and with the assistance of
Ole Brask and Ana Borgersen Biddle.

Published by Da Capo Press, Inc.
A Subsidiary of Plenum Publishing Corporation
233 Spring Street, New York, N.Y. 10013

Contents

Part I: The Music

Part II: The People

Foreword by Dizzy Gillespie

The first thing we must keep in mind about a musician is that the music he plays is a reflection of his true self. His music might not be what you, the listener, think he is, but truly, he can no more escape himself through his playing than we can escape the contingent world in which we are placed, except through death. You are what you are; that is reality, you can't escape it. And the reality of the musician—especially the jazz musician—is that the music is a continuance of himself.

A good example is Miles Davis. Miles talks rough—you hear him use all kinds of rough words. But when you hear the pathos in his music, that's a different story. His music reflects his true character. I once had a long conversation with his daughter, Cheryl. We talked about him—oh, did we talk about him! Seriously, I made a statement during that conversation. I said: "Miles is shy. He is super shy." A lot of people don't believe that, but I have known him for a long, long time. I'll give you an example of his shyness.

One night, we were both playing at the Village

Gate, and Sugar Ray Robinson and Archie Moore came in. Now, Miles is a big fight fan, so one would think that introducing the fighters from the stage would have been his moment. (I don't recall if Robinson was still champion at the time, but Sugar Ray is always the champ.) Anyhow, Miles, whose band was on the stand, came over to me and said, "Hey, Sugar Ray and Archie Moore are here." I said, "So?" and he said, "Well, won't you introduce them when you go on?" I said, "Hell, you're on now. You introduce them. You've got it!" But he didn't introduce them. He left it to me. That shows what I mean.

It also ties in with a fact about this book: like his music, a fine photograph of a musician reflects his soul. I'm very interested in photography and in how the camera can capture personality, and I especially like black-and-white photography. You can see depth in that. So I'm very excited about this book, because the photographs I have seen, especially those of Ben Webster and Jo Jones, really show their subjects' true selves.

At this writing, I'm getting ready to make a series of video cassettes. They will be lessons that clarify and explain our music—the music I had a part in creating in the forties. I hope that they will help to clear up a lot of misconceptions about the roles of Charlie Parker, Thelonious Monk, Kenny Clarke, and myself. They say now that Parker was a genius, but while he was alive, he was treated like a misfit by the society. As for some of the books about him, especially the so-called biography, they are fairy tales. Dan Morgenstern, I'm happy to say, doesn't write fairy tales.

Our music is a language, a great communicator. I could go to China with some music and take Chinese musicians who didn't understand one word of English and first let them play the music as they heard it, and then go over different spots with them and explain, "Now this passage goes baa-ih-dada-badiliya-bap-ah-dow," and let them try to mouth it first, and they wouldn't feel funny doing it. It would be much more difficult for a Chinese actor to comprehend the expressions a foreign director might want from him, but in music, communication is no problem at all. All you need is to be able to hear and mouth a phrase, and then translate it to your instrument. Our music is a language that transcends languages; a truly universal language.

The future of jazz? Jazz is alive and well and living in New York City. I'm not worried about the music going forward! We will always have our rebels who learn the rules and then break them. It has been suggested that the newer musicians don't have all the things to work with that we had, but whatever they have they are making do with, and they are making it. It's like religion: God sends to mankind what is best suited for the particular age. He knows what is best, and that is what he sends. It might not be what you want at the time, but in the long run, it is the best. And so it is for the musician. It was necessary, in our time, to have a lot of jam sessions, a lot of big bands, and a lot of interplay between musicians, but in this age, something else seems to be needed. The music continues to develop, so the creativity must not be hurting. The musicians will find what is best for them.

For example, I was playing in some midwestern town, and an ex-trumpet player who used to be on the road with bands and is an old fan of mine from the early days told me, after he had been in to see me two or three nights in a row, that he hadn't thought it was possible to expand on what Charlie Parker and I had once done. "But you've expanded on it, and it's beautiful," he went on. "I've been trying to get my son, who is sixteen and plays trumpet too, to come and hear you, but he just says, 'Aw, I'll wait until Freddie Hubbard gets here!'" I understand that boy. Each generation has its heroes, though there are some young people who want to hear where Freddie Hubbard came from and seem to enjoy hearing it, too.

It has been said that there are not as many original voices in jazz today as in the past. But we had a lot of Charlie Parkers and Dizzy Gillespies, just as we have a lot of John Coltranes now. Give them time! Look how long it took Coltrane to break away from the influence of Charlie Parker. And it takes each generation longer to get weaned, to cut the umbilical cord, because the message gets stronger all the time, and the musicians become more sophisticated. That's why, when someone comes up to me, as it often happens, and says, "Hey, man, I just want to hear some bebop; just give me what you and Yard used to play, not that other shit," I say, "Look, man, just because you lived in that generation, don't think you're the only one who knows about music." That sort of thing has been going on forever. During the transition from Louis Armstrong to Roy Eldridge, they didn't want to hear what Roy was playing. Then Roy's generation didn't want to hear what I was doing, and my generation didn't want to hear Miles. Yet it is all the same. It is the same music all the time. The elucidation is different—how you talk it, how you do it—but it is all one music.

It is one, like religion is one. If the word of God through Abraham is the same word of God through Moses and through Jesus and through Buddha and through Mohammed and through Bab and the Baha'u'llah, if the same holy spirit is in all of them, then it is one word.

I think you will enjoy this book about the one music.

Introduction
by
James Jones

I was eight or nine in the late twenties when I was first introduced to jazz. My brother was twelve years older, had been thrown out of at least two universities, possessed and played a C melody sax and a tenor sax, and at the time wanted more than anything in the world to be a professional jazzman who earned his living with his horn. He and some other like-minded souls in my small town in Illinois had formed a small band. This band played a lot of dances at local places, some of them as far as fifty or sixty miles away. They hoped to go on (though they never did) to bigger and better-paying dates even farther away, and Tuesday night was always band practice night at our house.

Being only eight or nine, I was classed as a kid and was banned from the practice room. I was relegated to the front porch, if I wanted to listen, to keep me out of the way and from under foot. The band practiced in our number one living room—what would have been called a parlor in an earlier day. This was already pretty big stuff, since my mother almost never let anyone into the number one living room. Most of our living was done in the number two living room, directly behind the number one living room. But since the big sliding doors between the two living rooms were closed when the band practiced, it was either the front porch for me, or the hall stairway, both hidden places where my brother could not see me and scream at me to make myself scarce. He was very serious, my brother. In the winter I sat on the hall stairs, in the summer on the front porch.

But mostly I remember the summers. I suppose because my brother was going to James Millikin then, I think, or one of those schools. In any case, I have very vivid memories of warm midwestern summer nights in the porch swing, moving it on its long chains in rhythm to their improvised hot choruses of *Avalon, San, Way Down Yonder in New Orleans,* or *Sleepy Time Gal.* The streetlamp over the brick street out in front would make concentric wheeling haloes of light in through the limbs and leaves of the maple trees in the front yard, as the swing moved. And I would sit and watch them over the brick balustrade as I listened.

The songs did not mean much to me then, at age eight and nine, but they sneaked into me just the same as I listened and became fused with my emotions about my childhood and those days. Years later, when I became a collector, I discovered on the Brunswick label copies of old solos by Trumbauer and Jimmy Dorsey which, note for note, my brother had played on those summer nights of my preadolescence. Apparently he had worked over the old 78s in his room alone, sweating over them until he had memorized them note by note, working out the fingering, even to the exact phraseology, until he could play them all exactly. That was an awful lot of work on his part. And it was weird to hear them twenty years later in the forties—after a Depression, a World War, and years of traveling around the country and the planet—hear them being played by Trumbauer and Jimmy Dorsey, just exactly as my brother had once played them.

Of course, I had not known at the age of nine that we were living through a sociological phenomenon. A cultural revolution that would someday be the subject for literally thousands of researchers, writers, music buffs, and students; a socio-cultural swing which they would call the Jazz Age. Neither did my brother. Had we known, I guess we would have kept better notes and observed more closely. But then I guess at the time not much of anybody else knew that. All that, the theorizing, comes a generation or so after the events. The people who are making the events are usually too busy living them to theorize them. In any case, that my brother, the scion of one of the oldest, best-off families of our town (this was before 1929), would be contemplating such an immoral profession as the tenor sax certainly denotes some kind of a sociological upheaval.

After the war, and already dedicated to writing, I spent a year in New York going to NYU on the GI Bill and met my first jazzmen. Somehow, by some process of inevitability, I found my way to Jimmy Ryan's. Some group or other, often Sidney Bechet's, was playing there every night; and on Sunday afternoons there were the famous Sunday jam sessions. I was poor enough so that I soon discovered, on my GI Bill money, that only the Sunday sessions were within my reach. I couldn't afford the evenings, where the waiters pushed drinks on you without mercy and priced them out of sight. On Sundays you could buy one beer and nurse it through the whole afternoon.

The jazzmen that I met were fabulous. Men like Baby Dodds, Pops Foster, Wild Bill Davison, Zutty Singleton, Eddie Condon, Bechet. Almost without exception they were men who had lived most of their lives on the wrong side of the tracks as I had after 1929, essentially antisocial beings who had had to learn to live with the American Puritan hypocrisy and snobbism as I was having to, sustained only by their talent and their art and artistry to rise up out of this welter of crap as I hoped I would be able to. They could spot a phony in less time than it took him to smile his smile. A pungent, flagrant sense of humor helped such men enormously, I was learning. They were enormously helpful people to be around on occasion, there at Ryan's.

Years later, when I was famous, I used to sit with Jimmy and deep in our cups we would discuss these "good old days." Ryan's was fading by this time, and Jimmy liked to talk about his "golden age." He remembered distinctly that he had picked me out of the welter of younger customers, had bought me many free drinks, had recognized that I had a big talent, and had prophesied my future fame and success. All of this was totally untrue. Already Jimmy was building the legend. But it seemed pointless to tell him that. Either he would refuse to believe me at all, or he *would* believe me, and then he would be hurt. So I simply agreed.

Sidney Bechet was one of the most potent, powerful people I have ever met. He did not look as though anything could bother him. Slow-moving, slow-spoken, soft-voiced, he was already a big man, with a big stomach. But that air about him made him seem even bigger. When he came out of Ryan's and walked across the street to Reilly's Tavern, it was as if some sort of primeval force had moved from the one bar to the other. He seemed to carry an atmosphere of peace and great tranquility around with him wherever he went. It was as if he had an actual physical aura of calm, which extended out around his body for six or seven feet, and if you moved inside it you were affected by it and became calm, too. For a young neurotic as I was then, who was physically brave but unsatisfied by it, who didn't know who he was, or where he was, or where he was going, or how he was going to get there, he was my ideal of what a man ought to be.

For some reason Bechet took a great liking to me and used to have me sit by him at his table at Reilly's, across the street. Rye was thirty-five cents a shot, and all the jazzmen went over there between sets for their drinks, instead of buying the expensive ones at Ryan's. At Reilly's, as at Ryan's, everybody deferred to Bechet. You just automatically did it, something about him made you. He talked a lot to me but he didn't say much, mostly clichés about what a man ought to do with his talent and with his life. But it wasn't what he said. It was the way he said it. A long time later I learned that everything he said was exactly true, and that whether it was a cliché or not did not make any difference, it was still true. But I suppose it takes everybody worth while a long time to learn that.

Years later when I was well known, in France where Bechet was a prince in his chosen domain and had married a white French woman, I ran into him a couple of times in Paris. He looked smaller to me then, but he still had that aura around him. He remembered me from Ryan's. He was glad I had succeeded, but told me that I must never let up because of that. We talked quite a long time both times. But our lives had taken different paths by then, he was no longer playing as much, I was not as involved in jazz, and we didn't run into each other again. We both seemed to know there was no need to look the other up. Not long after that I heard that he had died.

It was after my year in New York when I had dropped out of NYU and returned to the Midwest that I first discovered the music of Django Reinhardt, the French gypsy jazz guitarist. I was a minor collector by then (I was never more than minor), and a collector friend in Terre Haute who ran his own music store played for me a prewar 78 of the "Hot Club de France" with Django playing lead guitar and taking two solo choruses. It was one of his recordings of *St. Louis Blues,* the best one, I would learn later on, and I fell madly in love with it at once. He was asking fifteen dollars for it. That was an awful lot for me, but I could no more have rejected buying it than I could have spread my arms and flown around the room. We hunted through his entire shop and were able to find only one other, another "Hot Club de France" record, with Django playing only on one side. He let me have that one for ten fifty. One of Django's three sides was his *Honeysuckle Rose.* I took the three sides home as carefully as a farmer's wife with her day's egg crop or a miser with gold, to gloat over them and play them over and over.

These three sides of Django's were to have an enormous effect on my life and on my work. I was in the middle of writing *From Here to Eternity* at the time, feeling my way along, learning as I went. I had a theory about artistic expression, garnered partly from Hemingway, which, clumsily, I was trying to work out on my own and which, more or less, was that any perfectly expressed sentence or phrase conveys more on other levels and in other dimensions than it actually conveys on its own. So that it says more than anyone can prove that it *actually* says. It seemed to me that Django was already doing this in his music, with his masterful subtleties of phrasing and his great swinging beat.

So enamored of him and his music was I that in the novel I went to great length to write an entire long passage for the sole purpose of introducing a description of his music through the person of one of the guitar players, a sequence climaxing in a scene in which Prewitt and the other troopers write *The Re-enlistment Blues.* It was the only place in the book where I myself appeared as a character, under the name I often used for myself then of Slade, the naive Air Corps boy who goads them into writing it. I had been putting together ideas about the writing of this passage for a long time, but I almost certainly would never have done it, or written the lyric of the blues itself, without the discovery of Django and his music.

It was to have far-reaching repercussions. When

Introduction

the book became famous, I received a letter from a French jazz drummer named Dave Pochonet, also a Django fan, who offered to tape for me his full collection of Django sides. It was a magnificent gift, and I accepted with alacrity. When the big tapes finally arrived, I found they were nearly the entire collection of Django's recorded work, including rare radio broadcasts he had made.

It was these tapes, plus the little bit I had picked up about the mysterious gypsy and his bizarre unregulated life, that decided me even back then that I wanted to go to France and write a novel based on him and on jazz.

When my wife and I arrived in Paris seven years later, in 1958, it was a direct result of this. And a direct result of those original three sides I had stumbled on in Terre Haute, Indiana, in the late forties, in the middle of *Eternity*.

In Paris, where we had never meant to stay the whole sixteen years that we did stay, we spent a great many of our nights sitting up with American jazzmen in American jazz joints. There were literally almost fifty of these joints in Paris proper, and American jazzmen were continually passing through Paris on tour, playing concerts, working transatlantic Paris dates, and showing up to meet and jam with old buddies in the joints. In those earlier days Europe, led by Paris, had taken American jazz and American jazzmen to its heart. In typical French style, learned pundits were writing massive treatises about American jazz and its meaning. For the jazzman, especially if he was black, it was a great treat to be accepted as an individual and as a talent in a town where American-style racism had never existed. And everybody was hitting the Paris road by then.

All this time, I was researching (or thought I was) the book on Django. And I talked to everybody. I looked up Grappelli of the "Hot Club" (pronounced "Ott Cloob" in French); Joseph Reinhardt, his brother and "Le Ott Cloob's" second guitarist; Django's widow; and God knows how many American jazzmen who had known him or played with him. Nobody really seemed to know him. The gypsies, his brother, and his widow, didn't seem to know him either, or else just weren't talking. The gypsies seemed more concerned with getting money from me, or whoever was interested in Django, on a day to day, meeting by meeting basis.

I talked with Ellington about him, for whom he had once done, at the Duke's own personal invita-tion, an American tour. At the Carnegie Hall concert part of it, Django never showed up. He was found later wandering along Sixth Avenue looking with fascination in the windows of secondhand stores. The Duke only shrugged and smiled his sad, gentle smile at me; he had hoped to make the gypsy known, popular, and rich in America as, Duke felt, Django deserved.

Nobody seemed to know him—know who he was, or where he was at. They only knew that he played that incredible, beautiful music. In the end I was forced to abandon the book. But meantime we had become immersed in the Paris jazz scene.

One of the people we got to know well in his last days there was Lester Young. One of the places we often stayed the latest was Le Blue Note, off the rue de Berri behind the Champs Elysées. Lester was playing there regularly then. The owner-manager of Le Blue Note was a big American named Ben Benjamin, who had married a French wife, and who—provided he could get along with them day to day—always had the most celebrated jazzmen working for him. He had the best because he always offered to pay the best. But then he would fight with his jazzmen over the price of the drinks they had. Young fought with him nightly over the prices of the drinks he ordered.

"The Pres" still wore his celebrated porkpie hats, and when he dressed, slowly and carefully, to go out into the streets after his last set, it was always something of a major performance. Framed by the big fur collar of the long coat he loved to wear, his long gaunt face with the deep, purple, sick-looking hollows under the eyes would look out at you with a sort of princely helplessness.

I found his music as great as ever, though there were some who said it was not. But they never said it in his presence. He was a scrappy individual, who liked to carry a straight razor in his pocket which he loved to pull out and display, wide open. When he had his girlfriend Lady Razor with him, he said, nobody messed with him. I never heard of him using the razor. And scrappy or not, he had a marvelous sense of humor, and he loved females. He loved to sit at the bar between sets, trading quips with my good-looking wife. More than half the time she had him roaring with laughter.

The night before he returned to America the Blue Note gave him a farewell party. He had been saying for some time that he was homesick and anxious to get home, and that night he was happy.

When he put on the porkpie hat and long coat, he shook hands all around, even with Ben Benjamin. That was in March, 1959. A week later we got the news that he had dropped dead, at the foot of the gangplank in America.

Billie Holiday was another one we saw on her last trip to Europe. During her stay in Paris she hung out at the Blue Note because her old pal Lester was there. Once in a while she would sing. She had been giving some concerts in Paris at theaters, but we had been warned off of going to them because she wasn't up to her best, so we saw her only at the Blue Note. She wasn't holding her liquor well by this time, and only a little of it was enough to put her over the line. The last time I saw her, she came into the joint after a concert and asked for a drink.

Ben Benjamin had given his bartenders strict orders not to serve her any booze, and while all of us knew this, nobody had the guts to tell her, including "The Pres." Anyway, after asking politely two or three times, the Lady Day leaned her body languidly over the bar on an elbow and bawled at the top of her considerable lungs, "Hey, asshole! Gimme a drink!" She got the drink. And came and sat with us, fuming. She was soon to follow her pal Lester into death.

Looking back on it all now, it seems that the end of my deep involvement with jazz happened about this time. The deaths of Lester and the Lady Day seemed to presage the end of an era. At about the same time, I think, a basic change was coming over the jazz world.

Gillespie had come along with bebop. And at the other end of the string, Elvis had come up with his music that would be a forerunner for the long wave of rock 'n' roll—essentially a commingling of the jazz beat with country western. What was left in the middle was being taken over by the modernists, like Miles Davis and Monk.

That is not to say that we dropped out of it. We didn't. Nor should this be taken as any sort of value judgment. I still go out and listen to some of the greats of today. Occasionally.

But it isn't the same, for me, and I'd be lying if I said it was. The jazz people that I knew and loved, and the time they made that I also loved, are gone. Some are dead, some have faded off into an oblivion of illness or retirement, some are still playing in small bistros of another time. The attrition rate was high in the life-style that they lived.

Fortunately, a lot of those jazz people and a lot of stories about their times are captured and held down for us in this book. Jazzmen don't talk a lot about music to nonprofessionals. Nor do they like to talk much about themselves to the uninitiated. When they do, it is often because a few men like Dan Morgenstern are listening, quietly, encouraging them to articulate in words what they think in music, urging them to come out with what they feel about life and living it.

Ole Brask has been a lover of jazz since his early teens in Paris. His pictures of jazzmen began almost that early. With the faithfulness of love and appreciation, this great photographer and his camera have worked together with the same uncommon union of a musician and his instrument to catch for us the quality of the top jazzmen, both old-time and modern, whom he has known.

In *Jazz People*, Brask and Morgenstern, working independently and together—in the tradition of jazzmen—have captured much of the feeling and history of jazz that can be put between covers.

Part I:
The Music

Where Jazz Came From

Where It's Been, Where It Is

Where It's Going

We don't know where or when it started—the fusion of African and European elements that made possible the uniquely American music called jazz. We don't even know where that strange four-letter word itself (a word some jazz practitioners resent) really came from—its etymology is as obscure as the origins of the music. We do know that the music with the odd name, bred in the most humble circumstances, has become the first truly global art alongside the other form intrinsic to the twentieth century, the motion picture.

The message of jazz, direct and immediate, speaks straight to the heart, across cultural, linguistic, and political barriers. Louis Armstrong, the first and so far only rightful king of jazz, pinpointed the universality of this music in his inimitable way: "What we play is life and the natural thing. . . . Playing for the highest people to the lowest; that's the way it's supposed to be. I don't ever have to wonder about my public. Whether they're young or old, it's the same appreciation. They come in Germany with them lorgnettes, looking at you and everything, and by the time they get on the music, they done dropped them lorgnettes, and they're swinging, man!"

The fact that Louis Armstrong was born there—on July 4, 1900—is as good a reason as any for granting New Orleans the honorable title of birthplace of jazz, but there are others. Jazz evolved whenever African and European musical practices impinged upon each other, which is to say wherever black and white Americans came into contact. But there can be no question that some places offered a more favorable climate and fertile soil for the growth of the tender new plant than others.

New Orleans was a great port, a city with an international atmosphere relatively free from the racial bigotry elsewhere in the Deep South. French, Spanish, Caribbean, Celtic, Anglo-Saxon, and Germanic cultural currents merged with the African traditions retained by both the recently emancipated blacks and the Creoles ("free people of color") in the rich musical life of the city, with its French opera, German brass bands, Irish tenors, etc.

Even physically, the city favored music. Danny Barker, the New Orleans guitarist and historian, has put in perspective the seeming myth that Buddy Bolden (1868-1931), the semilegendary cornetist who has become the archetype of the jazz musician, could be heard for miles and miles around when he played his horn.

"The city has a different kind of acoustics," he explained. "There is water all around, and also water all under the city, and adding to this dampness, there was the heat and humidity of the swamps, of the bayous all around. And because of all this, because sound travels better across water, when you blew your horn in New Orleans—especially on a clear night—the sound carried." Bolden would be playing outdoors on such nights, perhaps at a dance on the shores of Lake Pontchartrain, following a picnic and excursion by one of the social clubs or fraternal organizations that proliferated in the city, especially among blacks.

These included such established organizations as the Masons, Odd Fellows, and Knights of Pythias, as well as such unique New Orleans "social aid and pleasure clubs" as the Zulus, the Tammanys, the Money Wasters, the Autocrats, the Turtles, the Original Swells, the Jolly Boys, and the Diamond Swells. All of them would enter floats in the Mardi Gras parade, trying to outdo each other, and all of them would hire bands for important social functions.

Not least among these were the burials of departed lodge brothers or club members. On these occasions, one of the city's best brass bands, such as the Eureka, the Onward, or the Tuxedo Brass Band, would accompany the coffin from the church to the cemetery and then march back to town. Bunk Johnson has described the music:

On the way to the cemetery . . . we would always use slow, slow numbers such as *Nearer My God to Thee, Flee as a Bird to the Mountains*. . . . We would use most any 4/4, played very slow; they walked very slow behind the body. . . . [After the burial] the band would come on to the front, out of the graveyard. Then the lodge would come out . . . and then we'd march away from the cemetery by the snare drum only, until we got about a block or two [away]. Then we'd go right on into ragtime—what the people call today swing—ragtime. We would play *Didn't He Ramble*, or we'd take all those spiritual hymns and turn them into ragtime—2/4 movements, you know, step lively everybody.

The practice of using marching bands to accompany funeral processions was initially imported from the Mediterranean region—Spain, southern France, Sicily, and Portugal. New Orleans blacks, however, uniquely adapted this custom by adding the joyful music on their way back to town from the cemetery. This unique adaptation provides us with one of the obvious sources of jazz. When the black bands marched, they put a swinging rhythm into the marches and quick steps borrowed from the traditional brass-band repertoire, or the hymns borrowed from church. This 2/4 rhythm became the rhythm of early jazz. In smaller combinations, the players also furnished music for dancing on weekend nights and played on wagons advertising the dances. When the paths of two such wagons crossed, the rival bands would lock horns and play at each other, so the people could judge which was better. In that custom, the proudly competitive tradition of the jam session was born.

Much too much has been made of the relationship between jazz and legalized prostitution in New Orleans. The fact is that the houses, which ranged from bastions of fin-de-siècle elegance to rude hovels, did not employ jazz bands. There would be

The Superior Band of New Orleans, c. 1910. Seated left to right: Walter Brundy, Peter Bocage, R. Payne. Standing: Buddy Johnson, Bunk Johnson, Louis ("Big Eye") Nelson, Billy Marrero

a pianist, perhaps a singer, and in the fanciest places, a string ensemble. Jazz did not begin as "whorehouse music," though there is no doubt that the many taverns and dance halls in and around the red-light district—that lively environment surrounding the licensed practice of the world's oldest profession—offered employment opportunities to the early jazzmen.

Most of these, however, were only part-time musicians. They were craftsmen or laborers who found music-making an enjoyable way to supplement their incomes. Buddy Bolden was a barber and for a while also published a popular scandal sheet. Louis Armstrong, poor even for a black youngster of the day, picked coal from the freightyard tracks and sold it from a pushcart; later he worked on the Mississippi levee as a stevedore.

The role of legendary ancestor of jazz fits what we know of Bolden to perfection. It was he, it seems, who first joined the strains of ragtime—a primarily pianistic music of Afro-American origin—and brass-band music to the blues, the secular folk music of the rural southern black population, characterized by "blue" tonality—a wavering pitch arising from the flattening of the third and seventh notes of the Western tempered scale.

The blues is the strain that runs through all American popular music and makes it unique. There are blue notes in the music of the black churches, which, in turn, have been transmitted to what is called white gospel, the religious music of rural white southerners. The blues permeates country-and-western music; the achievements of our best Broadway and Hollywood composers would be impossible without it; and rock'n'roll was at first just simplistic blues. Of course, the blues is part and parcel of all jazz styles, from the earliest to the most recent.

Bolden's music, as they said admiringly at the time, was *nasty*. It could be danced to in ways that had not yet made their debut in polite society. That would come gradually; after all, the cakewalk was still considered most risqué, and Irene and Vernon Castle would shock conservatives with the fox-trot more than a decade after Bolden's peak. In matters pertaining to popular music and dance, there has always been a distinct cultural lag between black and white America, though its duration has decreased considerably since the days of Bolden and his "slow drag."

The music Bolden mixed with the blues was basically ragtime, which, by the early 1900s, had been adapted to dance-orchestra instrumentation. In the early 1970s, ragtime was rediscovered by the American public—the impetus came not from jazz circles, but from concert pianists looking to expand their repertoire. It is, to the contemporary ear, a music redolent with Gay Nineties charm—an echo of an age of innocence. At the time of its greatest impact, however, it was viewed by musical traditionalists as barbaric, lewd, and vulgar. "Like a criminal novel, it is full of bangs and explosions, devised in order to shake up the overworked mind," reads a typical 1913 criticism. But this was mild compared to the reactions jazz would evoke in such quarters a bit later.

Ragtime had invaded most American parlors by the early years of the new century, but what went on in black dance halls in New Orleans was still a well-kept secret. Yet, what Bolden and his colleagues were putting together here was the music of the future.

Bolden, the legend goes, played stronger and louder than any other cornetist in New Orleans. If another band were playing nearby, all he had to do was point the bell of his horn in that direction, and, like a pied piper, draw the other dancers to the source of his sound. Eventually, he had several bands working on weekend nights under his name and would make the rounds to play a few numbers with each. But his behavior became increasingly erratic. During a Mardi Gras parade in 1907, he had a fit of madness, and some months later was committed to an insane asylum, where he spent the rest of his life—some twenty-four years—a victim of paresis.

The cornet—almost a twin of the trumpet and eventually displaced by it—was the dominant instrument in early jazz. The typical instrumentation that evolved consisted of cornet, which carried the melodic lead; clarinet, which embellished around it; trombone, which filled in the bass part of the harmony; and guitar, string bass, and drums—the so-called rhythm section—which provided the fundamental pulse. Piano came later—you couldn't very well carry one to a location job. The jazz-drum set was an ingenious combination of the military band's three percussion elements—bass drum, snare drum, and cymbals—operated by hands and foot. Later refinements included the high-hat—two cymbals brought together by a pedal—and by the early 1930s, the jazz drummer was a man whose job demanded the coordination and timing of an acrobat.

But for now the cornet was the glamorous instrument. After Bolden's involuntary abdication, there were contenders for his throne, chief among them Freddie Keppard (1889-1933), who had some of Bolden's power, and Joe Oliver (1885-1938), who captured Bolden's crown and henceforth became known as King Oliver. The fact that Oliver was not as loud but more subtle than Keppard says much about the rapid development of jazz. We can judge their respective styles from the evidence of phonograph records, a technological medium without which the history of the music would have turned out very differently.

Keppard could have been the first great black jazz musician to make records. He left New Orleans in 1912 with a group called the Original Creole Band; they first played in California, then began to tour the country in vaudeville, playing New York as early as 1915 and again in 1917 and the following year. During one of these visits, they were approached by the Victor Company—already the world's leading record label—and actually made a test recording. But Keppard didn't like the deal the band was offered. He wanted as much money as Caruso was getting. The Creole Band didn't record, and it wasn't until 1923 that Keppard's playing was first captured for posterity. By then, some say, it had already begun to deteriorate, for Keppard was a heavy drinker and liquor eventually killed him.

Oliver also got his first chance to record in 1923. Far from being in decline, he was leading the greatest band of his career, at the Lincoln Gardens in Chicago, the city that had become the new jazz center of the world.

According to the story that tells us early jazz was whorehouse music, the New Orleans musicians came to Chicago because the red-light district—Storyville—of their hometown closed down. It is quite true that Storyville was closed in 1917 by order of the Secretary of the Navy, who feared for the souls of young sailors. But the migration of musicians had begun long before. It was, in fact, a logical by-product of the northward migration of black Americans in the second decade of the new century. The outbreak of World War I, and America's eventual involvement in it, spurred the demand for labor in the industrial centers of the North. Between 1910 and 1920, the black population of Chicago more than doubled, from about 40,000 (2 percent) to over 100,000 (4 percent). By 1915, there were lots of New Orleans musicians in the Windy City, both black and white.

The assimilation of jazz by whites began early in New Orleans. As we have noted, the city was relatively easy-going in its racial mores, and certainly there were opportunities for musicians to listen to each other. Creoles of light skin color also routinely "passed" in white bands from the ragtime era on.

Among the early white New Orleans groups that traveled to Chicago was the Original Dixieland Jass Band—one of the first groups to apply that term, then spelled thusly, to music. (As a slang verb, it apparently had vague sexual connotations.) The band didn't make much noise in Chicago, where there was plenty of competition, but when it arrived in New York in early 1917 for an engagement at Reisenweber's, a popular restaurant, it made a lasting impact.

It was a matter of being in the right place at the right time. By 1917, dance styles, reflecting changes in social mores, were undergoing a revolutionary change, but New York had had no music to go with the new steps. For some years the Castles had been using the band of James Reese Europe (1881-1919), one of New York's leading black musicians, to accompany their dance exhibitions. Europe may have been the hottest thing in New York, but he was playing ragtime, not jazz, and the Original Dixieland Jass Band was hotter.

The dancers took to the band, and soon it was making records, becoming the first New Orleans jazz band to do so. This was in 1917. Ragtime had been disseminated via the piano roll and sheet music. Despite its rhythmic vitality and other innovative features, it was a composer's idiom, a written music. Jazz was a player's art, a music in which the sound of the instruments mattered almost as much as the notes being played, and the rhythm mattered even more. Neither sound nor rhythm can be accurately notated. The Original Dixieland Jass Band's records became the medium through which the new sounds of jazz, until now basically a regional music, spread throughout the United States, and before long, throughout the world.

The band's first disc for Victor, *Livery Stable Blues* and *Dixie Jass Band One Step*, eventually sold over one million copies—more than any single record by Caruso or John Philip Sousa's band, the leading sellers up to that time. Today the music sounds rather crude, and in the case of *Livery Sta-*

**Original Dixieland Jazz Band, 1917.
Left to right: Henry Ragas, Larry
Shields, Eddie Edwards, Nick La
Rocca, Tony Spargo (Sbarbaro)**

ble Blues, with its imitations of barnyard sounds, downright silly. But there is no denying the vitality of the band, and Victor's introductory publicity for the record gives us an idea of its impact on the ears and feet of the time:

> Only with the greatest effort were we able to make the Original Dixieland Jass Band stand still long enough to make a record.... You never know what it's going to do next, but you can always tell what those who hear it are going to do—they're going to "shake a leg." The Jass Band is the very latest thing in the development of music. It has sufficient power and penetration to inject new life into a mummy, and will keep ordinary human dancers on their feet till breakfast time.

Clearly, this was music meant for dancing, and there was little to interest the listener. The leader, cornetist Nick La Rocca (1889-1961), can hardly be said to improvise at all, and only the clarinetist, Larry Shields (1893-1953), varies his part to any significant extent. The rhythm and rough, energetic sound are what it's all about.

Before long, the superficial aspects of the Original Dixieland Jass Band's style were being copied by almost every dance band in town. Laughing trombones and cackling clarinets became the order of the day, and musicians who had never been farther south than Staten Island banded together under names redolent of magnolias and dripping with molasses.

The first black New Orleans band to record was that of trombonist Kid Ory (1886-1973) in Los Angeles in 1921. Its music, though less stiff and repetitious than the Original Dixieland Jass Band's, is not remarkably superior. But when King Oliver's Creole Jazz Band began to record two years later, there was a big difference. Here, for the first time on record, was jazz music to hear as well as "shake a leg" to. King Oliver's music captured the joyous spirit of New Orleans just at the time it was about to be superseded by something new—the assertion of the individual over the collective. In Oliver's music, all parts were in perfect balance (which is not to say that there were no technical imperfections in the music) and harmony. Each member of the eight-piece ensemble knew precisely what his function was.

At times, Johnny Dodds's clarinet would take the leading role, surfacing above the ensemble in solo flight. Then the two-cornet team would lead, or Oliver would take a solo, varying his sound by the use of mutes—an art of which he was a master and probably the inventor as well. He used found objects—a child's sandpail, a rubber bathroom plunger, a drinking glass—to create varied tonal colors.

By contrast, Oliver's fellow cornetist, a youngster named Louis Armstrong, played open horn, using no mutes, just letting his singing sound ring true. Together, they would devise intricate "breaks," harmonized two-bar interludes during which the rest of the band dropped out and the steady rhythmic pulse was suspended.

Armstrong had been brought to Chicago by Oliver in the summer of 1922. In New Orleans, Oliver had been "Little Louis's" mentor and, in a sense, surrogate father. When he left in 1918, he turned his job with the best band in town over to Louis. Now he felt that the young man was ready for graduate school. Or maybe he knew that Louis would inevitably find his way to Chicago and that he might as well have this brilliant player with him instead of competing against him. Though Louis wanted nothing more than to be a loyal, functioning member of the band, he was the force that would break the traditional mold. He was to become the first great soloist in the new musical language; meanwhile he helped bring the parent form to its final flowering.

There was another man—Oliver's exact contemporary—who would refine the New Orleans form even further and ultimately distill its essence. His greatest artistic success took place just after Louis's first breakthrough, but the history of an art does not proceed in neat chronological order. This man was Jelly Roll Morton (1885-1941), born Ferdinand La Menthe, a New Orleans Creole and one of the most complex and fascinating characters in early jazz. He began to play the piano in "sporting houses" while still in his teens, then drifted on to Biloxi, a gambling center, where he became a pool shark of considerable class. Working his way around the country, playing piano, hustling pool and other parlor games, acting in vaudeville and minstrel shows, Morton acquired a vast repertoire of songs and styles and the manner of a confidence man.

Blessed with a sturdy ego and great ambition, he modestly considered himself the world's best piano player and cultivated a talent for composition (he

King Oliver's Creole Jazz Band, early
1920s. Kneeling in foreground
playing slide trumpet is Louis
Armstrong. His future wife, Lil, is at
piano. The others, left to right, are:
Honore Dutrey, Baby Dodds, King
Oliver, Bill Johnson, Johnny Dodds

DAGUERRE
chicago

claimed to have written the first jazz arrangement, composed the first blues, etc., and it might well be so) and bandleading between such pastimes as running a hotel and club in Los Angeles, vacationing in Alaska, and trying his hand at fight promotion. He was proud of the diamond that adorned one of his front teeth.

In 1923, Morton finally made his first recordings, coincidentally also appearing on the first racially integrated recording date, a session with the New Orleans Rhythm Kings, the most proficient white band to come North in the early days. His piano solos were more impressive than his first band recordings, which seem like warmups for his great 1926 series for the Victor label, billed as "Jelly Roll Morton and His Red Hot Peppers." Using a traditional lineup of cornet, trombone, clarinet, piano, banjo/guitar, string bass, and drums—New Orleanians all except the cornetist—he recorded his own compositions and a few arrangements of other works. Morton was a genuine composer. His best pieces are beautifully organized and realized structures combining solo and ensemble work in ever-shifting patterns. When analyzed and broken down, his methods appear complex, but the music preserves the essential spontaneity of New Orleans jazz—in fact, it incarnates the spirit of that music. Morton was also a creator of lovely melodies, the equal, certainly, of the great ragtime composer Scott Joplin in this respect.

By 1926, however, jazz had ineluctably begun to move in new directions, and Morton's perfect realization of the New Orleans potential was born to be history, so to speak. Morton went on to make many more recordings, many of them excellent, but none as great as his 1926 output. By nature and temperament, he had to be up-to-date, and much of his later music reflects his attempts to come to terms with the new form of arranged big-band jazz, in which sections of two or more instruments take on the roles previously handled by individual voices, and the charm of the New Orleans collective is lost.

Morton eventually fell on lean days. The late thirties found him in Washington, D.C., running a rather sleazy establishment known as the Jungle Club, leading a mediocre group trying to play swing music. Here, he was occasionally visited by representatives of a new breed—the jazz-record collectors—who knew something about who Morton was, or rather, had been.

Eventually, Alan Lomax, who with his father,

John, had begun to make field recordings of American folk music for the Library of Congress, including much music made by black people, was introduced to Morton and decided to record some of this strange and seemingly boastful man's musical reminiscences. What began as an experiment turned into a two-month project resulting in a massive document of American musical history, idiosyncratic, not always absolutely reliable, but fascinating and invaluable. Playing the piano, singing and talking, Morton re-creates the past most vividly, tracing the transition from ragtime to jazz (for much of which he claimed responsibility), illustrating the styles of legendary musicians, and commenting on the mores and morals of a vanished society. Had he produced nothing else, these documents would assure Morton a place of honor in American music.

Inspired by this outpouring and aware that there was now a group of influential people interested in jazz history, Morton moved to New York and began to record again. But aside from some marvelous solo piano efforts, the results were an uneasy compromise between Morton's need to please his historically minded sponsors and his desire to prove his up-to-dateness—what would now be called relevance. The lovely new tunes he wrote were designed to be modern but in fact were full of old New Orleans charm.

Forced by ill health to leave New York for a more friendly climate, he made his way cross-country to California, where he died in 1941, once again a near-forgotten man. Three years later, the New Orleans revival was fully under way. Morton would have been its natural leader, and this time his need for relevance would not have been in conflict with his roots.

King Oliver, the other great figure of the final flowering of New Orleans, fared even worse. In New Orleans, his main work, before music became a full-time opportunity, had been as a butler, and he had the courtly manners of the old South. His main vice was eating—of a particular kind that would drive modern nutritionists wild. Mezz Mezzrow describes Oliver at table after a night's work:

> He steered me around to a bakery, where he bought three big loaves of hot bread, then over to a Chinese chop-suey joint. All he ordered was a big pot of tea for a nickel, and then he got fidgety and began to look all around the place. The waiters all seemed to be ducking him. Finally Joe cornered

Jelly Roll Morton in Storyville, c. 1903

Courtesy of Jack Bradley

Zutty Singleton, Red Callender, Kid Ory, Charlie Beale, Bud Scott, Louis Armstrong, and Barney Bigard, from the film *New Orleans*, 1947

the boss himself and said, "Man, what's your story, bring on that sugar."

I saw right away why all the sugar went into hiding when Joe showed up in that place. As soon as the sugar bowl arrived he tore a whole loaf of hot bread in half, poured most of the sugar into it, and ate it like a sandwich, sipping the tea to wash it down. He would eat two or three loaves at a time, with as many bowls of sugar. "Man," he told me, "this is what I call real eatin'. Moms always used to make sugar sandwiches for me when I was a kid."

By the time he was in his early forties, this diet had done in most of Oliver's teeth. Unfortunately, this was also a time of radical changes in musical tastes and styles, and Oliver had to move with the trend to keep up his reputation as King. He put together some pretty good big bands, one of which later became the nucleus for the famous Luis Russell band, but his own playing was no longer able to spark a band.

After considerable touring, he made his way to New York. Here, in 1927, he was offered a job as house band at the newly opened Cotton Club, but he dickered for more pay and lost out to an up-and-coming young bandleader named Duke Ellington. It was a fatal mistake; after some weeks at the Savoy Ballroom in Harlem there were just a few odd jobs, and then Oliver had to disband and send his men back to Chicago. In New York, all that kept him going was a long-term contract with the Victor label, which he filled with pick-up bands, and help in the form of studio work from his old New Orleans buddy Clarence Williams, a successful publisher and impressario.

In 1930, with the help of his trumpet-playing nephew, Dave Nelson, who also was a good arranger and organizer, Oliver put together a touring band. It was not a success. Oliver now settled in Nashville, forming a new band and touring the southern border states. His name still had some value, but the jobs were so ill-paying that Oliver took to carrying a gun, both to keep the musicians in line and to make sure he would collect from the ballroom operators.

Despite declining health, near inability to play, and constant problems with recalcitrant musicians and unscrupulous booking agents, he went on leading bands in obscure venues until his last band fell apart and he was forced to settle in Savannah, Georgia. Here he ran a fruit stand before being reduced to working as a poolroom attendant. He died in Savannah in 1938 and was buried in New York. Many musicians turned out to pay their respects.

Louis Armstrong insisted that Oliver's mistake had been to come to New York too late. "When he got there, everybody was playing him. Even I had been here long before him. And it was all his own fault, too. . . . time ran out on him. He looked around, and when he came to New York—too late."

Oliver's letters to his sister and friends are among the most moving human documents in the annals of American music. They formed the basis of the chapter on Oliver in the first significant American book on jazz, *Jazzmen* (1939). His last letter to his sister was written two months before his death in his fifty-third year. It begins: "I open the pool rooms at 9 A.M. and close at 12 midnite. If the money was only ¼ as much as the hours I'd be all set. But at that I can thank God for what I am getting. Which I do night after night. I know you will be glad when the winter say goodby."

When Louis Armstrong left Oliver's band in 1924, it was because he had been invited to join the big band of Fletcher Henderson in New York. Through his year with this group it was to become the most important of the early big bands, the pace- and style-setter for the dominant music of the next decade.

Henderson had schooled musicians in his band; almost all of his men had been to college and were good readers. His chief arranger was Don Redman, an erstwhile musical prodigy who played all the instruments in the band and then some. He was the originator of most of the devices that became standard practice for big-band writing. In the early twenties, a "big band" was usually nine or ten pieces. Henderson's had two trumpets (Louis made it three), one trombone, and two reed players who between them could cover about a dozen instruments, chiefly clarinets and saxophones. (Shortly after Louis joined, a third reed man was added.) The rhythm section consisted of piano, banjo (doubling guitar), bass (brass and string), and drums.

Brasses and reeds were usually deployed as sections, but of course the whole band could be used as a single choir. Redman allowed for improvised solo passages here and there, mostly of eight to twelve bars in length. The maximum on records was thirty-two bars—a full "chorus" of the tune being played if it was of standard Tin Pan Alley construction. The material was pop songs of the day, plus waltzes, maybe even a tango—anything that would please the dancers at the Roseland Ballroom, where Henderson was ensconced.

When Louis joined, the effect was immediate and explosive. It is described in some detail in the chapter on Louis. Let us note here that Henderson's music *after* Louis is what the band is remembered for. The young trumpeter from New Orleans brought about the final liberation of jazz from the remaining strictures of the marches and ragtime tunes the music had grown from. His conception of the beat was a flowing one—the thing called swing—best expressed in 4/4 time.

Along with his superior sense of rhythm, Louis had an incomparable tone on the instrument. His vibrato was neither too pronounced nor too controlled, his sound was full, round, and warm. His phrasing provided the basic vocabulary for jazz improvisation for the next ten years or more. Simply put, it was the syntax for a new musical language.

Louis Armstrong was the first great soloist in jazz, but there was one man with a possible prior claim to the title. He was from New Orleans, of course, and Louis had known him there. Three years older than the trumpeter, Sidney Bechet (1897-1959) had left his hometown for good in 1917. He started on clarinet but switched to the more powerful soprano saxophone in 1919, the year he left New York for Europe with Will Marion Cook's Southern Syncopated Orchestra, a troupe of some thirty players, singers, and dancers led by a man who had given up a promising concert career when a reviewer wrote that he was "the world's greatest negro violinist." He realized then and there that white society was not ready to accept a black classical musician as anything but a curiosity.

The Southern Syncopated Orchestra played all kinds of American Negro music; it had a whole section of banjos and mandolins. When it played blues and jazz, its star was Sidney Bechet. In the first intelligent appraisal of jazz published anywhere, a 1919 review in *Revue Romande* by the Swiss conductor Ernest Ansermet of a concert tour by the orchestra, Bechet was singled out:

> There is in the . . . Orchestra an extraordinary clarinet virtuoso who is, so it seems, the first of his race to have composed perfectly formed blues on clarinet. . . . Their form was gripping, abrupt, harsh, with a brusque and pitiless ending like that of Bach's Second Brandenburg Concerto. I wish to set down the name of this artist of genius; as for

Courtesy of Ralph Ginzburg

Sidney Bechet

Sidney Bechet

**Sidney Bechet on the corner of rue
Armstrong and rue Bechet in Paris**

myself, I shall never forget it—it is Sidney Bechet. When one has tried so often to rediscover in the past one of those figures to whom we owe the advent of our art—those men of the 17th and 18th centuries, for example, who made expressive works of dance airs, clearing the way for Haydn and Mozart who mark, not the starting point, but the first milestone—what a moving thing it is to meet this very black, fat boy with the white teeth and that narrow forehead, who is very glad one likes what he does, but who can say nothing of his art, except that he follows "his own way," and when one thinks that his "own way" is perhaps the highway the whole world will swing along tomorrow.

I have quoted Ansermet at length not only for his appreciation of Bechet, but for his perception of jazz as "perhaps the highway the whole world will swing along tomorrow." Even the formulation is apt. Bechet became more eloquent about his music later; in fact, his autobiography, *Treat It Gentle,* is an important contribution to the understanding of jazz.

Had he not spent years crucial in jazz development abroad, Bechet might have achieved a greater reputation in his homeland. As it was, he returned in 1921, deeply impressed young Duke Ellington, with whom he later played for a short time, and whose alto saxophone star, Johnny Hodges, he taught and influenced, and made some records in 1924-25 with Louis Armstrong that show the two as equals in terms of the art of constructing solos and playing with maximum expressiveness. They challenge each other, vie with each other, yet also understand and appreciate the principles of collective music-making.

Bechet left the United States again in 1925, heading for Paris with the show that launched Josephine Baker's international career. This time he stayed for almost six years, traveling as far east as Moscow (where he ran into Louisiana trumpeter Tommy Ladnier, on tour with another American band) and getting himself jailed for eleven months in France for a shooting fracas with another American musician, in which an innocent bystander—unfortunately a Frenchwoman—was nicked.

Back home during the depths of the Depression, he tried to launch a New Orleans-style small group with Ladnier; it lasted only a few months but made some marvelous records—the first to show Bechet's true powers. For a while, he and Ladnier ran a tailor shop in Harlem, but then Bechet returned to full-

time music with Noble Sissle's society dance band.

By 1938, the slowly growing interest in traditional jazz had reached the point where the first independent jazz record labels appeared. Bechet became one of the first to record for the new Blue Note label, formed by two German Jewish immigrants, Alfred Lion and Francis Wolff, who had first met in pre-Nazi Berlin through the shared hobby of collecting "hot jazz" records. Bechet made a stunning version of *Summertime,* which led not only to his rediscovery but also to a long-term contract with Victor Records. Prematurely gray and with imposing presence, Bechet was considered much older than he actually was, and he wisely did nothing to discourage the legend that he had worked with Buddy Bolden and such.

A few years after the end of the war, Bechet, who had to supplement his income with teaching, decided to visit France again. He liked what he saw, and in 1951 settled there permanently and became tremendously popular, not only in jazz circles, but in the French music halls. He had a number of hit records, and his wedding in Antibes was a major event of the 1957 social season on the Riviera, complete with parade and floats.

He appeared in films, and his most ambitious composition, a ballet score, was performed and recorded. He died in Paris in 1959; a bust of him was erected in Juan-les-Pins.

In *Treat It Gentle,* he wrote:

There's all the music that's been played, and there's all the music that hasn't been heard yet. The music of Scott Joplin, things he wrote. So many a piece of Will Marion Cook's. So many men who've spent their lives just making melody and who haven't been heard yet.

I'd like to hear it all one more time. I'd like to sit in a box at some performance and see all I saw years ago and hear all I heard way back to the start. I want to sit there and you could come in and find me in that box and I'd have a smile on my face. What I'd be feeling is, "the music, it has a home." As long as I got a heart to be filled by it, the music has a place that's natural to it. I could sit there and listen, and I'd smile. And when I've got to go I could go that way. I could remember all the richness there is, and I could go smiling.

Bechet and Armstrong played together again on a few occasions, in 1940 and 1945, but while the results were exciting music, the fine balance between individual and collective music-making that

Thomas ("Fats") Waller, 1942

had marked their earlier encounters was gone. In the ensembles, they vied for the lead. Jazz had become a soloist's art.

By 1940, Armstrong had been leading big bands for more than a decade; though they often had good (and sometimes even great) musicians in them, they acted purely as a foil for his playing and singing. It was inevitable now that the Armstrong example would break the collective mold. Once they had heard from Louis what could be done with jazz, other musicians were impelled to follow in his steps as best they could.

Before the final breaking of the collective ensemble mold, however, there was an association that led to some of the finest music of the Armstrong canon—some would say the finest. Louis's partner in these masterpieces, among them the famous *West End Blues,* was, like Bechet, his peer. But unlike Bechet's, his style had been shaped by the direct influence of Armstrong. Moreover, Earl Hines (b. 1905) played an instrument suited to accompanying as well as soloing—the piano.

The piano, about the only instrument that can truly play by itself, had been slow to shed the ragtime tradition. The first important jazz piano style, so-called stride piano, had a lot of ragtime in it still, but for the rather regular and somewhat dainty syncopated rhythm of ragtime, the stride players substituted a strong, swinging left-hand bass line, moving in a "striding" fashion. Stride piano flourished, especially in Harlem, from the late teens through the mid-twenties. Its foremost exponents included James P. Johnson (1891-1955), Willie ("The Lion") Smith (1893-1973), and James P.'s prize pupil, Thomas ("Fats") Waller (1904-1943). All three were also gifted composers.

Johnson, the least flamboyant personally but most brilliant pianistically of the three, was in his later years frustrated by the lukewarm reception given to the ambitious works in classical forms he had taken to writing. They have not been successfully revived (though the one-act opera he wrote with Langston Hughes, *De Organizer,* has surprisingly not yet been attempted). But his brilliant piano pieces, like *Carolina Shout,* the test piece for every stride pianist, and his fine popular songs, like *Charleston* and *If I Could Be With You,* live on.

Smith specialized in charming, melodic, pianistic tours de force that few others tried to perform. His harmonic sensibility had considerable influence on young Duke Ellington, himself no mean stride practitioner. Waller became one of the most successful black songwriters in the popular (as distinct from strictly jazz) idiom, with such evergreens as *Honeysuckle Rose, Ain't Misbehavin', Keeping out of Mischief, Black and Blue,* and *Squeeze Me* to his credit.

The stride players cultivated colorful public personalities. Smith, with his bowler hat, cane, and ever-present cigar, had a fast, Broadway-style line of patter. He earned his nickname during World War I in France, as a field artillery gunner of exceptional endurance and courage. His full name was William Henry Joseph Berthol Bonaparte Bertholoff (Smith was his stepfather's name). He was of Black American and Russian Jewish parentage—among other talents, he spoke fluent Yiddish and sometimes sang popular song lyrics in that language, in his own translations.

Waller, the son of a Harlem minister, undoubtedly learned from The Lion, though his actual teacher was Johnson. His gift for verbal improvisation was of the same order as his musical genius. Unlike The Lion, who became well known beyond jazz circles only in the post-World War II years, when he toured Europe and was a favorite at jazz festivals, Waller enjoyed great popularity from the mid-thirties on.

He made hundreds of records, mostly with the happy little band he called his "Rhythm," which included the splendid guitar of Al Casey, transforming even the most banal pop tunes into little gems of jazz and wit, egging on his musicians and burlesquing the silly lyrics by means of vocal and verbal exaggeration and invention. And he added spontaneous asides, such as this interjection during a ditty called *Spring Cleaning:* "What's that? No, madam, we can't haul your ashes for twenty-five cents! That's bad business!"

Waller appeared in several Hollywood films, stealing every little scene allowed him. Television would have been perfect for him, but he was dead before he reached forty. Fats stood well over six feet, weighed close to three hundred pounds, and was one of the champion drinkers and eaters of all time. He called scotch and water his "liquid ham and eggs," regularly ordered and devoured two of everything when dining out, and spread good times and laughter wherever he went. Though he was sometimes upset by the lack of appreciation for the more serious side of his talent—he was an exceptional organist and well versed in the classical

Al Casey

repertoire—those who conclude that Waller was a clown who wanted to play Hamlet miss the mark. The humor was genuine, not a mask.

The medium of the phonograph record captured Waller's personality exceptionally well, and he remains a real presence to listeners born long after his death. Louis Armstrong put it best: "Fats is gone now, but to me, he's still here with us. His very good spirit will keep him with us for ages. Right now, every time someone mentions Fats Waller's name, why, you can see the grins on all the faces, as if to say, 'Yea, yea, yea, yea, Fats is a solid sender, ain't he?'"

Earl Hines loved Fats Waller, and no Hines program is complete without a Waller medley. He credits Fats as a primary influence; James P. undoubtedly was another. But Hines's great achievement is that he freed jazz piano from its ragtime-inherited strictures, creating what has been called a "trumpet style" for the keyboard. His dazzling right-hand flights recall the inventions of Armstrong, and he punctuates them with plunging, unpredictable counter lines in the left. Sometimes both hands execute spiraling runs, whirlpools of sound that seem to suspend the rhythmic pulse, only to land smack on the beat once more.

Hines gave the piano its first prominent role in the large jazz band, executing fills with a touch powerful enough to hold its own against brasses and winds and perfectly placed in the rhythmic flow. He led his own usually excellent big bands from 1928 to 1947, bringing to attention many gifted instrumentalists and singers (Ray Nance, Trummy Young, Ivie Anderson, Billy Eckstine, and Sarah Vaughan among them), and influenced every pianist that followed, including the remarkable Art Tatum (1910-1956), technically the most gifted of all jazz pianists—perhaps of all jazz musicians. Tatum's harmonic audacity influenced the young turks who founded the bebop style, but that is getting ahead of our story.

In 1924, the year in which Bechet and Armstrong recorded together, a twenty-one-year-old cornetist from Davenport, Iowa, made his first records, with an otherwise rather undistinguished but very danceable band called the Wolverines. Bix Beiderbecke (1903-1931) had taught himself to play cornet to the records of the Original Dixieland Jass Band (again the phonograph!). He had taken piano lessons as a child after showing a precocious gift for music—at three, he was able to pick out tunes on

the piano after a single hearing; at seven, he participated in and was the undisputed star of a children's recital. But the lessons stopped. Young Bix quickly became bored with exercises.

He was bored with school, too, to the despair of his parents, good middle-class burghers of German ancestry. They finally sent him off to a paramilitary school, Lake Forest Academy. It was near Chicago, the capital of jazz, and thus his parents inadvertently sealed their son's fate.

Bix flunked out after a few months, having spent most of his time sitting in with Chicago jazz bands at night and sleeping (sometimes in class, sometimes in bed) during the day, or playing for weekend dances with a band he soon came to co-lead at the academy. His teachers were fond of him and loathe to flunk him, but he gave them no choice. Music was already his sole and totally absorbing interest.

Bix's approach to the cornet was unorthodox. He never learned the correct way of fingering the valves. The first really original white jazz musician was a maverick.

The Wolverines, the first significant professional band Bix played with, were very popular with the college crowd in the Midwest. They had the right rhythm to dance the Charleston to, but some of the dancers became listeners when they heard Bix. One of these was a young law student named Hoagy Carmichael. He wrote his first published song, *Riverboat Shuffle,* for Bix and the Wolverines, who recorded it. (Some later Carmichael, such as the verse to *Star Dust,* is pure Bix.)

The records led to an offer from New York. The band flopped in the big town, but not with the local musicians. Bix's sound alone was enough to captivate them, and on top of that, his ideas, so direct and logical, yet wholly unexpected, were the most remarkable since Armstrong's.

Bix had heard Louis on the riverboats that made their way up the Mississippi as far as Davenport and again in Chicago with Oliver's band. The two admired each other and sometimes played together (integrated jam sessions, while rare, were not unheard of by any means). But there was no direct influence; Bix's only hero on the cornet was Nick La Rocca of the Original Dixieland Jass Band, a limited but precise player. And maybe more. There is a moment on the Jass Band's record of *Singin' the Blues,* a piece that later became one of Bix's most famous solo vehicles, that lets us glimpse what it may have been that Bix heard. In any case, influ-

Bix Beiderbecke

**Bix Beiderbecke and the Wolverines
in the Gennet Recording Studios, 1924**

ences on major artists are important not for their intrinsic qualities but for what the mind being influenced makes of them.

For the next few years, Bix crisscrossed the Midwest, playing with various bands (a final effort to continue his formal studies at Iowa State University lasted exactly eighteen days, in February, 1925). The most important of his associations was with a St. Louis-born saxophonist and multi-instrumentalist, Frank Trumbauer (1901-1956), a first-rate musician with a sense of form and development that made him one of the first important jazz soloists, though he didn't have much swing. Most significantly, his conception was wholly compatible with Bix's, and he was a thoroughly schooled musician, able to give his younger friend many pointers.

Bix and Tram (as Trumbauer was known) became inseparable. They worked together in the band of Jean Goldkette, a French-born entrepreneur raised in Greece and Russia and trained as a concert pianist who by the late twenties had some twenty dance bands in his organization. The one with Bix and Tram was his showcase, and such stars as Joe Venuti and Eddie Lang, the Dorsey Brothers, and Don Murray were in its ranks. Eventually, it became too costly for Goldkette to maintain, and most of its personnel was taken over by Paul Whiteman, at even higher salaries.

Price was no object to Whiteman (1890-1967), who had been paid as much as ten thousand dollars for a single society engagement. He was the most successful bandleader in the world, the "King of Jazz." That notorious title has caused Whiteman's reputation a lot of unjust harm. The word "jazz," after all, was used in a quite different and much less specific sense during the "Jazz Age" (a term in itself a perfect example of this imprecise use). To most contemporaries, jazz simply meant peppy dance music in a contemporary style, coupled with an irreverent approach to life.

Whiteman, an ex-violinist of huge girth and gregarious appetites, ruled benignly but firmly over an ensemble that had grown from a modest nine pieces in 1919, when he first hit New York, to nearly thirty in 1927, when Bix, Tram, and the other genuine jazz players joined. For concert work, the personnel was augmented beyond this number, and the Whiteman repertoire encompassed everything from special arrangements of popular classics and commissioned works of extended scope (the most famous of these being George Gershwin's *Rhapsody in Blue* and *Concerto in F* and Ferde Grofé's *Grand Canyon Suite*) through novelty numbers to dance music of all kinds, superbly crafted by Whiteman's staff of arrangers, or by outside talent, including such black musicians as William Grant Still and Don Redman.

After the Goldkette bunch had joined, a real jazz flavor was occasionally imparted to the Whiteman sound, notably when Bix led the brass section or was featured in solo. And there were jazz holidays with small groups culled from the band (Whiteman was the soul of largesse with his musicians, but insisted that in "outside" recording work they employ only their colleagues, a circumstance that led to Bix being blamed by critics for having recorded only with his inferiors).

For twenty-four-year-old Bix, joining Whiteman seemed a dream come true. Contrary to the romantic piffle conveyed by early writers on jazz, he was not frustrated by the lack of opportunity to play jazz (and thus "express" himself) or by the need to read a lot of difficult music. He was only an average reader, to be sure, but by no means as poor a one as the romanticizers claimed. Besides, the Whiteman arrangers took special care of him, as did the leader. Bix was one of Whiteman's favorites. He was featured as much as anyone in the band, including men who had been with it from the start. And in 1927, there was not much more jazz solo space available to any white dance band musician. Bix had always been more than superficially interested in concert music, especially of the impressionist kind, and was eager for the opportunity to learn more about it. And he was making two hundred dollars a week—a fabulous salary for a young single man in those days.

The sad and simple fact is that Bix was already an alcoholic when he joined Whiteman, and the surprising thing is not that he couldn't keep up with the pace in Whiteman's band, but that he lasted as long as he did—nearly two years, excepting a four-month "vacation" for a Whiteman-paid cure. When his health broke down again in late September, 1929, Whiteman sponsored another cure, plus a rest at home in Davenport. Proud of his recordings with Whiteman, Bix religiously sent each record to his family; he was deeply hurt when by chance he looked into a closet at home and found it filled with his unopened packages. He got away as soon as he

Benny Carter

decently could. Whiteman didn't rebuff him when he visited with the band backstage and talked of rejoining. But it was clear that Bix would never hold a steady job again, though there were still moments of lovely playing, much of it now on piano.

Bix Beiderbecke died, officially of pneumonia, in August, 1931, in New York City in his twenty-ninth year. He left behind a handful of beautiful recorded cornet solos, four evocative piano compositions (*In a Mist, In the Dark, Candlelights, Flashes*), the first of which he also recorded, and a legend that refuses to die.

The subject of the most painstakingly researched biography in jazz literature, and the inspiration for a rather fanciful novel and an almost equally fanciful "memoir of the Jazz Age," plus countless articles and appreciations, Bix by all accounts was a pleasant, good-natured young man who loved music and couldn't stop drinking. (His only other known passion was for the works of P. G. Wodehouse.) His music, aside from the sinew and affirmation of life without which it wouldn't belong to jazz, has a quality of wistful yearning—the peculiar ambiance that continues to feed the legend.

Trumbauer didn't become a legend, but his musical influence was probably more decisive than Bix's. The cornetist was a compelling force in the formative years of the Chicagoans, those gifted white jazzmen are discussed in some detail in the chapter on Eddie Condon and his gang, and on Red Nichols and the other prominent and proficient jazz-tinged instrumentalists who ruled the dance-music roost in New York (the brilliant trombonist Miff Mole, the bass saxophone magician Adrian Rollini, the harmonically prescient pianist Arthur Schutt, the clarinetist, saxophonist, and arranger Fud Livingston, whose main ambition it was to record the perfect solo, and others once overrated and later neglected).

But Trumbauer deeply influenced two very great musicians, Benny Carter and Lester Young. The latter in particular has credited Trumbauer with inspiring him: "He always told a little story when he played, and I loved the way he slurred his notes." When Young revealed this in an interview in the mid-fifties, it was difficult for many jazz critics to come to terms with it. To them, Trumbauer was part of the Whiteman and white man's legacy, a branch of jazz they had become accustomed to dismiss. The truth is always surprising.

Benny Carter, who first heard Trumbauer on a record by the Benson Orchestra of Chicago in 1922, took the place of Fletcher Henderson's chief arranger and featured alto saxophonist and clarinetist, Don Redman, when Redman left to take over leadership of McKinney's Cotton Pickers—a band, incidentally, managed by Jean Goldkette—which he built into one of the best (and most typical) big bands of the decade.

This was the time when Henderson himself began to write arrangements for his band; he soon became so adept at it that he received credit for a good deal of Redman's pioneering work. Fletcher by now had in his ranks the greatest collection of gifted soloists in any large jazz ensemble. Coleman Hawkins (1901-1969) had been aboard since 1923. After exposure to Louis Armstrong, he crafted the first viable jazz style for the tenor sax. Clarinetist Buster Bailey (1902-1967), born in Memphis and raised on the music of W. C. Handy, the so-called "Father of the Blues" (he was in fact the first to systematically write down and structure into popular music form this folk idiom, and his *St. Louis Blues* remains a classic), joined shortly after Louis. Trombonist Jimmy Harrison (1900-1931) invented a style for his instrument that remained the touchstone until the advent of bop, and his successors in Henderson's rank were all in his mold. (Harrison died of cancer of the stomach; he loved to eat fried foods, pies, and ice cream. A seemingly innocent vice, but in his case apparently as deadly as Beiderbecke's very different poison.)

Henderson's post-Armstrong trumpeters included the lyrical Joe Smith (1902-1937), a black counterpart of Bix, famed for his sweet tone and Bessie Smith's favorite accompanist, and Tommy Ladnier (1900-1939), a New Orleans-bred player in the King Oliver tradition, disdainful of high notes. Benny Carter's several tenures with the band saw him develop into one of the foremost alto sax stylists and arrangers in jazz.

Henderson's band lacked professional discipline, and its records, though studded with brilliant solos, fail to do it justice—according to those who heard it in person. Among them was no less an authority than Coleman Hawkins, who claimed that on a good night the band could "stomp all other bands into the ground." The combative tone of this comment is not surprising when one recalls that those were the days of "battles of the bands." Often as many as four crack outfits would play opposite each other in a big ballroom, such as Harlem's famous Savoy, "the

Coleman Hawkins. At left: Buster Bailey

Coleman Hawkins

Buster Bailey

home of happy feet," with the winner declared by popular acclaim.

Such battles were prevalent from the late twenties on, long before the so-called Swing Era began. Ironically, that prime period for big jazz bands found Henderson in trouble for most of its duration. The Henderson crew was famous for its fancy, powerful cars and reckless driving between engagements. In 1928, Henderson's big Packard roadster ran off the road, and the bandleader suffered a severe concussion. After this incident, his interest in business matters and discipline declined even further, though he continued to be a great talent-spotter and arranger.

The up-and-coming Duke Ellington orchestra did better on records. Its leader understood the special requirements of the medium—such as setting up a proper balance of instruments in the studio and crafting pieces that would sound complete rather than compressed within the three-minute-plus limit of 78 r.p.m. discs.

Hawkins left Henderson in 1934 to go to Europe. That was the year in which a young Chicago-born clarinetist, Benny Goodman, who had been making a good living as a studio musician in New York, decided to form a big band of his own, spurred by his friend John Hammond, a wealthy young jazz enthusiast. Goodman (b. 1909) had joined drummer Ben Pollack's band in 1926; it was one of the best and most jazz-oriented white dance bands of the twenties. Pollack had been with the New Orleans Rhythm Kings. He hired Jimmy McPartland, a Bix disciple; Jimmy's chum Bud Freeman, a fine tenor player; and Glenn Miller (1904-1944), a studious trombonist and arranger who eventually became the most successful dance-band leader of the Swing Era, gave it all up to volunteer for army service, built the best of all service bands, and disappeared forever in a small plane headed for Paris from England.

When the Depression forced Pollack to disband, some of his key sidemen got together and formed a cooperative band that eventually found a good front man in Bing Crosby's kid brother Bob. The Bob Crosby band, with a musical policy of skillful adaptation of modified New Orleans style to the big-band idiom, enjoyed a fair amount of success during the Swing Era. Its best-known alumni include the New Orleans clarinetist Irving Fazola of the beautiful tone; another New Orleanian, the sterling tenor saxophonist Eddie Miller, still active

Bessie Smith on 1924 sheet music cover

in his hometown in the mid-seventies; trumpeter Billy Butterfield; and trumpeter Yank Lawson and bassist-arranger Bob Haggart, who in 1966 formed the good if hyperbolically named World's Greatest Jazz Band, which continued the Crosby-Pollack tradition.

Pollack's greatest find was the Texas trombonist and singer Jack Teagarden (1905-1964), who settled in New York in 1928 and surprised both black and white musicians with his ability to play authentic blues. He soon discovered that his style and conception closely resembled Jimmy Harrison's, and the two became fast friends, often jamming together all night, with Harrison's roommate, Coleman Hawkins, accompanying them at the piano. (By the late twenties, contact between black and white musicians had become more frequent and far-reaching; after all, Henderson's band played at the Roseland Ballroom "downtown," the best white bands played opposite, and the musicians shared lockers and dressing rooms.)

Teagarden would have done better for himself if he hadn't joined Paul Whiteman's band on a five-year contract in 1933, shortly after leaving Pollack. By then, Whiteman's band had become the musical backwater it decidedly wasn't in the twenties, and Teagarden missed out on entering the big-band sweepstakes until rather late in the game. He formed his own large group in 1939 and until late 1946 struggled to keep his head above water in the big-band pool, going bankrupt several times. The quality of his bands declined, and it wasn't until he joined Louis Armstrong's new All Stars in 1947 that his career picked up once again. After leaving Louis in 1951, he led his own "All Stars"; they seldom were, but the small-group format suited Jack, who, like Louis, was able to play well with the worst sidemen.

With his relaxed, seemingly effortless playing and lazy vocal delivery, Teagarden sometimes appeared to be half asleep on the stand. But this was deceptive—his style demanded the utmost in control, and he was a superb craftsman, a quality reflected in his hobby of tinkering with all sorts of machinery, including model trains. He developed his unorthodox technique because he started playing trombone before his arms were long enough to assume the correct slide positions; it became the envy of every legitimately schooled trombonist.

Benny Goodman left the Pollack band in 1929. His career and personality are discussed in some detail in our chapter on Giants of the Golden Age. The groundwork for his eventual success as a leader of a jazz-oriented big band was laid—in addition to such black bands as Henderson's—by a now largely forgotten cooperative ensemble, the Casa Loma Orchestra (which had begun its career under the Goldkette aegis).

Perhaps because it contained no particularly notable jazz soloists, with the exception of clarinetist Clarence Hutchenrider, it evolved a highly disciplined ensemble style largely based on the device of the riff. (A riff is a short musical phrase, rhythmic rather than melodic in essence, and made effective by repetition, which had its origins in the call-and-response patterns of African and black American music.) It found great popularity among college audiences. The style was the creation of Georgia-born arranger-guitarist Gene Gifford (1908-1970); perhaps significantly, Gifford later became a maker of blueprints. The Casa Loma's popularity, however, was also based on the band's ability to play smooth, romantic ballads, made the more effective by the silken tenor voice of vocalist Kenny Sargent.

By 1934, almost every big band had Casa Loma-styled riff arrangements in its library; even Henderson recorded its theme song, *Casa Loma Stomp*. Goodman was no exception, but he soon discarded this tricky, somewhat mechanical stuff in favor of first-rate arrangements commissioned from Henderson and other gifted black and white arrangers.

Henderson, recommended to Goodman by John Hammond, needed the work. His own band was suffering from the economic consequences of the great Depression, which hit the music business hard (the annual production of phonograph records, more than 100,000,000 in 1928, dropped to 2,500,000 at its nadir in 1931), but black bands the hardest. Henderson even disbanded briefly in 1934, but was soon back in business, his reputation boosted by Goodman's success. (Goodman made sure his arrangers received label credit on the records and mentioned Fletcher's name when introducing his numbers, in person and on the air.) By the end of 1935, Henderson was leading one of the best bands of his career, with such stars-to-be as Roy Eldridge, Chu Berry, and (a little later) Sid Catlett in his ranks, plus alumni Buster Bailey and John Kirby.

The advent of the Swing Era, like the breakthrough of New Orleans jazz in 1917 and the Char-

Eddie Miller

leston craze in the twenties, was made possible by new styles in dancing. The so-called jitterbugs, direct descendants of the Lindy Hoppers, citizens of Harlem who had created a new acrobatic dance in honor of Charles Lindbergh's transatlantic flight in 1927, wanted fast and strongly rhythmic music to dance to. The swing bands provided it, with slower, more romantic changes of pace also readily available.

Swing music differed from the popular dance music of the twenties in having a stronger jazz base. Not just the soloists but also the arrangements reflected a jazz bias. And something new began to happen. People stood in front of the bands to listen instead of just dancing. They wanted to know the names of the soloists and adopted the musicians' private slang. They collected musicians' autographs, snapped up the new records each week, and perhaps even tried to play like their idols in high-school and college bands. The serious among them read the musicians' magazines, the old but changing *Metronome* and the new *Down Beat.* They voted for their favorites in these magazines' popularity polls (held annually from 1936 on) and argued heatedly about the relative merits of their favorites. Some thought Artie Shaw rather than Goodman deserved the title "King of Swing."

Shaw, a clarinetist like Goodman, but with his own attractive tone and style, was also a former successful studio musician turned bandleader. Born in New Haven in 1910 and a professional by the time he was fifteen, he was one of the most visible of swing stars by 1938, when he recorded his first hit, *Begin the Beguine.* (Goodman made hundreds of records, but never had a real hit except *And The Angels Sing;* Shaw had a string of them.)

A temperamental man with an intellectual bent, Shaw hired Billie Holiday as his band singer, perhaps inspired by Goodman's pioneering efforts at racial integration (Benny had hired pianist Teddy Wilson, then vibraharpist Lionel Hampton, as members of his featured small groups). In 1940, Shaw made the great Armstrong-inspired trumpeter and singer Oran ("Hot Lips") Page (1908-1954) a regular member of his band—the first black musician to be both a featured star and regular section member of a white big band. (Fletcher Henderson, having disbanded once again, had been Goodman's regular band pianist in 1939 but wasn't featured, while Hampton's occasional drum chores with the Goodman big band were just stopgaps.)

Shaw was the *enfant terrible* of the band world. At the height of his success in 1939, he walked off the stand in the middle of an engagement and fled to Mexico, cursing the ever more persistent jitterbugs as empty-headed fans. Just as suddenly, he broke up the band with Page (one of the best of his career) to enlist in the navy. His personal life was flamboyant. He was married eight times to beautiful women, including Lana Turner, Ava Gardner, Kathleen Winsor of *Forever Amber* fame, and finally Evelyn Keyes, who lasted. His autobiography, *The Trouble with Cinderella,* was published in 1952. Well written, it pulled no punches and offered revealing glimpses of the inner workings of a successful swing band, as well as a surprisingly tender portrait of Willie ("The Lion") Smith, with whom Shaw often sat in in Harlem and whom he credits with teaching him important things about life and music.

Shaw was an exceptional clarinetist, a musical perfectionist, and an experimenter—among other things, he was the first to add strings to a jazz band. He gave up music as a career in 1955 and hasn't touched a clarinet since.

Goodman's and Shaw's closest rivals in the swing popularity race were the Dorsey Brothers, clarinetist and alto saxophonist Jimmy (1904-1957) and trombonist Tommy (1905-1956). Both worked with many famous bands of the twenties, having been taught all the instruments by their father, a Pennsylvania coal miner and amateur musician. Later, they carved out studio careers and co-led their Dorsey Brothers Band, first only on records, then (from 1934) on a full-time basis.

Famous for their fights, verbal and sometimes physical, the brothers had a violent argument on the bandstand of the Glen Island Casino in May, 1935. It began with a difference of opinion concerning the proper tempo for a tune and ended with Tommy stalking off the stand. From then on, each brother led his own band.

Tommy's was the more jazz-oriented. It included such players as Max Kaminsky, Bud Freeman, and Dave Tough from the ranks of the erstwhile Chicagoans, and, briefly but tellingly, the great trumpeter Bunny Berigan (1908-1942), who shared initials and alcoholism with Bix Beiderbecke but was inspired by Louis Armstrong. Bunny achieved swing fame through his caloric solos on several Dorsey hits, notably *Song of India* and *Marie,* and soon formed his own big band, though he was temperamentally quite unsuited for leadership. (Musically it was another story, and his *I Can't Get Started,* on which he also sang, remains one of the key recordings of the Swing Era, still to be found on juke boxes after almost forty years.)

In 1939, Tommy hired the great black arranger and trumpeter-singer Sy Oliver. In the same year, he coaxed a young singer named Frank Sinatra away from Harry James's new band. With Sinatra, Tommy's fame hit its peak. He was a marvelous trombonist, not a great "hot" player, but an exquisite delineator of melody, with tone production and breath control that every musician admired. Sinatra says he learned to phrase and breathe correctly from watching Tommy.

Buddy Rich, a sensational young drummer who had worked with Bunny Berigan and Artie Shaw, joined in 1940, and Goodman's star trumpeter Ziggy Elman also came aboard. Tommy was a demanding leader, and the band was highly disciplined, but he always gave his jazz talent elbow room. Charlie Shavers (1917-1971), the black trumpeter who had been the spark plug of bassist John Kirby's extraordinary sextet (known as "The Biggest Little Band in the Land," it also included Buster Bailey) joined Dorsey in 1945, following in the footsteps of Hot Lips Page and Roy Eldridge.

Sinatra's popularity, made possible by his exposure in the Tommy Dorsey Band, was ironically one of the factors that led to the eventual decline of the bands. By the late forties, the singers had taken the play away from the bands in terms of audience appeal and record sales. But Tommy was one of those who held on.

Brother Jimmy, meanwhile, had reached his peak appeal through singers as well. In his case, it was the boy-girl team of Helen O'Connell and Bob Eberly that caught the public's fancy.

Jimmy gave up the race in 1953, joining forces with Tommy, who graciously gave him co-billing. Once again, there was a Dorsey Brothers Band. It enjoyed considerable success on the new medium of television with a weekly variety show, which, among other things, introduced the phenomenon of Elvis Presley to the home screen (while in motion, he was carefully presented from the waist up only). In 1956, Tommy Dorsey choked to death in his sleep after a heavy dinner and drinks. Less than seven months later, Jimmy died of cancer.

For obvious reasons, black bands, though often musically superior, ran well behind the top white organizations in the popularity race. The best location jobs (long runs at good hotels—every hotel had a ballroom featuring bands in those days), sponsored radio programs (a big financial plum), and the most favorable recording contracts primarily went to white bands, as did the film appearances that could boost a band's popularity like nothing else.

Still, many black bands did well enough to sustain long careers. One of the hardest-working and most popular was Jimmie Lunceford's, known as "The Harlem Express," though it had been founded in Memphis, where the leader had been an instructor at Fisk University. Lunceford had his Joe Glaser in the dedicated manager Harold Oxley, himself a former bandleader. Like Glaser with Armstrong, Oxley kept the band working almost 365 days a year, with one-nighters the bulk of the bookings. But the band earned good money. Lunceford was not a great musician; aside from an occasional flute excursion, he didn't play in the band at all. But he was a shrewd leader and great disciplinarian, with a feeling for the right material and most effective presentation.

Only Duke Ellington managed to keep his musicians longer than Lunceford. Most of his men were well educated, and he stressed decorum. The instruments gleamed; the uniforms were spotless and "sharp." The band was splendidly drilled; suddenly, all the trumpeters would toss their instruments in the air, clap their hands, and catch the horns on the next beat. Many of the players doubled as vocalists, and at one stage the whole band doubled as a glee club.

The secret of Lunceford's success, however, was his ensemble style, the creation of his great arrangers. The primary architect of Lunceford style was Sy Oliver (b. 1910), who joined in 1933, just in time for the band's important New York debut at the Cotton Club. Oliver's work manifested an unerring sense for the right tempos, superior craftsmanship, wide-ranging dynamics (a lot of swing bands knew only loud and soft), and a sense of humor. Others included the band's pianist, Edwin Wilcox, who joined in 1929 and was with the band until Lunceford's sudden death from food poisoning on the road in 1947.

The band's sections were a marvel of unity, the saxes breathing as one, the trumpets specializing in high-note effects (for better or worse, Lunceford was responsible for popularizing this eventually over-used trick). The rhythm was unique, a 2/4 on

**Benny Goodman. At right:
Red Norvo. Jo Jones at drums**

Roy Eldridge, Russell Procope, Chu Berry, and Dicky Wells in front of the Savoy Ballroom, Harlem, 1935

Photograph by Timme Rosenkrantz. Collection of Duncan Schiedt

top of 4/4 pulse paced by Jimmy Crawford's solid drumming. It was a dancers' delight; one of Lunceford's best numbers was called *For Dancers Only*. There was also room for solo work, notably from altoist Willie Smith (1910-1967), later with Harry James and Duke Ellington and one of the leading stylists on the instrument, and trombonist Trummy Young (b. 1912). Both were also excellent rhythm singers and entertainers.

If Lunceford's band was the essence of showmanship, another highly successful black band emphasized the natural drama of the music itself. Count Basie's crew came roaring out of Kansas City in 1936. That town had been a jazz mecca since the late twenties, due to both its geographical position as the juncture of South- and Midwest-band routes and to the regime of "Boss" Tom Pendergast, which didn't bother enforcing such things as closing hours for public places or prohibition laws, or anything else that might interfere with the enjoyment of night life.

Basie's band is detailed in the chapter on Giants of the Golden Age. By all odds the greatest of its many stars was Lester Young (1909-1959), a key figure not only in the history of the tenor sax, but of the music itself. Lester's father led a touring family band in the still surviving minstrel tradition; the nucleus was Lester, his younger brother Lee, and his sister Irma. At one point, in their preteens, all played saxophone. Lester was also taught trumpet, violin, and drums by his father, who had attended Tuskegee Institute and was a strict and demanding parent. There was much moving about during Lester's childhood, with first New Orleans, then Minneapolis, among the few more than temporary bases of operation.

For extra-musical reasons ("By the time you had packed up, all the pretty girls were gone"), Lester disliked playing drums, but his father insisted. When he was seventeen, Lester rebelled against his father's plans to tour the Deep South, which he had learned to hate. He left the band without an instrument of his own, was taken under the wing of an obscure bandleader named Art Bronson, who bought him a baritone saxophone, and for the next six years barnstormed around the Mid- and Southwest. His associations included a brief stint with the declining King Oliver. ("He was a nice old fellow, a gay old fellow," Lester recalled years later. Oliver was all of forty-eight at the time; young Lester had no idea of his past importance.)

Musicians were beginning to talk about the

young saxophonist, and while he was playing in Count Basie's first band in Little Rock, Fletcher Henderson, who had heard and liked him in Kansas City, sent for him to take Coleman Hawkins's place. The Henderson musicians, used to Hawk's robust style, could not accept Lester's smooth, understated elegance, and he quit the band after three months, making sure Fletcher gave him his release so the music world would know he hadn't been fired.

In 1936 he rejoined Basie, this time at the Reno Club in Kansas City (sawdust on the floor, nickel beer, fifteen cents for a shot of whiskey), and left town with the band, making his recording debut in October with a small group including Basie, Jo Jones, and Walter Page—three fourths of what later became the greatest rhythm section in jazz. The records, in particular *Lady Be Good* and *Shoe Shine Swing*, featured Lester well and created a sensation among young musicians. (At twenty-seven, Lester made his record debut relatively late. He was ready.)

He stayed with Basie until December, 1940. In the interim he had made his famous series of records with Billie Holiday, who gave him the nickname "Pres" (short for President, in a day when

the holder of that office was a man the people looked up to). He countered with "Lady Day." Both names stuck. Lester also dubbed trumpeter Harry Edison "Sweets"—he had a way with words as well as with music.

Lester left Basie because the band, which earlier had served as such a perfect springboard for Lester's inspired flights, had begun to rely more and more on written arrangements rather than the loose "heads" (that is, memorized routines for section work) that characterized its initial style. Many of the men were poor or indifferent readers, and rehearsals dragged on and on. Lester had always been a quick student. "It was like school," he said. "I knew my lesson, but the other kids didn't, so I'd go to sleep. Then the teacher would tell my mother."

As a pretext for quitting, he refused to attend a rehearsal called for a Friday the thirteenth. He formed his own little band, soon teamed up with his drummer brother, then toured for the USO, and in December, 1943, rejoined Basie at the instigation of Jo Jones, remaining until September of the following year, when he was inducted into the army.

The next nine months were a nightmare for the sensitive and gentle musician. First, he underwent

Lester Young

**The Basie Band, 1941. Standing at
left: Count Basie. Seated at far right:
Lester Young. Others: Walter Page
(bass); Buddy Tate, Tab Smith, Jack
Washington (saxes); Jo Jones (drums);
Freddie Green (guitar); Vic Dickenson,
Dicky Wells, Dan Minor (trombones);
Buck Clayton, Ed Lewis, Harry Edison
(trumpets)**

minor surgery, and when he was returned to duty, a redneck officer, who had taken offense at what he thought was a photograph of a white woman in Lester's footlocker (it was a picture of his then wife, who, like Lester himself, was light-skinned), saw to it that he was court-martialed for possession of marijuana (Lester had naively answered a question about pot smoking in the affirmative on his induction questionnaire).

Lester was sentenced to a year's detention—the army term for jail. Fortunately, he was released for reasons of health (and also due to the efforts of friends on the outside) after serving only a few months, but the experience sufficed to turn an already introverted and shy man increasingly from the non-musical world toward refuge in alcohol and marijuana.

Nonetheless, he still had some of his greatest music in him. He now began a long association with Norman Granz, producer of Jazz at the Philharmonic. The Jazz at the Philharmonic tours sometimes teamed him with Coleman Hawkins, whom he once termed "the first president."

Lester's influence among young players had grown during the war years. His style was now so widely copied that he made a conscious effort to change it; the gradual decline of his health wrought other, less-calculated differences. To the end, however, Lester retained his mastery of time and phrasing and his wonderful sense of melody. And he never lost his sense of humor. (As a defense against boors and simpletons, he had long ago developed the habit of answering unwanted questions with such phrases as "bells" or "ding dong"; these also served as greetings for special friends. The boors thought he was daft and left him alone, which was exactly what he wanted.)

He died in his room at the Hotel Alvin, a comewhat-may establishment at the corner of Fifty-second Street and Broadway, overlooking the entrance to Birdland, at the time New York's leading jazz establishment. Death came within less than a day of his return from a two-month stay in Paris.

Zutty Singleton, the great New Orleans drummer, also lived at the Alvin, and he and Lester were good friends. At Lester's funeral, I was right behind Zutty in line to view the body. Zutty gazed at Lester for a long time, started to move on, then returned for another look.

"The last time I saw Lester alive," he explained later, "he looked so sad, and he told me, 'Zutty, I'm

Jo Jones and Milt Hinton

tired. I just want to rest.' Here he looked so peaceful, I just had to turn back once more. He found his rest now."

Lester was the prototypal hipster. He walked on crepe soles, gliding through life like a graceful sleepwalker. Porkpie hats became fashionable long after he had introduced them. His detached yet knowing attitude became a model for a generation of "cool" people.

Lester created a revolution in jazz long before any official revolt was announced. It was a quiet revolution, a profound change in sensibility, a new way of employing rhythmic and melodic freedom, a different approach to the production of sound. Lester soared over the crescendo of the Basie band in full cry with beautiful, logical, astonishing, and perfectly placed phrases. His playing was the essence of streamlining—a design concept which, perhaps not coincidentally, made its public appearance at the time of Lester's record debut.

Irony and understatement were relatively new to jazz when Lester first demonstrated them (the underrated trumpeter Frankie Newton [1906-1954] and the unique Pee Wee Russell [1906-1969] were among the few who had sometimes employed them). He could hear around corners. Among those who truly understood what he was about was a kid from Kansas City named Charlie Parker.

The only child of an itinerant sometime entertainer and railroad cook, who left his family when the boy was nine, and a hard-working, devoted mother, Charlie Parker was born in Kansas City, Kansas, in 1920 but soon moved to its bigger namesake across the river. He played baritone horn in his high-school band, but his mother didn't care for the cumbersome horn and got him an old alto saxophone. At first, he showed no great aptitude for music. At fourteen, he joined a school kids' band called the Deans of Swing, and bassist Gene Ramey remembers him as "the saddest thing in the band."

The story goes that it was humbled pride that led young Parker to become a serious musician. At an early age, he had begun to sneak out at night to frequent Kansas City's humming entertainment district. To make ends meet, his mother had taken an additional job cleaning Western Union offices in the late night and early morning hours; this made almost nightly absence from home easy and undetectable.

That a bright, inquisitive, and more than somewhat spoiled boy should be exposed to temptation in such an environment is not strange; that he should give in to seduction by evil elders is not strange. What is strange is that a boy well on the way to becoming a heroin addict at fifteen was able to go on to conquer the world with his music.

According to his own testimony, Charlie knew two (or rather, one and a half) tunes when he decided to sit in with the pros at a typical Kansas City jam session. The tunes were *Lazy River* and part of *Honeysuckle Rose.* But it was *Body and Soul,* one of the harmonically most complex of popular tunes, that was being played when Charlie courted disaster. "I was doing all right until I tried doing double tempo on *Body and Soul.* Everybody fell out laughing. I went home and cried and didn't play again for three months," he recalled.

A bit later on, the intrepid but not much improved altoist joined a bunch of Basie bandsmen at a session. When he started to play, drummer Jo Jones, a tough critic, sailed his big cymbal all the way across the dance floor. It landed with a crash that chased the boy out. But this time he didn't cry. He took a job with a band playing at an Ozark Mountains resort, carrying with him the few then available records by Lester Young and a plentiful supply of saxophone reeds. When he returned from the mountaintop three months later, he was a musician. He had also become a father, having married a somewhat older girl the year before. He was all of seventeen.

After playing with some of the most interesting older musicians remaining in Kansas City, altoist Buster ("Prof") Smith, one of his strongest influences, and tenorist Tommy Douglas, a fine technician, Parker joined what was to become the best Kansas City band since Basie. It was a young band, led by pianist Jay McShann, who combined Basie and southwestern blues, as Basie had added blues spice to his Harlem stride and Hines roots. McShann's mates in the rhythm section included two players who would go on to make names for themselves, drummer Gus Johnson and bassist Gene Ramey, who became like an older brother to Parker (and eventually, in the late forties, like a father—he was appointed Parker's legal guardian, a service which, incidentally, he also performed for Lester Young).

By late 1940, the band was recording, first for a Wichita radio station (the transcriptions miraculously survived, were recovered almost twenty years later, and eventually were issued on commercial recordings in 1974), then for Decca Records, at that time the major company most interested in contemporary black sounds. The band's singer, Walter Brown, made a hit with the public. This, of course, was a break; on the other hand, it boxed the band into a recording situation that did not allow it to use its best material. There are only four instrumentals among the eighteen sides recorded by McShann during Parker's tenure, which lasted until 1942.

The band had played New York by then, making quite an impression at the Savoy and being heard on the air by musicians who were astonished at the alto soloist featured on *Cherokee,* a tune with demanding chord changes played at a then unheard-of tempo. If they were working nearby, they made it their business to check the band out in person.

The soloist was Charlie Parker, and he already had a unique style. He had absorbed some of Lester Young's key lessons and added to them his own quite different, much more vehement temperament. His control over his instrument was as surprising to his contemporaries as Louis Armstrong's flights had been some fifteen years before. It took Parker's way longer to seep into the marrow of all jazz than it had taken Louis's. Times were different; so was the message. But the two had one thing in common: their way of singing the music affected all players and singers on all instruments, and only they accomplished that.

Revolutions aren't made by one man, nor do they originate in one place. It has been said and often written that the music to be given the strange name of bebop, later simplified to just bop, was born in Harlem in the years 1941-42, at some specific places, primarily one called Minton's Playhouse (still in existence), where special jam sessions were going on.

Revolutions, in retrospect, can be seen as evolutionary processes, albeit accelerated. Bop, which once fell so oddly, even abrasively on the ear unaccustomed to its speech, is now heard as a natural, logical outgrowth of mature swing, traceable to simultaneous stirrings and discoveries in places throughout the land of jazz. Yet the Minton's myth remains, and there is something to it.

By the early forties, New York had become the jazz capital. It had always been the place to make one's mark for good, or to fail, even when New Orleans or Chicago or Kansas City was the place for

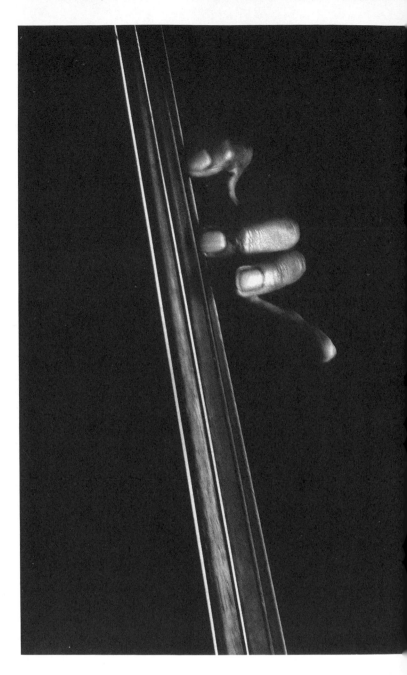

creative activity. Now it was both a testing ground and a proving ground. There was also a war going on, a war that would have as deep an impact on the future of jazz as it did on all things human.

The regularly employed musicians at Minton's were an oddly assorted lot, but they had in common an adventurous spirit and a venue that made it possible, even desirable, to indulge in experimentation. The place was owned by a former musician and official of the musicians' union and managed by a former bandleader, Teddy Hill, who was sympathetic to jazz and its makers. The house band consisted of Joe Guy, a trumpeter who emulated Roy Eldridge—then the model for almost all young trumpeters—and was an inveterate "jammer"; Thelonious Monk, a pianist of already very personal cast, musically and behavioristically (of whom more in our chapter on Modern Masters); Nick Fenton, a reliable, tireless bassist; and Kenny Clarke, the senior member of the group, born in 1914 and a veteran of several swing bands of note, including Teddy Hill's. (He had been fired by Hill for his unexpected placement of bass drum accents, a bebop practice that became known as "dropping bombs" and was introduced by Clarke. Hill had to play for the dancing public; he had no aesthetic objections to Clarke's way. Nor did the pioneer Sidney Bechet, with whom Clarke had worked and recorded.)

On the bandstand stood a beat-up amplifier of the primitive type then in existence. It was a fixture, always at the ready for its owner to plug his guitar into when he was able to drop in, between or after jobs with Benny Goodman. The owner of the guitar and amplifier was the man who for all practical purposes had joined the two. Charlie Christian was born in Texas in 1916. He was playing with an obscure group in Oklahoma City when John Hammond dropped in at the recommendation of several musicians of proven taste. He heard a spectacular and wholly original player, a totally new voice, in terms of both sound and conception, a guitarist who phrased and swung somewhat like a tenor sax—the tenor sax of Lester Young.

Steeped in the blues, Charlie Christian was a fountainhead of awed inspiration, first of all to guitarists, whom he either scared or seduced (some abandoned well-established styles to follow his way), then to players of all sorts of horns. Horns because his was a single-line conception, like that of an instrument able to play only one note at a time.

To be sure, he was an exceptional rhythm guitarist, who could strum chords with the best of them. But when he soloed, he used chords only to punctuate or amplify a single-note line thought.

And he had terrific swing. Hammond, with the help of a tenorman in the band who had jammed with Christian (his name is Jerry Jerome), smuggled Charlie's amplifier onto the bandstand at the Los Angeles ballroom where Benny Goodman was appearing. He knew that Benny would probably say "no" if asked to let a totally unknown young man sit in on a strange instrument during a public performance and wanted to present him with an accomplished fact.

It worked. Benny, appearing after intermission to perform with his small group (including Lionel Hampton and Fletcher Henderson), spotted the guitarist and the odd contraption too late to have them removed without a public scene. Biting the bullet, he beat off *Rose Room*, a tune singularly well suited for extended improvisation. Eventually, he gave Charlie his chance. What he heard transfixed him, and Charlie got the green light for chorus after chorus. Then, carried away, Benny embarked on a lengthy excursion himself. That *Rose Room*, they say, lasted twenty-five minutes—nothing big today, when jazz players habitually "stretch out," but unheard of in 1939 at a public performance, where a little over three minutes was the rule and a bit more than five the general limit.

Benny hired Charlie Christian on the spot and made him part of his sextet. Both in its original incarnation, with Hampton and Charlie making it the first group in which electronically amplified instruments were prominent, and later on, when Ellington trumpet star Cootie Williams and the jumping tenorman Georgie Auld gave it a three-horn front line and Count Basie often sat in on record dates, it was the best small group Goodman ever had.

Playing with Benny made Charlie famous, and he was making more money than he had thought possible before joining, but the urge to stretch out was there. At Minton's, he could indulge it. His presence in the rhythm section was inspirational, and his solo flights affected all within hearing range. Charlie Christian became a founding father of bebop long before it was so named.

By the time the new music was making its public debut, Charlie Christian had been dead for almost three years. A victim of tuberculosis (that is to say, of poor nutrition as a child and other environmental factors), he died at Seaview Sanitarium on Staten Island on March 2, 1942, not yet twenty-five. In 1976, young guitarists were still discovering Charlie Christian with delighted surprise.

Among those who regularly visited Minton's were Roy Eldridge, Hot Lips Page, and a young trumpeter with Cab Calloway's big band, Dizzy Gillespie. (Dizzy's full story is told in the Modern Masters chapter.) Initially inspired by Roy, Dizzy was on his way toward his own style and fascinated by the possibilities of altered chords. This was precisely what had led Charlie Parker to the discovery of his own way of playing, so when the two met, sparks flew.

Charlie seldom played at Minton's, preferring another Harlem establishment, Monroe's Uptown House, where the surroundings were less spartan. Besides, he had a job there, appearing in the nightly floor show, doing his McShann specialty, *Cherokee*. Here the great Ben Webster, Duke Ellington's tenor sax star, heard him and spread the word about a young musician who might well change the way the saxophone was played.

So, while Kenny Clarke was amending the role of the drums in jazz from pure timekeeping to irregular accenting (jazz drummers had long ago begun to make polyrhythmic comments, but they always maintained a regular pulse underneath; with Clarke and his followers, that pulse can become implicit), Dizzy and Charlie were at work on altering the chordal structure, with Monk supplying the proper accompaniment, both rhythmically and harmonically, and Charlie Christian supplying ideas and fire.

It has been written that they, and others who sympathized but couldn't always keep up, devised these departures from jazz convention to discourage less-sophisticated players from sitting in and cluttering up the proceedings, and even that they were working on changing jazz so that white musicians would no longer be able to compete with blacks, but both theories are far-fetched. There were less involved ways of dealing with unwanted visitors to the bandstand. As for the racial angle, white players, if good enough, were welcome at Minton's and elsewhere in Harlem. In those days, jazz was still by and large a fraternity in which the enemy was not a race but a state of mind—the "square" mentality.

When Dizzy and "Bird," as Parker was beginning to be known (the genesis of that nickname may be found in the Modern Masters chapter), left the Harlem session life to join Earl Hines's big band (Parker on tenor sax because that was the only open spot), bebop was still an unborn idea. In the Hines band, there wasn't much new music to play, though Dizzy contributed an exotic composition, *A Night in Tunisia*, that became a bop classic. But between stage shows or dance sets, Dizzy and Bird assiduously practiced complex exercises from music books used by classical virtuosos, running them down in unison at breakneck tempos.

When Hines's singer, Billy Eckstine, who had left to go out on his own, decided to form a big band, he invited Dizzy and Bird to join. Both accepted, and though neither lasted long in what became the first big band of bebop, they put their stamp on it. A host of stars-to-be passed through the Eckstine ranks in a few years, absorbing the tradition of the masters. Because of Eckstine's great popularity, his band could get away with playing music above the public's head, but eventually the price of keeping a big band together became too steep, and the singer, who genuinely loved jazz, had to disband.

Parker had no use for big bands; he had never cared to play in them. Dizzy, on the other hand, was a big-band fan and throughout his long career has put such groups together whenever the opportunity arose. Now, in early 1945, Dizzy and Bird were together in a small band, playing on Fifty-second Street, Swing Street, the heart of New York's jazz scene.

For a scant two city blocks, West Fifty-second Street was a beehive of musical activity. It had begun with good piano players in a speakeasy frequented by musicians and continued after repeal with a madcap group, the Spirits of Rhythm, featuring the legendary scat singer Leo Watson. Then it branched out. By 1942, almost every doorway in the block between Fifth and Sixth avenues led to music, most of it good, and quite a few notable clubs could be found further west, across Sixth.

The Street, as it was known among aficionados, was hospitable to bands of every size and description, provided they could play. There was traditional jazz at Jimmy Ryan's—some of the Chicagoans, or Sidney Bechet—but at the Sunday afternoon jam sessions, Dizzy Gillespie might be among the participants. Count Basie's big band squeezed into the Famous Door to show New Yorkers what it had been unable to show at Roseland. Billie Holiday held forth at Kelly's Stables, opposite Coleman Hawkins's band. Stuff Smith, the mad fiddler, was at the Onyx Club. Art Tatum made fantastic music at the Three Deuces amid the chatter and clatter. Musicians from every good band in town converged on the Street after their jobs were over (hotel bands quit at one A.M., the Street ran until four). And then there was always after-hours in Harlem, if you weren't tired.

Dizzy had played the Street before; he could adapt to any musical situation and had subbed in John Kirby's tight little sextet and jobbed with clarinetist Joe Marsala from Chicago, a Jimmie Noone disciple. Bird was not a known quantity, but it didn't take long. Sure, the jazz Dizzy and Bird played together was new and startling, but they were never treated as foreigners. In fact, Bird appeared on several conventional record dates; on one, he and tenorist Dexter Gordon, an Eckstine alumnus, teamed with Buck Clayton and New Orleans guitarist Danny Barker. The music came out good.

But there *was* something radically different about bop: it was the first jazz style designed for listening, with no thought for dancers (not to say that some people, especially "uptown," didn't try to and like to dance to bop), and it was the first jazz style to present itself without the customary amenities extended to the public. I don't mean that the early boppers did what later became standard practice in terms of bandstand manners. They *did* announce the tunes and introduce the members of the group, and Dizzy was an excellent showman and entertaining master of ceremonies. Even Bird made announcements; the idea of the bop pioneers as surly rebels insulting their audiences is poppycock, though it is regularly spouted by both friends and enemies of the music.

The absent amenities were in terms of the music itself. It made no concessions, no compromises. It was, for the first time, other than at jam sessions, music presented to the public as it would have been presented to fellow musicians. Those who put it down as "musicians' music" were on the right track, if for wrong reasons.

Most bop repertoire consisted of originals, pieces composed by members of the band and not yet in common currency. Almost all of these originals were based on well-known popular tunes, made unrecognizable to the untrained ear (and that included the ears of many uninitiated musicians) by

new melodic lines based on the underlying chord structure of the tune rather than on variations on its melody. The solos thus became variations on variations. Much of the music was also based on the blues, but this too was transformed by means of altered chords, though once the improvisation began, the blues structure usually revealed itself.

It wasn't bop's fault that it emerged at a time when big bands were declining, for various social and economic reasons. Nevertheless, by 1947, musicians and writers hostile to what now had unquestionably become the jazz of the day, even to the point of seeping into the music of such established bands as Benny Goodman's, roundly condemned it and blamed it for "ruining the business." On the other hand, bop musicians often felt that such hostility to their music, rather than the decline of the market in general, was responsible for their not being able to find enough work.

The natural tension and suspicion between the established and the new was thus heightened by outside factors. In addition, many older musicians had returned from military service to find their jobs taken by youngsters who had moved up swiftly in the ranks of the best-paid bands while they had been away. And a peculiar thing had happened in the jazz world. As the future began to assert itself, not always politely, the past was being rediscovered. For most of its life, jazz had been taken for granted. It was a phenomenon—like that other young art, the film—that existed for a practical purpose. It had a social function; its behavior was dictated by the needs of the musicians on the one hand, by their desires on the other, with the former by far the dominant factor.

From the very early days on, the music had been evaluated in print. There were reviews of bands in *Variety* and its counterparts, in daily papers, and in the Negro press. By the mid-twenties, commentators on popular culture, mostly with appalling ignorance of its true nature, pontificated about jazz—though what they understood by that term must be accepted with the same compassion we have applied to Paul Whiteman's kingly title.

As we have seen, some literate musicians had an inkling of the potential of jazz—for example, Ernest Ansermet's Bechet appraisal. But such insight was rare indeed. The jazz musicians themselves, of course, seldom had any abstract notions about what they were doing; the doing of it was sufficient, and the music had no history as yet.

By the end of the twenties, the first interest in jazz among intellectuals began to manifest itself in France, England, and even America. Reviews of records and performances in English music papers of that time were more literate than in their American counterparts, though English reviewers were almost entirely unaware of the importance of black musicians, who were approached, if at all, as exotic and/or barbaric. The French were more sensitive to the black contribution, but at first not much more. It must be remembered, however, that little black jazz was available in Europe until the end of the decade.

Of course, there were also European attempts at playing jazz. In the twenties, these were mainly confined to imitations, sometimes quite good, of the Bix-Trumbauer-Red Nichols school. A bit later, Armstrong became a strong influence, and in the mid- and late thirties, the presence in Europe of Coleman Hawkins and Benny Carter made itself strongly felt on the work of local players.

But there was one European musician who was truly original and even influenced American practitioners. This was Django Reinhardt, a Belgian-born gypsy who played guitar and banjo from the age of twelve and was already a professional six years later, in 1928, when he was severely injured in a fire. His left hand was so badly burned that doctors recommended amputation, but Django refused, and after long, hard work he was able to regain the use of three fingers. This handicap turned out to be a blessing, for he developed a unique way of fretting and was even able to play octaves on the guitar, long before Wes Montgomery.

In 1934, Django began to make records that showed his mettle, with a group known as the Quintet du Hot Club de France—the first jazz string ensemble, consisting of two guitars in addition to Django's, a violin, and string bass. The group's music had a charm all its own, and its gifted violinist, Stephane Grappelli, was still reflecting it in

Django Reinhardt and Le Quintet du Hot Club de France, 1939. Left to right: Stephane Grappelli, Eugene Vees, Roger Grasset, Django, Joseph Reinhardt

Courtesy of Max Jones

his work of the seventies. But there was only one Django. He died in 1953.

In America, the first known intellectual stirrings concerning jazz took place at the Ivy League colleges. Such young men as Squirrel Ashcraft and Bill Priestley, who played piano and cornet respectively, adored Bix and wondered about his significance in the general scheme of things. A young dancer named Roger Pryor Dodge was fascinated by the playing of Ellington trumpeter Bubber Miley, another doomed soul. And a young writer named Charles Edward Smith, who was to become the first important American jazz critic, corresponded in the very early thirties with Ashcraft concerning the relative merits of black and white jazz.

By the time Smith coedited *Jazzmen,* a book that was published in 1939, Wilder Hobson had brought out his pioneering study, *American Jazz Music* (also 1939), and the year before, Winthrop Sargeant's intriguing *Jazz: Hot and Hybrid* had appeared, all of them successors to the first books on jazz that were more than curios: Robert Goffin's *Aux Frontières du Jazz,* published in Brussels in 1932, and Hugues Panassié's *Le Jazz Hot,* published in Paris in 1934.

At first, all this activity had little effect on the music. But by the late thirties, some of the critics were supervising recording dates, among them a young Englishman named Leonard Feather, who settled permanently in the United States in 1939, Panassié, and Smith. *Jazzmen*'s most significant chapters dealt with the music and musicians of New Orleans, and its whole focus was on black New Orleans jazz as the parent style, the pure, commercially undiluted "real jazz." Panassié, though more contemporary in his orientation, had changed his mind about a lot of things since his first book was published. His second, *Le Vrai Jazz* (1942), already implied a harder line in its title and unequivocally advocated the natural jazz superiority of black musicians.

As Smith and his co-workers began to listen to and search for old jazz and blues records, and as they went to New Orleans and elsewhere to seek out and interview older musicians, they hit upon the not so far-fetched idea that this almost vanished music (even in New Orleans older musicians in 1938 were trying to play swing and Louis Armstrong) could be re-created for recording purposes. Heywood Hale Broun went to New Orleans and recorded the oldest musicians still playing, some of them men who had worked with the legendary Buddy Bolden. He issued the music on his own small label, Delta.

Meanwhile, the son of the Turkish ambassador to the United States had located Jelly Roll Morton in Washington and brought him to a studio to make his first commercial records in eight years. (The young Turk's name was Nesuhi Ertegun, and he and his brother Ahmet eventually founded Atlantic Records, at first a modest jazz label, which branched out into rhythm-and-blues with Ray Charles and other hit makers. The multi-million-dollar operation was bought by Warner Communications, one of the by then ubiquitous conglomerates, in the late sixties.)

Smith brought Morton to New York for more records, still for a small label, then persuaded Victor, the biggest of them all, to give their erstwhile artist another chance. And Panassié was invited by the same company to record whomever he liked at three New York dates. The results were the first deliberate efforts to re-create older jazz styles, involving Bechet, Mezz Mezzrow, and Tommy Ladnier.

In 1939 as well, the legendary Bunk Johnson (1879-1949), a New Orleans trumpeter from the old days, who played in Bolden's last band and retired from music in 1931, was located with the help of Louis Armstrong in New Iberia, Louisiana, working in the fields and teaching music for the WPA. A trumpet was donated by Louis, lengthy correspondence ensued, and in June, 1942, Bunk made his first records, in New Orleans. He was sixty-two years old, and all the jazz world thought it fabulous that so old a man could still play the trumpet at all—not to say so surprisingly well. Thirty years later no one thought twice about Louis Armstrong still playing at seventy.

Thus the New Orleans revival began. Kid Ory was discovered running a chicken farm in Los Angeles; by 1944, he, Jimmie Noone, and other New Orleans veterans were broadcasting regularly on Orson Welles's radio show, Welles having become a New Orleans fan.

And while all this was happening, and plans were being made to bring Bunk to New York (he had already played in San Francisco and proven himself to be not a gentle, lovable old father figure, but a fiercely proud, complex, egocentric, and mulishly stubborn man), the musicians' union promulgated a recording ban that lasted from August 1, 1942, until the fall of 1943. Then Decca Records signed, opening the gates for an unprecedented number of small, independent labels that sprang up before the giants, Columbia and Victor, decided to give in almost a year later.

Thus, a crucial period of jazz development is largely undocumented by commercial recordings (in subsequent years, lots of material recorded for transcriptions, taken off the air, or recorded surreptitiously at concerts, sessions, and clubs has seen the light of day, but it didn't materialize until many years after the fact), creating an additional communications gap inimical to the new jazz.

By 1945, Bunk was playing in New York with unprecedented attention from the press (he made "colorful copy" and the revivalists proved adept at press-agentry) while Dizzy and Bird held forth on Fifty-second Street. The battle lines were drawn, not between the musicians, who by and large believed in live and let live, and still adhered to the old convention of not speaking ill of one's colleagues for publication, but between the new breed of jazz scribes.

And so the artificial and, in retrospect, ridiculous holy war between boppers and "moldy figs" (as the traditionalists soon were labeled) commenced. In the arguments between archaic and futuristic music the present was forgotten, and such still-in-their-prime players as Roy Eldridge, Art Tatum, Coleman Hawkins, and many others hardly seemed to exist as far as the verbal battle was concerned.

Young white musicians appeared, here and abroad (particularly in France), who strove to copy the music of King Oliver, Johnny Dodds, Morton, and others. (Nobody tried to copy Bunk Johnson, who had the remnants of a good tone, but to all but the most fanatic retrogressionists seemed limited from the standpoint of inventiveness.) Most of them took on amateur status or disappeared from the music after the revival had peaked, but a few excellent professionals did emerge from this unusual start—the first jazzmen directly inspired by the historical past. (Bob Wilber, who studied with Sidney Bechet, and the pianist Dick Wellstood are outstanding examples.)

Few black musicians, aside from those in Bunk's New Orleans orbit, participated in the traditional revival. But there was one outstanding exception: the trombonist and bandleader Wilbur De Paris.

Born in 1900, De Paris was working in his father's carnival band at the age of seven. Later, he toured the famous (and notorious) TOBA circuit of black tent and theater shows in the South; the ini-

tials stood for Theater Owners Booking Association but were interpreted by performers as "Tough on Black Asses." For more than twenty years, De Paris was a solid section trombonist with a succession of big bands, including Louis Armstrong's and Duke Ellington's, seldom taking a solo. But in 1948, he formed his New New Orleans Band, featuring his gifted younger brother Sidney on trumpet, and developed a repertoire of pieces by Morton, Oliver, and other early masters, plus pieces of his own in the classic idiom.

The band was in residence at Jimmy Ryan's on Fifty-second Street from 1951 until early 1962. It toured Africa in 1957 for the State Department and continued to work steadily until Sidney's death in 1967. Wilbur ran a rehearsal studio in New York and put bands together for special occasions until his death in 1973. He was a gentleman of the old school, a serious student of jazz history, and a leader who knew just what he wanted from his musicians. His music was a hybrid, but one of the few viable results of the traditional revival; another was the band of clarinetist George Lewis, who became known as a Bunk Johnson sideman and acquired a devoted following after Bunk's final retirement.

Eventually, the shrillness of the traditonal versus modern arguments subsided. In 1950, Charlie Parker recorded standard popular tunes with a string section and toured with Jazz at the Philharmonic (as indeed he had in 1946, after his break with Dizzy in California). Bunk had gone back home, suffering a stroke in late 1948 and dying in July, 1949. He made his last recordings in New York in December, 1947, the first and only ones without supervision by revivalist critics or boosters. He picked mostly Swing Era musicians (he referred to the New Orleanians handpicked for his official bands as "emergency musicians") and chose a repertoire in part consisting of tunes from *The Redback Book of Rags* (to be played as written, he pointed out), and, in another form of heresy (New Orleans jazz, to be genuine, must be collectively improvised, the doctrine goes), pieces like *Out of Nowhere, Some of These Days,* and even *Marie Elena*—in other words, products of the despised Tin Pan Alley commercial song mill, of which good old and true New Orleans jazz was supposed to be the antithesis.

The Bunk episode had tragic overtones: Bunk went home a broken old man; one of his discoverers and staunchest boosters committed suicide, in part

Sidney G. Paris Family Band, 1916.
Top left: Wilbur De Paris. Lower right: Wilbur's brother Sidney

Sidney G. Paris' Family Band, a Feature with Roy Gray's Amusement Co., Season 1916.

Wilbur De Paris

because of Bunk's taunts. Yet it had contributed much of value: a body of music that would otherwise have gone undocumented and a wealth of historical material, much of it suspect but all of it revealing of the man and his times and the forces that made them.

Bunk and Charlie Parker never played together, but Parker and Sidney Bechet did, at the first major jazz festival held anywhere, in Paris in 1948. The two saxophonists respected each other, and one of Parker's later recordings with strings was *Summertime,* which he heard Bechet play in Paris. And Dizzy confounded California traditionalists by sitting in with a revival band at a benefit for an ailing New Orleans musician in Los Angeles. The critics chattered on, but the musicians sometimes listened to each other.

The younger boppers, unfortunately, were not inclined to hear the past. Disciples always being more dogmatic than their teachers, they were more affected by the journalistic exchanges. Beyond that, many of them adopted standoffish attitudes toward the public, stemming in part from inexperience in performing (this was the first jazz generation not to receive extensive big-band training before striking out on its own), partly from behavior patterns peculiar to drug addicts.

"Do what I say, don't do what I do," was Charlie Parker's despairing counsel to those who thought that by emulating his affliction they might apprehend his genius. Social factors as well as Charlie Parker's example caused the at one time frighteningly high percentage of addiction among musicians; there was, after all, an increase of hard drug use in the society in general. But there is no doubt that the Parker mystique played a major role.

Parker himself had a remarkable constitution. He was one of history's greatest consumers. He consumed everything in huge quantities: food, drink, drugs, pleasure. His exploits loom larger than life (even so, his purported biographer found it necessary to distort and invent, perhaps because the habits of pulp-fiction writing are hard to break), and no doubt some of the tales are just that.

But anyone who has had contact with Parker can testify to his enormous energy and his gargantuan appetites. In terms of drugs, he was able to withstand synergistic reactions with astonishing control. Alcohol, barbiturates, and heroin taken in succession did not immobilize him or greatly impair his motor functions. However, he did *not* play better when he was high; one can readily distinguish a stoned Parker from a relatively sober one, and there is no question which is superior.

Eventually, his level of consumption killed him when he was thirty-five. Some critical opinions to the contrary notwithstanding, he had showed no impairment in creative powers, only in physical strength. The circumstances under which he died—apparently of a heart attack, in a friend's hotel suite—brought about an autopsy. The medical examiner estimated Parker's age as about fifty-five.

Dizzy Gillespie never fell victim to the heroin habit. His disposition has always been sunny, and as the elder statesman of bop he sets an example of tolerance and understanding as well as of continued creativity. He still puts big bands together whenever he can, he still tells jokes, he still does his charmingly indecent little dances, and still plays the trumpet with more wit, imagination, and daring than any other practitioner of that demanding horn. In a sense, Dizzy is proof of the durability of bop, for though the music he played in 1976 was not stylistically locked into the bop tradition, it was nevertheless a direct continuation of its essentials.

Meanwhile, three of his most gifted disciples are gone. Fats Navarro (1923-1950) was the first, a victim of heroin and tuberculosis. Clifford Brown, greatly influenced by Navarro as well as by Dizzy, was senselessly killed in a car crash at just twenty-six, in 1956. Lee Morgan (1938-1972), Brownie's most promising heir, was shot in a nightclub.

Miles Davis, the first trumpeter after Dizzy's breakthrough who didn't try to copy him, celebrated his fiftieth birthday in 1976. As we point out in the Modern Masters chapter, Miles contributed not just one but a series of styles, from cool to electronic; he has refused to stand still, even at the calculated risk of abandoning something perfect for something rough and problematic.

Miles, of course, was once famous for turning his back on audiences. But he never did much of that; he just didn't believe in remaining on stage while someone else was playing, or in acknowledging applause. Or perhaps "believe in" isn't the right phrase; "had no patience with" might be closer to the mark. That his anti-show-business posture became a show in itself is no refutation of the integrity of his original impulse. When he saw how the public responded, he realized that he had found a performance personality that suited his character.

Miles was one of the most popular jazzmen of the mid-fifties, a period of renewed interest in the music among a sizable segment of the general population. Though the category-minded would classify this as the era of cool jazz and hard bop, there was in fact a wide variety of jazz being played and listened to. There were Ellington (whose career took a great upswing after his 1956 Newport Jazz Festival appearance), Monk, Dave Brubeck, and Erroll Garner (see the Modern Masters chapter). There was Stan Kenton, a dedicated, articulate, hard-working pianist-arranger-bandleader, and the only man to enter this tough field after 1940—the year he unveiled his first band in California—and survive into the seventies. His music, once self-proclaimed as "progressive jazz," despite its occasional bombast and pretense has served to introduce many to jazz, and has been of high musical quality as well as fine craftsmanship, especially when he led a band that included Lee Konitz and Zoot Sims. There was Gillespie (who in 1956 became the first jazz musician to tour for the U.S. State Department). And there was Louis Armstrong, who made new converts and conquered new lands for jazz in his fifth decade of professional performing.

At the end of the fifties, another new wave arose. This time the music was truly radical, not just seemingly so. Ornette Coleman (b. 1930) instinctively broke with the Western tonal tradition that had hitherto ruled jazz, and John Coltrane (1926-1967), a saxophonist who had come to the fore through his work with Miles Davis, broke with tonality in stages, through a process of deliberate searching for new modes of expression.

As had been the case since the arrival of bop (or to a more limited extent, since the placing of the holy grail in New Orleans), critics and journalists played a role in the development of the music first labeled "avant-garde," then "the new thing," and lastly and most fittingly, "free jazz." (Coleman was the first to hit upon this apt title and recorded an album with that name, but when a concert by his group was thus advertised in Cleveland, many of the people who turned up refused to pay for tickets, and the promoter had to cancel the event.)

Speaking of nomenclature—if we seem to have overlooked the once prominent "West Coast jazz," it is only because there was no such thing, except in the imagination of record producers and jazz writers. In spite of that, there were albums like "East versus West" and other such nonsense. It is true, however, that the main reaction to cool jazz, which is what most of the West Coast product was, arose in New York, where such hard bop phenomena as Art Blakey's Jazz Messengers and Horace Silver's groups were headquartered. On the other hand, the non-hard Modern Jazz Quartet was also a New York (that is, eastern) phenomenon, while the Clifford Brown-Max Roach Quintet, a prime representative of hard bop, was formed in California. Geography, once a significant factor in jazz, no longer played an important role in the age of instant communication.

As Coltrane's experiments became more radical, culminating in a "free" jam-session record called *Ascension,* the jazz audience once again seemed divided between those who embraced such abrasive music, some of which was a self-confessed expression of political anger and racial bitterness (though only a relatively small number of musicians deliberately so labeled their musical output), and those who rejected it, with very few neutrals in between.

Coltrane's sudden death in 1967 (he was forty and died of primary hepatoma—cancer of the liver) robbed the free-jazz movement of its spiritual leader and standard-bearer. Coltrane had established himself with the jazz public through his work with Miles Davis, and in his earliest days on his own, with the hit recording of *My Favorite Things,* a Rodgers and Hammerstein ditty from *The Sound of Music* which lent itself to Coltrane's modal tendencies and near-Eastern soprano saxophone sound. (It also served to establish the soprano as an equal among the saxes for the first time in jazz history; despite Bechet, it had always been a maverick.)

On the strength of such initial successes, and the uncommon cohesiveness of his famous quartet, with the remarkable Elvin Jones on drums and the gifted McCoy Tyner and Jimmy Garrison on piano and bass, Coltrane carried a comparatively large segment of the jazz audience with him into *terra incognita.* Once he was dead, it became more difficult to lead them on in that direction—which was toward increasingly ecstatic, incantatory, extended improvisation. But even Coltrane's followers had begun to balk at some of his final experiments, especially after he had let Jones and Tyner go in favor of lesser talents, including his pianist wife. At any rate, the free-jazz movement continued in many individual directions, some leading to dead ends, others to electronic music, still others back to simplicity and tonality.

Parenthetically, it must be noted that since bebop, jazz solos have become more and more extended in time. Again, this is a development related to technology. In the late forties, the long-playing record was introduced, and this made it possible for jazz musicians to stretch out on record. At first, longer performances were modest in duration, but eventually, entire sides of LP albums were devoted to single-minded musical excursions lasting twenty minutes or more.

A few musicians thrive under such freedom from temporal restrictions—Coltrane at his best was one, Sonny Rollins and Dexter Gordon, in a more traditional mold, are others. But the work of lesser lights often became redundant, and the absence of a steady rhythmic pulse or other firm guideposts only made listening more of a problem. There was, of course, a genuine influence from the musical traditions of the East, notably India, with their entirely different conception of time. But contemporary Western civilization doesn't yet offer most of its members that freedom from temporal restrictions that some may consider a blessing, and the prolonged perorations to which too many musicians were prone in the heyday of free jazz have happily subsided.

Instead, the lesson that total freedom is as (or more) restricting than rigid rules seems to have been learned. All sorts of music coexist in the house of jazz as the seventies pass midpoint, from rediscovered roots to excursions into space. Rock has made inroads, basically rhythmic but also in terms of sound, which for a while threatened to make jazz overwhelmingly electronic and amplified. But the beauties of acoustic piano are being rediscovered, and light ensemble textures are surfacing once again. And there is, as always, a host of gifted young players, if perhaps not as many strongly individualistic musical personalities as in the past.

Predictions are useless in the arts, and jazz—for better or worse—is an art. It has become conscious of being so, not necessarily an advantage but certainly a responsibility. This consciousness has been used as a cloak for the most transparently insincere concoctions, and it has misled many an honest journeyman of music into thinking bigger than his talent allows. But it has also led to the realization of ambitious ideas and projects unthinkable in the "good old days" of jazz as a socially functional music.

In all its astonishing diversity, the not yet century-old musical phenomenon called jazz shows no inclination to falter. The directions it has taken do not always lead straight ahead, and may not appeal to earlier generations of fans or players, but to a degree uncommon in our century, the music has resisted dehumanization. "Jazz is speaking from the heart. You don't lie," said Bunk Johnson. He learned that lesson at the dawn of jazz. That it still holds true is something the music can take pride in.

Part II:
The People

1

King Louis

Louis Armstrong was a phenomenon. His face, his smile, the sound of his voice, the tone of his trumpet were instantly recognizable throughout the world. To those familiar with Louis only as the genial entertainer of his late years, the claim that he is one of the few artists of our age who truly changed the world may seem odd. Yet it is indisputable. His genius transformed jazz from an interesting and even remarkable folk and dance music to an art form, a medium for individual expression. To this day, there is not a single important artist in jazz who has not learned from Louis—directly or indirectly, knowingly or unknowingly.

Jazz was not the only music changed by the advent of Armstrong. All American music—"serious" and "popular"—has been affected by him through and through. The way in which brass instruments are played and scored for, in symphony orchestras or rock bands, derives from his extension of their range and expansion of their expressive potential. The way our popular singers phrase—from Bing Crosby on—would be unthinkable without Louis. And the concept of swing, in which our popular music has been immersed for so long, was almost unknown before him.

In Louis Armstrong were combined the physical equipment almost ideal for playing the trumpet— that most demanding of all brass instruments—and a temperament almost perfect for withstanding the psychic strains and pressures of first making one's way to the top, then of staying there. And this rare, synergistic combination was leavened with the magic of genius. What he did and was is remarkable enough in and of itself, but when we consider that he was, among other things, a black man in a white-ruled world, he takes on an almost mythical dimension.

As befits a myth, Louis Daniel Armstrong was born on the first Fourth of July of the twentieth century, in New Orleans, a city with a unique disposition toward music-making. He was raised in circumstances poor even by the standards of that day for a black child, but he never looked back in anger. "I sure had a ball there growing up in New Orleans as a kid," he said some sixty years after the fact. "We were poor and everything like that, but music was all around you. Music kept you rolling." He meant it.

The family was unstable: his father soon vanished; his mother came and went, and with her a succession of "stepfathers." A grandmother was the only permanent point of reference. Louis got his music from the street and from church. He was bright in school, whenever he managed to get there. In his early teens, he formed a vocal quartet that sang in the street for pennies, and he did odd jobs: selling newspapers, pushing a coal cart—the merchandise picked from the railroad freightyard tracks and offered to the ladies of the evening to heat their "cribs." There was never a thought of spending any of his hard-earned money on himself, such as for the purchase of a musical instrument. Every penny was needed for the barest necessities.

On New Year's Eve of 1912, Louis found a pistol in a drawer at home; it had been left there by a "stepfather." Fortunately, it was loaded with blanks. He took it to the street, and on a dare, fired it. The noise was greater than he had anticipated, and after six shots he was arrested for disturbing the peace.

In January he was sentenced as a juvenile offender and sent to the Colored Waifs' Home. For once, it truly was for his own good—as the sentencing magistrate had claimed. The home was not a bad

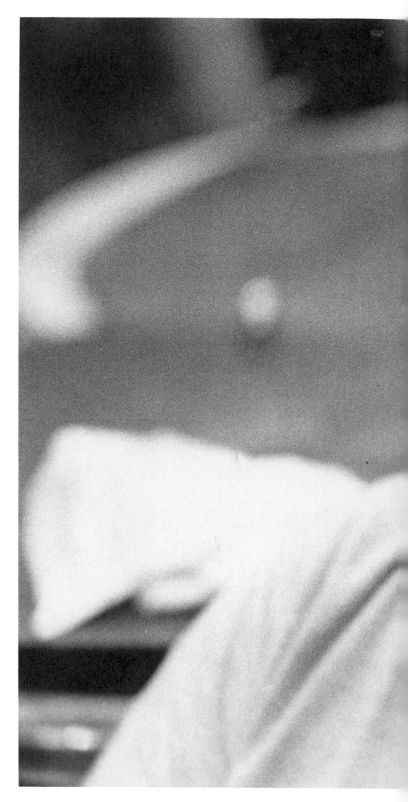

Louis Armstrong

place. Like every institution in New Orleans, it had its own band. Louis first played drums, then graduated to bugle, and under the special tutelage of band director Peter Davis learned the rudiments of music as well as the fundamentals of trumpet. He was discharged in June, 1914, and resumed the kind of work he had done before, collecting scrap iron, delivering milk, and as he grew stronger, unloading banana boats and doing other longshoreman's work on the levee.

But he listened to music often and well. Eventually, the great Joe ("King") Oliver took him under his wing, tutored him, played duets with him, and when he got good enough—which, consensus has it, was very soon—sent Louis out on jobs he could not fill himself. By 1917 he held steady playing jobs in and around the red-light district, learning what he didn't already know about the ways of the world. It was good training; in later years, nothing human could surprise him.

In 1918 he married Daisy Parker, a very jealous girl who sometimes threw bricks at him, but he knew well enough how to keep from "being hit" and stayed with her until 1922. In 1919 he took his tutor and idol's place in the best jazz band in town, trombonist Kid Ory's. He also began to work on the Mississippi excursion steamers, which had bands that required good reading ability. A mellophonist named David Jones helped him improve his skills, and for a couple of years, Louis worked regularly on the boats, sailing out of St. Louis as far north as Davenport, Iowa—where young Bix Beiderbecke heard him—and Minneapolis/St. Paul.

In the fall of 1921, he returned to New Orleans and worked in taverns and with the city's best marching bands. Then, in the summer, came a wire from Chicago that changed Louis's life—and the course of music. It was from King Oliver, and it asked Louis to join his band. Had it been anyone else, Louis said later, he might not have accepted. He had seen too many musicians leave home with money in their pockets and "have to hobo their way back. Wasn't nobody going to get me to leave New Orleans but King Oliver. His calling for me was the biggest feeling I ever had musically."

Whenever he was interviewed in later years—which could be almost daily on those exhausting tours of Europe, Asia, or wherever—he would refer to the moment of receiving that telegram as the happiest in his life. His mother—he had been supporting her and his sister as well as his wife and an

adopted child for some time—fixed him "a big trout sandwich" for the long train ride, made sure he had on his long underwear, and Louis was on his way.

On his last night in New Orleans, the bouncer at the tavern where he was working told Louis he liked his playing and wished him luck up North. And then he said: "Always keep a white man behind you that'll put his hand on you and say, 'That's my nigger!'" For the time and the place, it was sound advice.

Louis was overwhelmed by Chicago, by the hustle and bustle, the many people. There seemed to be no one there to meet him at the station, and he was almost ready to go right back when a redcap Oliver had left word with took him in tow and delivered him at the Lincoln Gardens. The band sounded so good to Louis that he again decided to go home, but Oliver spotted him and dragged him to the stand.

Oliver's band was already the awe of Chicago's aware musicians. When Louis joined, Oliver devised a way to keep them even more astonished. He knew that Louis had a natural harmonic gift which allowed him to invent the most perfect second part for any melodic lead line. So, instead of taking a solo "break"—two unaccompanied measures of his own invention—Oliver, while the rest of the band was playing, would lean over to Louis and move the valves of his cornet to the notes he had picked for the next break. Louis, knowing what was coming, would make up the second part, and the two confounded their listeners with what seemed to be musical telepathy.

There were many other things to learn from Oliver, and the fact that all but one of the members of the band were from New Orleans made the transition period easy. That one, the pianist, was from Memphis. Educated at Fisk University, pretty, vivacious, and Louis's senior by some two years, Lillian Hardin had been working with jazz bands for almost five years without considering it much more than a pleasant way of making a good living, "buying clothes and ice cream and whatever young girls do."

It was when Louis got an occasional chance to play in his own way—a way still very much influenced by Oliver, but with a much stronger tone (when the band made its first records, playing into the primitive horn setup of premicrophone days, Louis had to stand way behind Oliver so as not to unbalance the recorded sound) and a more spirited "swinging" beat—that she began to get an inkling of the real potential of the music. The fact that she had fallen in love with Louis helped.

Louis was still devoted to Oliver, the father figure, and had no thoughts of leaving him. To Lil, who had become the second Mrs. Armstrong in early 1924, it seemed obvious that the King was keeping "Little Louis" under wraps in order to neutralize a potential rival. Furthermore, she had discovered that Oliver was holding out money from the band. So in 1924, when Fletcher Henderson, leader of the most distinguished black dance orchestra in New York, offered Louis a job at a higher salary, she urged him to accept and he did.

Henderson's music was a far cry from the New Orleans collective of Oliver's Creole Jazz Band. It was arranged music, played by sections—brass, reeds, rhythm—and used for its material not the blues, rags, and stomps favored by Oliver, but Tin Pan Alley songs of the day, including tangos and waltzes. The Henderson band played at the Roseland Ballroom on Broadway, for white dancers only.

For Louis, this was a chance to better his musical skills. There had been no reading with Oliver and he was rusty; besides, the notation used on the riverboats had not been very sophisticated—mostly lead sheets to learn new songs from. Henderson's arrangements were among the most demanding in the field. When Louis joined, a rehearsal was in progress. A medley of Irish waltzes had been called. Henderson remembered: "There was a passage that began triple fortissimo and then it suddenly softened down on the next passage to double pianissimo. The score was properly marked 'PP', but when everybody else softened down, there was Louis, still blowing as hard as he could. I stopped the band and told him—pretty sharply, I guess—that in this band we read the marks as well as the notes. I asked him if he could read the marks, and he said he could. But then I asked him, 'What about PP?' and he answered, 'It means *pound plenty!*' " Everybody collapsed.

As for Louis himself, he recalled that when a fight broke out between the trombonist and the tuba player and the curses began to fly, he knew he wasn't so far from home after all.

Louis's impact on the Henderson band and on all of New York dance music was tremendous. One can divide the band's recorded output into pre- and post-Armstrong. The former is of only limited interest; the latter shows that Louis's rhythmic, melodic, and harmonic superiority first stood out like a red dot in a white field, then gradually began to transmit itself to the sensibilities of the best of the other players and eventually to the arrangements themselves, permeating the whole style and approach of the band.

Trumpet (or cornet) players may have reacted to Louis more strongly than other musicians, yet Rex Stewart's response was not untypical: "I went mad with the rest of the town. I tried to walk like him, talk like him, eat like him, sleep like him. I even bought a pair of big policemen's shoes like he used to wear [a New Orleans sartorial touch Chicago had not erased] and stood outside his apartment waiting for him to come out so I could look at him. Finally, I got to shake hands and talk with him."

Louis stayed with the band fourteen months. When asked why he quit, he would say that he had become homesick for Chicago and his wife. A plausible enough reason, but not the only one by any means. The Henderson band had a half-dozen soloists, and Louis had to be content with his share, though he was clearly the best. That was okay; he was prepared to be one of the boys. But he also liked to sing, and Henderson rarely gave him the chance. Roseland had a weekly talent contest night, and when the customers proved shy, the boys in the band would sometimes do specialty numbers. On one occasion, Louis sang and brought the house down. Henderson still did not respond; only on one of the many records he made with the band does Louis sing, and then only a few bars of "scat"—that imitation, or rather, intimation, of instrumental sounds and phrasing that he would soon perfect and popularize.

One of the last times I saw Louis, who was always loathe to say negative things, a mutual friend asked him about the Henderson days. For once, Louis didn't hold back. He said that Henderson, a college-educated, light-skinned Negro, had never really accepted him for what he was and could do. Louis didn't mind sharing trumpet solos with Howard Scott, who could play, but he resented having no more solo space than a Henderson favorite, Elmer Chambers, with his "nanny goat sound" and jerky ragtime rhythm (and here Louis gave a devastating vocal imitation of Chambers's corny phrasing), who also played most of the lead trumpet parts. And Henderson wouldn't let him sing, though the public loved it, because, deep down, Louis's gravel

Marable's Capitol Revue (aboard S.S. Capitol, c. 1920). Left to right: Hy Kimball, Boyd Atkins, Fate Marable (best-known bandmaster on the Mississippi), Johnny St. Cyr, David Jones, Norman Mason, Louis Armstrong, Norman Brashear, Baby Dodds

voice embarrassed him, though he did let Louis do a Bert Williams imitation. Henderson was too "dicty," too high-toned to let Louis reveal his full talent, and Louis apparently never forgave him, though he sent a huge floral arrangement—in the shape of an organ, pipes and all—to Henderson's funeral, and, for the record, had always spoken well, if not very warmly, of the man.

Louis also left the band because he didn't like the lax discipline and widespread drinking. Louis was no martinet or prude—anything but—but he approached his work with a thoroughly serious professional attitude. Though he came from the South's most catholic and permissive city, he was imbued with the Protestant work ethic—in this as in many other ways he was a typical American.

Henderson's reaction to Louis's singing brings up an important point. Long before "black is beautiful" became a slogan, Louis was aware of its truth. He took pride in being what he called "pureblooded" black, and believed that his ancestors had come from the Gold Coast. When he visited Africa, he managed to find reminders of his family there, much to his satisfaction.

All his life he never put on airs. Though he became a millionaire, he saw no need to move from the comfortable, modest home he had bought in Queens in 1942 at the time of his fourth and happiest marriage. He loved his fans and never gave a concert or made an appearance anywhere without patiently signing autographs and exchanging pleasantries with his admirers. If a producer or club owner tried to prevent the fans from gaining access to him, Louis became angry. He was as gracious to the humblest among them as to the Prince of Wales.

There were some who confused this kindness— the ultimate in good manners, and Louis was one of nature's noblemen—with servility, and these people also found it hard to accept his natural physical features and behavioral traits for what they were. His marvelous teeth, the subject of admiring articles in dentistry journals and one of the tools that made possible his playing strength, made some people uncomfortable when flashed in that famous grin. His gravelly voice, part nature's gift, part the result of years of singing, hard trumpet breathing, and smoking, seemed exaggerated to them, just as his mirth-laden "mugging"—so similar to West African facial and bodily expressions—seemed to them proof that Louis Armstrong was an "Uncle Tom."

This false perspective was reinforced by aspects of Louis's behavior that were rooted in his early upbringing. He was polite to his elders—black or white—yet if he addressed a white man as "mister," this was proof of Tomming. He was not a political activist; few black performers of his generation were. Yet he was suspected of being a conservative. But he supported many good causes, not with empty words, but with hard cash. He just did not believe in mixing ideology with his music, which he considered "my living and my life," a means to make people happy—no more, no less. "I just play," he would say.

When he did speak out on an issue, it was tremendously effective. It happened when he took Eisenhower to task for his refusal to support desegregation efforts in Little Rock. He said that Ike "had no guts" and added that "the government can go to hell." During his extensive international tours of 1955 and 1956, he had been received with such intense admiration and love that the *New York Times* had claimed "America's secret weapon [to be] a blue note in a minor key" and "its most effective ambassador . . . Louis (Satchmo) Armstrong," while Edward R. Murrow devoted an hour-long documentary to the man he called "Satchmo the Great." This made his words count. He backed them up by expressing reservations about a scheduled State Department tour of Russia: "The people over there will ask me what's wrong with my country. What am I supposed to say?" (Unfortunately, the chance to go to Russia never arose again. It was one of the few spots on earth he didn't visit. But in 1975, four years after his death, the New York Jazz Repertory Orchestra toured the Soviet Union for the State Department with a program of Armstrong's music in which some of his most famous recorded solos were transcribed for three trumpets. No single horn could do them justice.)

Such public outbursts were rare, but in 1956, when Louis, on tour in Denmark, watched the television coverage of the march on Selma, there was another. "They would beat Jesus if he was black and marched," he told an interviewer. Again he made headlines all over the world. No other spokesman for black Americans was as effective until the advent of Martin Luther King.

His detractors—and even they were usually apologetic when offering their barbs—probably didn't know that Louis Armstrong was the first black artist to have a sponsored commercial radio show (in 1936, for Fleischmann's Yeast); the first black performer to make his own introductions on the air (in New Orleans, in 1931, because a bigoted announcer refused to present him); and the first black jazz musician to have featured speaking roles in Hollywood films. In addition, he was responsible for an incalculable number of human break-throughs. Getting the Armstrong message was soul-opening.

Blacks and whites fearful of Louis Armstrong's essential negritude should have been shaken into recognition by the enthusiastic reception he received in Africa. Unlike many other black American artists, he had no communications problem there. His music and manner were instantly understood and relished, if not entirely, then certainly essentially. Louis Armstrong knew who and what he was far better than those who criticized him, and they were a pitiful minority. Thousands cheered him wherever he went.

Louis was stubborn and even a little perverse in his refusal to change a single line in his theme song, *Sleepy Time Down South*, written for him in 1931 by a team of black songwriters (including the famous actor Clarence Muse). After all, Paul Robeson had recorded this song. The only adjustment Louis made in over forty years was changing "darkies" to "folks." All the other antebellum South clichés stayed in, to the chagrin of even some loyal fans. Yet he refused for years to play in New Orleans because he had been prevented from performing for thousands of black fans during a visit there in 1931—marring an otherwise triumphant homecoming, complete with a parade through the streets and a cigar and a baseball team named after him. You had to take Louis as he was—whole.

We have gotten away from our story. Louis returned to Chicago to find that his wife had gotten him a job at the unheard-of pay of seventy-five dollars a week (Henderson had paid him fifty), and his name outside the club in big letters. He thought it a bit ostentatious, but what he hadn't reckoned with was the impact of his records, both with Henderson and others, notably Bessie Smith, the world's greatest blues singer, and Sidney Bechet, the New Orleans soprano saxophonist who was his only peer as an instrumentalist.

Soon, he was so much in demand that he could hold two jobs. One was playing for silent films with the prestigious Erskine Tate Orchestra at the Vendome Theater, where the stage show included semiclassical features like the intermezzo from *Cavalleria Rusticana* and the overture to *Poet and Peasant* as well as jazz specialties (Louis had heard "classical" music in New Orleans; playing it further broadened his horizons). The other was at the Sunset Café, where the manager was a crabby, shrewd man named Joe Glaser. His parents had wanted him to study medicine, but his love for the sport of kings had gotten him involved with the underworld. Glaser had an ear for jazz and blues and an eye for black talent.

Louis had begun to make records under his own name in 1925, with a studio group made up of friends from the Oliver band and wife Lil as musical organizer. The Hot Five discs became the rage among musicians, being the first recordings to give Louis a chance to do his stuff relatively unimpeded. As in the case of the Original Dixieland Jass Band eight years before, the medium of the phonograph spread the message. Musicians now could play and replay Louis's great solos, study them, and learn them by heart. A musical revolution was taking place.

Wingy Manone, a New Orleans trumpeter and singer of Sicilian ancestry, and Jack Teagarden, a Texas trombone player and singer of Dutch and German stock, first met in Albuquerque in 1925. They shared a love for Louis Armstrong's Hot Five records. Wingy says Jack was particularly crazy about *Oriental Strut*.

"He decided nobody else could top that, and said we ought to preserve it for posterity. We had heard that if you buried things out there on the Mesa they would be petrified, like all the old trees and stuff that had turned to stone.

"So one day Jack and I took Louis' record of *Oriental Strut* and drove out to the Mesa with it. We dug a big hole and laid the record away, and as far as I know, it is still there today."

Small wonder Joe Glaser put on the Sunset marquee the words "Louis Armstrong—The World's Greatest Trumpeter." Those were days of fierce competitiveness among musicians, and some challenged Louis's right to that title. One of his first unintended victims was his mentor, King Oliver, who was working across the street. Then came another New Orleans noble, Freddie Keppard. Later, there were younger men, like Jabbo Smith, who had learned well from Louis and had great speed but none of Louis's power, or Louis Metcalf in New York, who made himself a crown of gold paper

**Louis Armstrong's Hot Five, c. 1926.
Left to right: Johnny St. Cyr, Kid Ory,
Louis Armstrong, Johnny Dodds, Lil
Hardin Armstrong**

Zutty Singleton

and challenged Louis only to have to tear up the crown.

Most musicians didn't challenge; they listened and learned. Among them was a young pianist from Pittsburgh, Earl Hines, with whom Louis formed a musical partnership that resulted in some of the greatest music ever put on record. For the first time since his brief encounter with Sidney Bechet, Louis had found someone who could challenge and stimulate him. After almost fifty years, such masterpieces as *West End Blues* and *Weather Bird* stand unsurpassed. Jazz was coming of age, and Louis Armstrong was its guardian.

Contributing to the success of Louis's recordings with Hines was the drummer in the group, Zutty Singleton, a friend from New Orleans. Zutty's rock-solid time and inspiring beat were ideally suited to hold the Armstrong trumpet aloft during its most extravagant flights. Off the stand, the two were inseparable. They worked together, with Hines along, at the Sunset as well as in the studio, and after a while hit on the idea that they might be big enough to open their own club. The venture failed, and after a month, Louis and Zutty were back at the Sunset. But New York beckoned— Louis had gotten involved with the girl who would become his third wife, and she had never been there. Nor had Zutty or most of the other men in the band.

They piled into the Hupmobile Louis had bought with the proceeds from a book of trumpet solos he had sold to a music publisher (another first) and barely made it to the big town. As they got to Forty-second Street, the car's radiator boiled over, "the cap came off, and a cop came over and searched the car for shotguns 'cause he'd seen the Chicago license plates," according to Louis. The cats were sharp dressers, of course; Louis had long since lost his New Orleans look.

New York was ready for Armstrong, but did not have much use for his band. Characteristically, he tried to carry his friends as long as he could. But to no avail; pretty soon, he was doing a featured "single" in a Broadway revue, *Hot Chocolates*, with a score by Fats Waller that included *Ain't Misbehavin'* and *Black and Blue,* both to become jazz and Armstrong classics.

The treatment of *Ain't Misbehavin'* set the pattern for the new Armstrong. He was now fully developed as instrumentalist and singer; his unique vocalizing had come into its own via the Hot Five and Hot Seven recordings. He would start with a statement of the melody on trumpet, paraphrasing it slightly, imbuing it with his majestic tone and innate swing. Then would come the vocal, complete with spontaneous asides and outbursts of scat, and then a concluding trumpet solo, freely improvised, and topped off with a high-note cadenza.

Nearly thirty, he was the first full-fledged virtuoso produced by jazz, and he relished his powers. In later years, he spoke with disapproval of this stage of his career, claiming he had forgotten his public in order to please the musicians, "doing crazy things with the horn." But he was also developing his stagecraft and learning how to get the most out of—and into—a song, no matter how unpromising it might seem.

Idolized by his fellow musicians, jamming after hours almost every night, doing the town in the company of Alpha, his new love—a pretty girl who loved high living—Louis was enjoying life. But he was becoming a hot show-business property. After a sojourn in California, where he was featured at a favorite haunt of movie stars, Frank Sebastian's Cotton Club, and suggested to the young drummer in the band, Lionel Hampton, that he should play the vibraharp on some records they were making, thus helping to launch a remarkable career, Louis found himself back in Chicago, with a new manager and a big band of his own, ready to go on tour. (During his stay in California, he was jailed briefly for possession of marijuana. Louis was a pioneer all around.)

His ties to his hometown were still strong; half the men in the band were New Orleanians, and he would remember it as the happiest band he ever led. It lasted just about a year and made some fine recordings, including the first of many *Sleepy Time Down South*s and Louis's first big hit, *You Rascal You,* an irreverent ode to a rival which included such lines as

> When you're laying six feet deep
> No more fried chicken will you eat

> and

> I'll be standing on the corner high
> When they bring your body by. . . .*

From then on, humorous "novelties" became part and parcel of the Armstrong repertoire, serving as

vehicles not only for laughs but also for incongruously ravishing trumpet solos. Such unconventional aesthetics presented the budding school of jazz criticism with no end of problems. His audience, still mainly black, didn't have any.

Louis's manager, a rough man named Johnny Collins, was ambitious but irresponsible. His affection for his client seemed genuine, but it did Louis little good. A tour of the South was fraught with troubles, including a narrow escape from rednecks incensed by the presence of Collins's wife, who was in charge of the band's transportation and sat up front in the bus, next to the driver, guitarist, and "straw boss" Mike McKendrick.

This sight so displeased the Memphis constabulary that they arrested the entire band on the trumped-up charge that the bus had not been legitimately chartered. Collins got them out of jail. Louis had become a radio favorite, and broadcasts were scheduled throughout the tour. That night the band broadcast from a Memphis hotel, and Louis made a dedication to the chief of police. It was *I'll Be Glad When You're Dead, You Rascal You.*

Louis had left Chicago because of problems involving rival factions of gangsters. Then even more than later, the underworld had considerable interest in the music business, and the manner in which business was conducted was often quite unceremonious. Louis found himself staring down the business end of a .45. Its owner wanted him to leave his Chicago job and return to a certain New York nightclub right away.

It wasn't the last time Louis had such problems. His first trip abroad, a three-month tour of England in 1932, was untroubled. But his second visit to Europe, starting in London in August, 1933, resulted in a final break between Louis and Collins. Louis seldom discussed unpleasant things and years later confined himself to stating that Collins was "a fantastic cat . . . always something would be wrong, always trouble with the promoters, trying to make me declare bankruptcy—fantastic stuff. Mixing me up in stinking publicity stunts. Finally in England I was finished with him."

It appears that Louis fired Collins, who retaliated by taking Louis's passport with him to America. It is said he vowed that Louis would never work in his homeland again. Louis remained in Europe until early 1935, taking the longest vacation of his entire career—from spring to fall of 1934. When he returned home, lip trouble was given as the reason for

Arvell Shaw

six months of inactivity, preceding the formation of a new band under the aegis of a new manager—the same Joe Glaser who had put Louis's name out in front at the Sunset Café in 1926.

Glaser was the incarnation of the advice the New Orleans bouncer had given Louis on the eve of his departure from home. Until Glaser's death in 1969, the two men's fortunes were intertwined in a relationship unparalleled in show business. Though he never disclosed the details, Louis was convinced that he owed his renewed career to Glaser, and perhaps he was right. In any case, there would be no more troubles of this sort for Louis. Glaser, who was connected with a major booking agency when Louis approached him, formed his own company in 1937 and built it into the most powerful agency in the jazz and black talent field.

Fiercely loyal to Louis—who came first among all his clients, and they knew it—Glaser nonetheless worked him very hard. In the early days of their relationship, he would travel with the band whenever Louis toured the South; later, he made sure the road manager was able to stand up under pressure. But the schedules were grueling—hardly any time off; backwoods locations as well as big hotels; recording sessions squeezed in between long stints on the road, etc.

Though Glaser obtained such plums as sponsored radio shows and film roles for Louis, many observers felt that in later years his old-fashioned ways were a hindrance rather than an asset to Armstrong's career. After the big-band format had been scrapped in 1947, and the Armstrong All Stars, with such luminaries as Jack Teagarden, Barney Bigard, Arvell Shaw, and later Earl Hines had been formed, Louis's popularity rose to an all-time high. By the late fifties, he was "Ambassador Satch," the world's most beloved entertainer, yet when the All Stars, which now included Trummy Young and Edmond Hall, were not hopping around the globe (with schedules comparable to the ones at home), they were keeping up the same old pace of touring the highways and byways of the United States. Glaser seemed incapable of turning down a booking, even when filling it meant a detour of hundreds of miles and an added strain on Louis and the band.

Louis hardly ever complained. He was an old

Trummy Young

trouper, and he loved his work, his "living and his life." He took pride in his stamina and endurance, which were truly exceptional. (One talent that stood him in good stead was his ability to go to sleep, real sleep, at a moment's notice, anywhere, anytime, and wake up just as quickly.)

And he took extra special care of the parts of his body he considered most important—his lips and his stomach. For the latter, he swore by the restorative powers of Swiss Kriss, a herbal laxative which he consumed religiously, sent to all his friends for Christmas, and sang the praises of consistently. He signed his correspondence "Swiss Krissly yours" and adopted the slogan "Leave it all behind you."

For the lips, there was a special ritual before each performance. His trusted valet, Doc Pugh, would open a leather case containing little cans of the special lip salve made for him in Germany, bottles of a solution with which he bathed his lips, and scrupulously sterile applicators, cotton balls, tissues, etc. The ointments were applied with particular care to the astonishingly calloused center portion of his upper lip that had to bear the brunt of the mouthpiece pressure. Scar tissue accumulated through decades of playing had hardened to the consistency of tough leather, but the "chops" could still get sore.

Louis's famous record date with Duke Ellington was made on two consecutive days bracketed by the return from a strenuous road trip and the beginning of another, and between numbers, Louis was constantly bathing his battered lips. Nevertheless, he played beautifully and familiarized himself with material he had never done before in minutes. He even had words of cheer for Ellington, who was complaining of a headache during the second session, which ended in the late afternoon. By early evening, Louis was back on the band bus, still treating the "chops."

At the end of a famous 1966 interview in *Life,* he said: "Some cats want pats on the back, and they want you to kneel down because they did this and did that, and they are so and so. But I still feel I'm just an ordinary human being trying to enjoy the work I live. It's something to know you still can make that call when the man says, 'All on.' That's enough wonderment for me. A lot of them are gone, dropped out. Ain't but a few left, a few of us."

Yet there were times when he rebelled against the killing pace. I heard him quote Bert Williams's old adage: "In show business, you've got to die to prove that you're sick." But he wasn't feeling well when he said that; as soon as the trouble had passed, he was ready for the old grind again.

Glaser might have set Louis up in residence at a Las Vegas hotel, with occasional tours of major spots at home and abroad. He might have gotten him a television series—what a host Louis would have made, with his rapport with people of all sorts and his charisma! But Glaser was still thinking in old-fashioned terms of one-nighters, moving the band from big time to small time in a single jump on the bus. In part, it was Louis's own fault. The proof is that he didn't change after Joe's death—he still wanted to work as much as he could, no matter how precarious his health. "The show must go on" remained his creed, and it seems a miracle that he died in his sleep at home, his wife of twenty-nine years by his side (his fourth marriage, to dancer Lucille Wilson, was the one that lasted; "She understands that the horn comes first," he said), rather than on a one-nighter somewhere in North Dakota.

He never forgot what had happened to King Oliver—the tragic fall from great heights. Oliver died from many causes, as Louis saw it—neglected health (you can't play the trumpet without good teeth and a good constitution), missed opportunities, and a broken heart. "A broken heart is the lowest thing a man can die with," Louis said. "I won't die with that."

So he took good care of himself, despite (or because of) the grind of the road, and never turned down a movie spot (no matter how dire the film— and he was in some dogs as well as some good ones) or an interview ("You've got to keep your name before the public"). In a way, though he had an innate sense of his worth and dignity, Louis Armstrong never really knew how great he was. His immense popularity, he felt, was due to hard work, luck, and "keeping your name before the public." He knew he was an artist, "but I always let the other fellow talk about art." He was proud of the fact that what he called "our music from New Orleans" had earned worldwide fame and recognition, but he seemed unaware of the extent to which the survival of that music was due to his own contributions.

In his younger, combative days, when he was ready to lock horns with any comer, he must have known how great he was, but later he felt that he had just been out to impress fellow musicians, an unimportant pursuit compared with the real work of pleasing the public. The success of *Hello, Dolly!*

brought him more satisfaction than the recognition of *West End Blues* as an imperishable masterpiece of the art of jazz. (His joy in the success of *Hello, Dolly!*, which knocked the Beatles out of first place on the top-selling record charts in May, 1964, was shared by many of his colleagues. When Louis and the All Stars did a one-night stand in July at the Metropole, the rough-and-ready Times Square jazz spot, his fellow musicians threw a party for him at the Copper Rail, their favorite watering hole across the street. There were banners reading "You Beat the Beatles!" and the luminaries present included Duke Ellington, Eddie Condon, Ben Webster, Sonny Greer, Lionel Hampton, Bud Freeman, Pee Wee Russell, Buck Clayton, and many more, representing a jazz generation that felt vindicated by Louis's achievement. The fact that it was totally unanticipated made the victory even sweeter.)

Perhaps he had no faith in the assurances of immortality given by those "other fellows" he let talk about art. But then, he was not the first artist to take himself less seriously than critics and intellectuals. What he did take seriously was his work, the constant hard work that had brought him so far from singing for pennies in the streets of a New Orleans slum.

There is no explanation for genius, but one of the best summations of the impact of Louis Armstrong, of his essence, is pianist Jaki Byard's reaction to his first encounter with Louis: "As I watched him and talked with him, I felt he was the most *natural* man—playing, talking, singing, he was so perfectly natural the tears came to my eyes. I was very moved to be near the most natural of all living musicians." To Louis Armstrong, his art and craft were nothing more or less than the disciplined expression of his nature. He was a phenomenon.

2 The Duke and His Men

"When I was a child," wrote Duke Ellington in his memoir *Music Is My Mistress,* "my mother told me I was blessed, and I have always taken her word for it. . . . Royalty is inherited from another human being, blessedness from God."

Edward Kennedy Ellington was indeed blessed. He was born in Washington, D.C., in 1899 and raised in the security and warmth of a loving middle-class family which gave him (the only child until he was almost a man) a sense of essential moral, ethical, and social values and an inviolable feeling of personal worth. (Those who perceive the Afro-American experience as unfulfilling would do well to study the life and work of Duke Ellington.) He was blessed not only with prodigious artistic gifts, but also with a talent for life and living. His temperament precluded catching what he called "the bug disease," that is to say, allowing the irritations of daily existence to bug him, to gnaw at his innards.

Though far from naive in the ways of commerce—he had only briefly been a professional musician when he decided to take an advertisement

Duke Ellington Orchestra, 1934. Ellington seated in center, with Sonny Greer kneeling at his right and Freddy Jenkins at his left. Standing, first row: Barney Bigard, Marshall Royal, Johnny Hodges, Harry Carney, Wellman Braud; second row: Joe Nanton, Juan Tizol, Lawrence Brown, Arthur Whetsol, Fred Guy

Duke Ellington and Sonny Greer, c. 1933

Duke Ellington in 1934 on the sound stage of _Belle of the Nineties_ in Hollywood

in the Washington, D.C., phone book larger than any other orchestra leader's, though he didn't even have a regular band as yet—Ellington realized early on that he couldn't be both artist and businessman. So he put his shrewdness to work in finding clever and, as far as possible, honest management for himself.

His first manager was Irving Mills, a song publisher-plugger and lyricist and a man about town, who got him good recording contracts (jazz musicians, especially black ones, were routinely gouged by record companies well into the forties, and some would say until the present) and the crucially important job at the Cotton Club in 1927 that launched the band to fame. Five years later, Mills understood that the prestige and publicity of a European visit, complete with a command performance for the King of England, meant more than money.

Ellington eventually broke with Mills, chiefly over the matter of rights to the massive catalogue of Ellington compositions, some of which Mills claimed to have co-composed, but the parting of the ways was civil. "In spite of how much he had made on me," Ellington wrote years later, "I respected the way he operated. He had always preserved the dignity of my name . . . and that is the most anybody can do for anybody."

It wasn't only for the sake of his art and sanity that Ellington made the decision to let others handle his business affairs. It was also to gain what he once described as the most valuable thing in life: time. Nearly all of the thousand or so copyrighted compositions that constitute Ellington's published *oeuvre* were completed under the deadline pressure Ellington found it impossible to work without. Masterpieces were written on trains or planes (Ellington had long refused to fly, but once he had tried it he became a passionate air traveler), during breaks in recording sessions, in hotel rooms in the early morning hours after his performance work and socializing was done, or otherwise on the run. No other composer in history, not even Mozart, created his works under such extraordinary circumstances.

For more than fifty years, Ellington worked almost fifty-two weeks of each year. Music was his vocation and avocation, his work and play. In later years, when, as the world's busiest bandleader, he was asked when he planned to retire from what seemed an ever more strenuous schedule, his re-

Collection of Duncan Schiedt

The Cotton Club, New York City

sponse was: "Retire to what?" Retirement was for the unfortunates who didn't like their life's work. Ellington was in love with his.

Though he was an exceptional pianist, it was rightly said that Ellington's instrument was his band. When he wrote a piece, he wrote with specific instrumental colors in mind, and each of these colors was a specific and unique individual on the personal palette that was his band. In later years, Duke would admit to intimates that it was becoming increasingly difficult to find musicians with individual personalities to write for. The young musicians could play anything set in front of them, he noted, but didn't have the unmistakable sounds or styles of the earlier generation. To have an orchestra of his own is every composer's dream; in modern times, Ellington was the only one to realize it. The price came high, but he wasn't interested in saving money.

The key men he kept gathered around him longer than any other bandleader had to be well paid for their services, and to meet the swollen payroll he had to keep the band working steadily. When it became increasingly difficult economically to maintain a big band, Ellington had to rely more and more on touring abroad, which often paid better than working in the United States. He loved to travel, but it was hard on the men.

The band's longest tour, in 1971, consisted of five weeks in the Soviet Union, immediately followed by a month in Europe (mostly one-night stands) and three weeks in Latin America (including many remote locations). The band then landed in Chicago, played a dance there the same night, the next day traveled by bus to a one-nighter in Muncie, Indiana, and the following night opened a two-week Christmas holiday stand at the Rainbow Grill in New York's Rockefeller Center. The two opening night sets ran two hours each instead of the customary seventy-five minutes. Ellington didn't want to let his many friends in the house down. "A few weeks ago," he said about a similar tour, "I slept in my own bed for the first time in six months." He was then in his seventies.

Ellington always did things in style. In the 1930s, when travel in the South (and certain other parts of the United States) could be not just unpleasant but downright dangerous for black musicians, the Ellington band traveled in its own Pullman car. It would pull in at a siding for the duration of the band's stay in the area. The musicians would be taken to and from the job in cabs or private cars and enjoyed their meals in the privacy of their own railroad car. Card playing was the favorite pastime during such stays.

While he commanded complete respect from his men, Ellington was not a disciplinarian. There was no sight in banddom comparable to Duke's crew starting a night's work. Depending on the circumstances, only half the troops might be present on the stand as the opening number got under way, and not all of these might be ready to play. Ellington himself would not materialize until the second number, and if the event was a dance, not until well into the program.

Johnny Hodges, who played alto saxophone like an angel, usually managed to look utterly bored. When called upon to come up front for a feature, he would move at minimal speed. Only faithful Harry Carney, who joined the band at seventeen in 1927 and remained until the end, surviving Ellington by less than five months, would always be on time and never look blasé. Hodges and Carney were perhaps the most remarkable among the many confirmed individualists who contributed to Ellingtonia. Both hailed from Massachusetts, Hodges from Cambridge, Carney from Boston. Each had a sound that was like a signature: totally and unmistakably original and unique.

Carney filled the big baritone saxophone with his mighty breath. He was the anchor of the most remarkable ensemble sound in jazz, the emblem of continuity, an Ellingtonian for forty-seven years. And Harry was not just a musical cornerstone. For decades, he was Ellington's sole companion on the road trips. When the rest of the band would go by bus, Ellington would ride in Carney's car. Carney was perfectly cast for this role. He loved to drive, was careful and alert, and didn't talk when Ellington didn't feel like making conversation.

This was not a chauffeur-boss relationship by any means. Ellington was not a passenger but, as he called himself, the navigator. It was his duty to chart a course and to stay on it, and he took considerable pride in his knowledge of the United States highways and byways. How many million miles this twosome togged will never be calculated. They never had an accident of consequence and always got to the job. Sometimes they were the only ones who did. Once the bus lost its way to a Rhode Island location and tenor saxophonist Paul Gonsalves, who had not yet joined the band but was there to listen,

Johnny Hodges

Paul Gonsalves

recalled with delight how Carney and Ellington duetted for more than an hour, keeping the dancers happy: Carney with his huge sound and Duke literally stomping time, his feet compensating for the absent drummer.

Carney was the kindest of men. It was he who warmly greeted the lowliest fan, remembered his or her name, and generously provided information about the band's itinerary, interesting future projects, etc. Yet he never committed an indiscretion. When Harry joined the Ellington band in 1927, he was on summer vacation from school but already owned a car and all his instruments and had six thousand dollars in the bank. He never did get back to school and never took another vacation of any significance.

Johnny Hodges joined a year later than Carney. He soon became a primary color in Ellington's tonal palette, one of the key stylists on the alto saxophone, and one of the greatest of jazz musicians. Short of stature and unassuming in appearance, he nonetheless projected an aura of dignity and aloofness. In fact, he was a down-to-earth, warmhearted man with a well-developed sense of the ridiculous and a fatherly manner (he was in the habit of addressing even his contemporaries as "young man").

In matters musical, he had definitive opinions and was not reluctant to express them. Once, at a concert-dance, when Ellington called an arrangement bestowed upon the band by an ambitious composer with modernist leanings, the ensemble began to struggle through it, producing odd and un-Ellingtonian sounds. Hodges stopped playing, held up his part for all in the band to see, and slowly and deliberately tore the music paper in half. The piece was never called again.

It was always a special delight to attend an Ellington performance at Harlem's Apollo Theatre. Hodges was a particular favorite here, as indeed anywhere, and when the time came for his features, the audience would begin to react even before he had played his first note, which was invariably greeted with a sigh of contentment. From then on, there would be an ongoing "conversation" between player and audience, the latter responding to his phrases, anticipating them, exhorting the player but never interfering with the flow of his music.

When Johnny played the blues, there would be shouts and exclamations, and when he played a ballad (and no one could play a ballad like Johnny Hodges) there would be oohs and aahs and little moans from the ladies. Ellington, Hodges, and Billy Strayhorn—Duke's alter ego in the roles of composer, arranger, and pianist, and his great friend and support—created some of the most beautiful romantic music of our time. Of all time.

Another audience favorite was Paul Gonsalves, the great tenor saxist who had performed the near-impossible feat of adequately replacing Ben Webster in the band, following Al Sears, who didn't try. A native of New England like his section mates Carney and Hodges, Paul was descended from Cape Verdeans, though he good-naturedly accepted the nickname "Mex," based on misinterpretations of his complexion and last name, which was frequently misspelled "Gonzales." His real friends never called him anything but Paul.

Painfully shy when cold sober, Paul needed fortification to face the world and often fortified himself a bit too much. He was the most likable of men and genuinely seemed to like almost everybody (Ellington said that Paul never harbored an evil thought) but could become quite stubborn when

Harry Carney

rationing of fortifying substances was suggested. Withal, he was a remarkable athlete and had tremendous stamina, on and off the bandstand.

Paul loved to play and was one of the last of the true jammers—musicians willing to take out their horn (or borrow someone else's) and blow under almost any musical conditions. And he always managed to play well, even near the end, after he had suffered a stroke and his other motor functions seemed somewhat impaired. It was Paul who ignited the band's famous performance of *Crescendo and Diminuendo in Blue* at the 1956 Newport Jazz Festival, and it was the recording of this performance (as well as its impact on attendant critics) that launched a strong comeback for the band. Not that it had been in a musical slump, but Duke had fallen victim to the periodic (and idiotic) critical reassessments of jazz by people unable to accept the fact that an artist active for more than a few decades might still have something valid to offer.

Paul's twenty-seven choruses of up-tempo blues, set between brilliant ensemble segments, brought the audience to its feet, and from then on, what had been spontaneously inspired had to be re-created at will. It was all part of the jazzman's art and craft, and Paul was up to the task, though his own predilection in the realm of self-expression ran to pretty melodies performed at slow or middle tempos. Ellington compromised by devising a feature on *Body and Soul* for him that began as a ballad and then jumped to triple time. This and *Crescendo* were sometimes called when Paul had been a bad boy and wasn't in shape to meet the challenge. This was one of the many ways in which the leader kept his men in fighting trim.

Ellington never fired anyone; he let them fire themselves. Paul, of course, was one of his very special people, and when punishment was applied, it was only a reminder, not a threat. Lesser lights who consistently violated professional standards soon found repeated public humiliation more than they could bear and would exit quietly.

Some departures were more spectacular. The famous bassist Charles Mingus, in his semi-autobiography *Beneath the Underdog,* describes how Ellington discharged him after an incident during a show at the Apollo (for the full story, see the Modern Masters chapter). Mingus, a newcomer to the band, had been chased across the stage by a knife-wielding veteran Ellingtonian. Mingus recalls that Ellington fired him with such charm and grace that he left feeling he'd been granted a particular favor.

Others quit of their own volition because they felt they might do better outside the Ducal fold. Financially, some may have done so; musically, they almost never did. Ellington had a profound grasp of each player's strengths and weaknesses that enabled him to present his soloists in the most flattering way possible.

It is no insult to Barney Bigard, who brought a touch of New Orleans and one of the loveliest sounds ever coaxed from a clarinet to the band, to say that he never sounded better than with Ellington—not even with Louis Armstrong, whom he subsequently joined. And Cootie Williams, the brilliant trumpeter with Duke from 1929 to 1940 and then with Benny Goodman (for one high-paid and musically quite effective year), came back to Ellington after twenty years on his own and only then regained his true artistic equilibrium.

An exception to this rule is trumpeter and sometime vocalist Clark Terry, who made his mark with Ellington from 1951 through 1959. He was no tyro; his prior affiliations included Charlie Barnet and Count Basie. Yet, as he told Duke's biographer Stanley Dance, "everything previous was like elementary school. Ellington was like college." Terry has used his Ducal education well, and since leaving the fold has established himself as one of the most original trumpet stylists in jazz. He has led his own bands, big and small, and has carved out a secondary career for himself as instrumental clinician (that is to say, someone who visits colleges and high schools and gives seminars for young musicians, something Terry is particularly good at; his rapport with kids is marvelous). With a little luck, Clark Terry might become as famous as he deserves to be. Meanwhile, he is doing just fine.

Hodges, too, strayed from the fold, but not for as long as Cootie. He left in 1951 to start his own small band, enjoyed not inconsiderable success, but nonetheless returned four years later. The bonds were too strong. Much of the music he had made in his absence was Ellington music, and many of his musicians were ex-Ellingtonians.

Hodges's sudden death from a heart attack at sixty-four in 1970 was a serious blow to Ellington, who had barely recovered from Billy Strayhorn's passing (and the grueling illness that preceded it) three years earlier. That blow, though momentarily stunning, was one from which Ellington bounced

Barney Bigard

back with renewed creative vigor—he now had to work for two. But Hodges was an irreplaceable sound and an irreplaceable inspiration. Strayhorn's final work, a feature for Hodges, *Bloodcount,* had been a masterpiece. Ellington had just completed a piece for Hodges in which he was to portray his early idol and inspiration Sidney Bechet. It was Paul Gonsalves who was called upon to fill those big shoes, and the tribute to Bechet became a requiem for Johnny Hodges.

The relationship between Ellington and Strayhorn was unique in the annals of music. Co-composer, arranger, sometime pianist, confidant, and Ellington's musical right arm, Strayhorn was drawn into the Ellington orbit in 1938, when, as a shy young man of twenty-three, he mustered up the courage to visit Duke backstage during an engagement in Pittsburgh and played and sang some of his compositions for him. (Among them was *Lushlife,* a song of sophisticated, almost decadent resignation that became a hit for Nat King Cole more than ten years later. That it should have been written by a largely self-taught young man whose cultural horizon had been circumscribed by Dayton, Ohio, Hillsboro, North Carolina, and Pittsburgh was thoroughly surprising, not to say inexplicable.)

By the following year, Ellington had sent for Strayhorn, at first intending to make use of his talents as lyricist and pianist. It was soon discovered, however, that Strayhorn was a gifted composer and arranger for instrumental music, with an uncanny ability to apprehend and realize Ellington's ideas. During their twenty-eight-year collaboration, it was sometimes difficult to know where Ellington left off and Strayhorn began; their joint efforts were seamless entities. However, there was a distinctive Strayhorn personality which Duke allowed to flourish in such famous contributions to Ellingtonia as *Chelsea Bridge, Raincheck, Passion Flower, Daydream,* and, as Duke was always quick to point out when it was credited to him, the band's theme song for more than thirty years, *Take the 'A' Train.*

In his autobiography, Ellington wrote: "He was my listener, my most dependable appraiser. . . . any time I was in the throes of debate with myself, harmonically or melodically, I would turn to Billy Strayhorn. We would talk, and then the whole world would come into focus. . . . He was not, as he was often referred to by many, my alter ego. Billy Strayhorn was my right arm, my left arm, all the

Clark Terry

Billy Strayhorn and Duke Ellington

eyes in the back of my head, my brainwaves in his head, and his in mine."

When Hodges left the band in 1951, he took with him a man who had been an Ellington sidekick since 1919. When Duke was still a yearling and not yet wise to the ways of New York it was Sonny Greer, a drummer from New Jersey whom he had met and worked with in Washington, who took him around, showed him the ropes, and introduced him to such heroes of the keyboard as Willie ("The Lion") Smith.

The conclusion that some of the Ellington ambiance derived from Sonny Greer is inescapable. Like Duke, Sonny is an incurable optimist and a gentleman with courtly manners. To this day, he gets dressed up even to go to the corner store for a loaf of bread. There was (and is) no sight in the world of jazz to equal that of Sonny Greer enthroned behind his percussion array high above the rest of the Ellington band. His equipment included chimes, gongs, tympani, cymbals galore, tom-toms, and exotic temple blocks. His bass-drum front was splendidly hand-painted, and every bit of brass or chrome sparkled and shone.

Sonny used all this stuff; it wasn't just for display. Ellington described him as "the world's best percussion reactor—when he heard a ping, he responded with the most apropos pong." And Sonny described himself most aptly as the "mixologist" of the band. His effects were unique, always fitting, and an inseparable part of the Ellington sound.

He left, I think, because he realized that big-band drumming had undergone substantial changes over the years and that the band might be in need of something new. That something turned out to be Louis Bellson and his crackling precision and swing. Sonny turned his attention to small groups and is still plying his trade with vigor and exquisite taste, and once again in Ellingtonian surroundings. In the mid-seventies, he was working in a trio with Russell Procope, for nearly thirty years Ellington's lead alto saxophonist and clarinet soloist in the Bigard tradition, and leader Brooks Kerr, a pianist in his early twenties who knows more Ellington music than Duke himself was able to recall. "Ask Brooks Kerr," he would say when questioned about pieces from the band's early years.

The men who passed through the Ellington ranks were an extraordinary group of musicians, from Sonny Greer, Otto Hardwick, Arthur Whetsol, Bubber Miley, and Tricky Sam Nanton to Law-

Jimmy Hamilton

rence Brown and Rex Stewart through Ben Webster, Jimmy Hamilton (of the impeccable clarinet and raunchy tenor sax), Cat Anderson (of the stratospheric trumpet notes and exceptional adaptability), Clark Terry, and Willie Cook to Ernie Shepard, Norris Turney, Money Johnson, John Lamb, Joe Benjamin, and so many others—not to forget the greatest singer the band ever had, Miss Ivie Anderson.

Special mention must be made of Jimmy Blanton, dead of tuberculosis at twenty-three, whose two years with the band (1939-41) sufficed to change forever the role of the bass in jazz, if perhaps not to fully realize the potential of his authentic genius. And we cannot forget Ray Nance, who came aboard in 1940 to replace Cootie Williams and not only brought a similarly warm, strong, and soulful if totally personal trumpet voice to the band, but also added the special talents of violinist, singer, dancer, and entertainer. "Ray never played a bad note in his life," said Duke Ellington.

Nance was able to bring all his talents to bear on what was to be Ellington's only successful venture in the musical theater, a medium for which he seemed so well suited. This was *Jump for Joy*, produced and presented in Los Angeles in 1941. Ellington was proud of the fact that it was the first black "special significance" show. It was subtitled "A sun-tanned revue-sical" and made its points with style and wit. "I think a statement of social protest in the theater should be made without saying it," he reflected years later. Always a fighter for human rights and dignity, he reserved the right to choose his own weapons in the struggle against racial bigotry.

Though he wrote incidental music for several plays, including works by Shakespeare and Eliot, his further ventures with musicals failed to get off the ground. But then, his whole life's work, in a sense, is musical theater, a huge canvas of American life—in particular, the life of black Americans—and beyond, for the world traveler drank in all the many sights and transformed them into beautiful, moving sounds.

Ellington once described himself as "the thinker-writer, the shaper, the mixer, the player, the listener, the critic, the corrector," an apt summary of some of his many roles within his own creative realm. It does not include the public man, the showman, the presenter, the gracious, charm-

Cootie Williams

Jimmy Hamilton, with Johnny Hodges, Russell Procope, and Harry Carney

ing, elegant, and commanding presence that to many was Duke Ellington. Few men so public remained as private, for despite his frequent interviews, not infrequent writings, and gracious accessibility, the core of the man remained submerged.

He made no secret, however, of his love for the company of pretty women, and he was a great flatterer. What he said of his father—"He knew exactly what to say to a lady, high-toned or honey-homey"—held doubly true for himself. "When you were playing piano there was always a pretty girl standing down at the bass clef end," he found out early on in his musical career, noting that he gave up athletics once he had made this important discovery.

Yet he had almost nothing to say about his wives. The first, a motherly-looking woman, bore him his only child, a son, Mercer, in 1919. She was no longer part of his life by the time he found success in New York. Much later, there was a quiet lady—she had been a dancer—who waited discreetly for him at recording sessions and was very occasionally seen in the background at social events. It was astonishing to learn from intimates that she was Mrs. Ellington.

Ellington allowed his son to help with the band in later years. (Mercer had wanted to become an engineer, but his father steered him to music. He showed genuine talent as a composer and arranger but only limited ability as an instrumentalist.) He sat anonymously in the trumpet section and acted as the band's road manager and troubleshooter. The handling of any unpleasantness was usually delegated to him. His father never introduced Mercer to the public—perhaps he resented admitting to a gray-haired son. Intermittently, Mercer led several good but short-lived bands of his own.

There were moments when Ellington appeared frivolous, when his loyalty to his adoring fans and his dedication to showmanship seemed to override his best creative impulses. But such moments passed; besides, he had the capacity for genuine enjoyment of sometimes outrageous show-biz presentations. And he meant it when he told his fans that he "loved them madly." It was part of the tradition he grew up with and of his joy in giving pleasure. There was always time to be serious, and if there wasn't time enough for public performances of new and demanding works, he made sure these were recorded. Not at the whim of some record-

Ray Nance

Johnny Hodges and Jimmy Jones

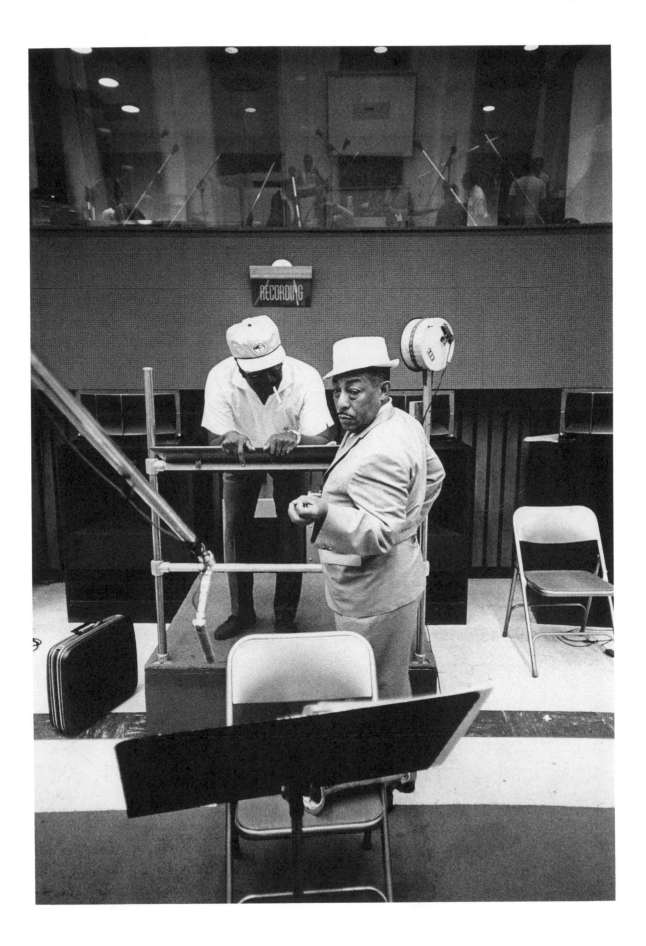

Duke Ellington

company executive, but by and for himself and for posterity.

This facet of the Ellington legacy has just begun to be tapped. Concomitantly, Mercer Ellington is keeping the Ellington band alive. Not as a copy, which would be impossible in any case, but as a living repository of Ellington music, which, after all, was always in a state of flux.

A true believer, Ellington regarded his Sacred Concerts as the most important work he had done. While these large-scale works for chorus, orchestra, and vocal and instrumental soloists are genuine, moving, and typically Ellington, it is possible that posterity will judge them differently, singling out instead those remarkable and unparalleled three-minute masterpieces for unique orchestra shaped to the strictures of the 78 r.p.m. phonograph record.

Whatever the ultimate verdict, the work of Duke Ellington is, as he wanted it to be, "beyond category." He despised categorization in music and life and resisted the label "jazz" on this account, preferring "the American Idiom" or "Music of Freedom of Expression." He needn't have worried. He was in a class by himself. In fact, he was blessed.

3 The Condon Mob

"He had straw-colored hair, slicked down with 'Stacomb' and parted in the middle. He wore a Norfolk suit with four buttons and a half-belt, knickers, very expensive shoes, and the inevitable (I learned later) bow tie. He was the sharpest thing I had ever seen outside of John Held's drawings in *College Humor*." Thus Arny Freeman, brother of the famous tenor saxophonist Bud Freeman, described the impression made upon him by Eddie Condon at their first encounter, in prohibition-era Chicago.

Though he was an excellent rhythm guitarist, Condon's claim to jazz fame rests not so much on his playing as on his gifts as a proselytizer for and organizer and presenter of the music he loved. He was a champion talker (his speed and manner of delivery had much in common with James Cagney's, and the resemblance was also physical, in terms of stature and body English) and drinker (his recipe for a hangover cure began with the words "Take the juice of one quart of whiskey"), resourceful, scrappy, afraid of no man, and one of the best friends jazz had in its corner.

The youngest of nine siblings, he was born into a warm, loving Irish-American family (both paternal grandparents had been born in County Limerick; they met and married in America and had eleven children; on the maternal side were the McGraths, born and married in County Tipperary, whose seven children were all born in the new land). Eddie was born in 1906 in Goodland, Indiana, where his father kept a saloon. Two years after the birth of his last child, the state went dry. John Condon moved to Momence, Illinois, and set himself up in the tavern business there, but the scourges of Demon Rum caught up with him again. Undaunted, he emigrated to Chicago Heights and founded yet another friendly saloon. When the Volstead Act became law, he finally accepted his fate and became a policeman.

Eddie's first instrument was the ukulele; it was soon replaced by the banjo. He played his first musical job at fourteen, and left home one month before his sixteenth birthday to pursue the career of a professional musician. He played with Bix Beiderbecke before very many musicians had heard of that remarkable cornetist and pianist, and by 1924 had settled in Chicago, where he soon came to know many of the gifted white youngsters who, like himself, had become entranced by the new music called jazz.

Some of them became his lifelong friends: cornetist Jimmy McPartland, who idolized Bix and followed him in the Wolverines; tenor saxist Bud Freeman; two drummers, Dave Tough and Gene Krupa, who would become spark plugs of some of the Swing Era's greatest bands; Joe Sullivan, christened Dennis Patrick Terence Joseph and one of the best jazz piano players of his or any day; Frank Teschemacher, a Kansas City-born fiddle player converted to sax and clarinet who would have become one of the luminaries of the music had he not been killed in a car accident two weeks before his twenty-sixth birthday; and Pee Wee Russell, the lanky, painfully shy clarinetist who never did play in or even pass through Chicago in the twenties but was Bix's roommate when both were in Frank Trumbauer's band at Hudson Lake near South Bend, Indiana, in the summer of 1926.

Condon and the members of what became known as the Austin High Gang (though only McPartland, Teschemacher, and bassist Jim Lannigan actually attended that Chicago school) made frequent pilgrimages to Hudson Lake that summer. Bix was

their hero. But they also worshipped Louis Armstrong, whom they had first encountered with King Oliver's band at the Lincoln Gardens, and admired Johnny Dodds, Jimmie Noone, Baby Dodds, Zutty Singleton, and the other great black musicians from New Orleans who were active in Chicago.

Along with such other slightly older or slightly younger native or adoptive Chicagoans as clarinetist Mezz Mezzrow, cornetist Muggsy Spanier, pianists Art Hodes and Jess Stacy, clarinetist Benny Goodman, and drummer George Wettling, they were among the first Americans to consciously and openly idolize and emulate black men (and women—Bessie Smith was another love of theirs). Though they wanted to play their own music, they knew it would have to be patterned on their black heroes' styles in order to be any good. They worked with some of the best dance bands in the city, but often quit because there wasn't enough jazz to play or got fired because they played it nonetheless.

Some were more rebellious than others. Mezzrow—perhaps the least gifted musician among them but certainly a man with a gift for life—eventually convinced himself that he was really black. He found Beiderbecke's music a bit too decadent and European-influenced—a subject on which he discoursed at length in his autobiography, *Really the Blues,* published in 1946. One of the most remarkable (and readable) books ever written about jazz, it was a best-seller in France and is still in print in the United States at this writing.

Full of tall tales about Mezz's exploits (Nat Hentoff dubbed him "the Baron Münchausen of Jazz"), the book is also a vivid and engrossing chronicle of a unique era in the history of jazz and America. Mezzrow, who organized the first racially integrated band in the United States (in New York in 1937) and became famous for the superior quality of the marijuana he sold ("Mezz" and "Mezzerola" became synonyms for good grass in the Harlem of the thirties) went to jail when the drug laws were changed, but he declined to change his way of making a living. (Since he also refused to update his music and for a while was sidetracked from playing anything at all, having acquired an opium habit, he didn't earn much of an income from music.)

He met and deeply influenced the French jazz critic Hugues Panassié—the first important writer on jazz in Europe and America—and participated

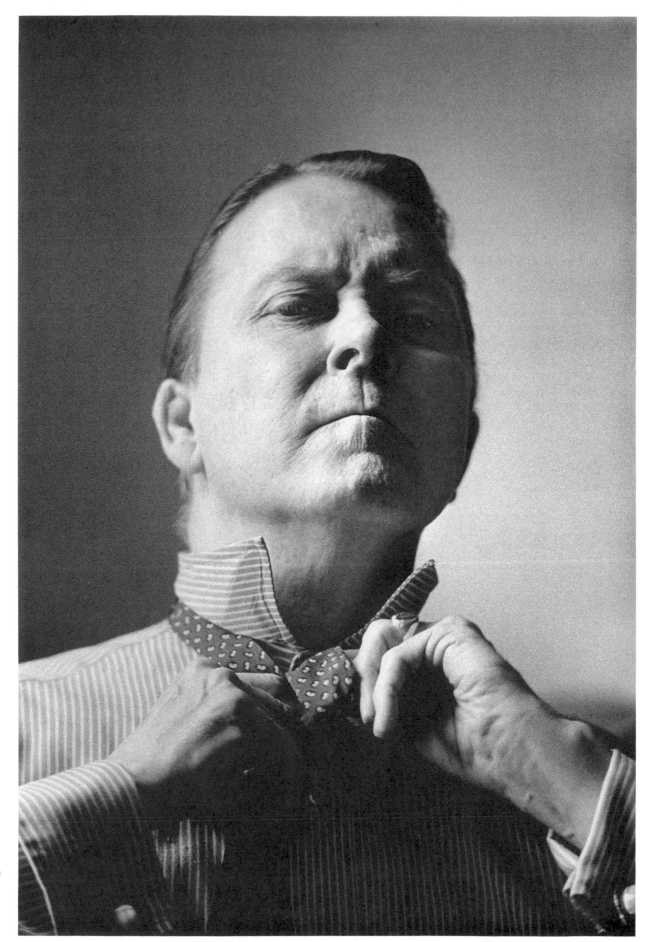

Eddie Condon

in the recording sessions organized by Panassié during a stay in the United States in the late thirties. After the war, Mezz started his own short-lived record company, King Jazz, dedicated to what he considered to be the only true jazz. This meant a modified New Orleans style deeply rooted in the blues. Nine out of every ten numbers recorded for King Jazz were blues.

From 1948 on, he spent more and more of his time in France and eventually settled there, becoming a well-known figure in the Paris cafés and at the race track and occasionally touring in the provinces with a band handpicked to his liking. He died broke and unregenerated in Paris in 1972, not quite seventy-three years old: the first "white Negro" and the archetypal hipster.

Condon was never as dogmatic about jazz as Mezz, though just as evangelical, and their ways parted fairly early, not long after both had moved to New York in 1928 in search of recognition for the music. The year before, in Chicago, Condon and his friend and fellow Irish tenor Red McKenzie had persuaded two major (and one minor) record companies to give their music a chance. The records involved most of the Austin High Gang plus Mezz, Muggsy, and McKenzie, an ex-jockey who wasn't a bad singer. (Condon was not so good and later would make no bones about the fact. "I sing here," he wrote in the notes to a reissue of an early effort. "I was young and didn't know any better. I do now.") They didn't sell very well, but musicians took notice of them, and they became the slender foundation on which so-called Chicago style was built. Whether there actually was such a style has been a subject for debate among critics for decades; most of the players have disclaimed any aspirations toward founding a school. The music was often a bit rough, but it had more of the real spirit of jazz than anything played by white musicians before, excepting perhaps the excellent New Orleans Rhythm Kings, the Austin Gang's inspiration before they discovered King Oliver.

In New York, whence they had ventured mainly on the strength of Condon's convictions and gift of gab, the Chicagoans frightened the resident white musicians and most club owners and other potential job givers, though they landed a brief engagement backing singer Bee Palmer at the Palace Theater. Cornetist Red Nichols, the leading white jazz figure in town—he controlled lucrative studio- and pit-band jobs and made innumerable recordings—hired the wild men for a few recording sessions and

George Wettling

odd jobs and even toured New England with a band including Condon, Freeman, Tough, Mezzrow, Russell, Sullivan, and trumpeter Max Kaminsky, a Chicago-minded Bostonian. It was by all odds the best band of his long career, but Nichols's martinet ways and reluctance to give Kaminsky any solos led to an abrupt disbandment, vividly described by Mezzrow:

"One stormy night only a few couples came [to see the band], and they must have arrived by boat. Red told Maxie to take charge, and as soon as he was out of sight I yelled 'Let's jam some.' Everybody was for it, and when we got going on *Sweet Sue* it was such a relief to shake Red's arrangements out of our hair that we got in a pretty good groove. Just as we finished and laid back feeling happy, Red came tearing into the hall and jumped up on the stand. 'The whole goddamned band's fired,' he barked. 'You're all on two weeks' notice.' "

That, pretty much, was the Chicagoans' lot. They found it difficult to compromise with the requirements of even jazz-oriented dance bandleaders and became adept at keeping starvation from the door, devising ingenious methods of smuggling permanent "visitors" past suspicious hotel desk clerks,

sleeping five in rooms designed for two, snitching milk from wagons and doorsteps, and drinking hot water mixed with ketchup in the Automat.

One night, Condon and Kaminsky were locked out of their hotel. They owed fifty-five dollars and had just enough money for breakfast; it was four in the morning and unbelievably cold—fourteen degrees below zero, a record low for New York. The clerk refused to let them sit in the lobby. They decided to call Artie Shaw, a bachelor clarinetist with a fancy apartment on Fifty-seventh Street. Let Condon tell the rest:

Shaw had offered us a job in a band he was planning to take to South America; we didn't think he would care if we joined up early. Maxie called him.

"I'll make it short, Artie," he said. "It's fourteen below and we're in it. Have you got any unused floor?"

I watched Maxie's face as he listened; it went slowly through disillusion, irritation, and disgust. "Aw, forget it!" he said suddenly, and hung up.

We stood without saying anything, trying to think. Finally I caught a name which had been eluding me.

"Landseer Apartments!" I said. "Gene Krupa

Max Kaminsky at Jimmy Ryan's, with Sal Pace, Bobby Pratt, and Freddie Moore

opened tonight at the Paradise with Buddy Rogers. He's staying at the Landseer."

I called him; I didn't tell Maxie that Krupa had just been married and was on his honeymoon. I was afraid he wouldn't let me ask if he knew it.

"Sorry to bother you, Gene," I said, "but Maxie and I have just been locked out of the Lismore and we wondered—"

Krupa interrupted me. "Come right down," he said. "I'm sorry I haven't a better place but this was all we could find. I'll fix the daybed for you in the living room and leave the door open."

He waited up for us, gave us a drink and tucked us in.

Gene Krupa, the man who, for better or worse, put the drum solo on the jazz map, was one of the kindest, nicest men in the music business. Life rewarded him strangely. In 1943, when Krupa's career was at its peak—after he had left Benny Goodman to form his own big band and it had become a big success (among other reasons, because it featured the trumpet and vocals of Roy Eldridge, the first black musician to be a regular member of a white band as distinct from a special attraction, like Teddy Wilson and Lionel Hampton with Goodman)—he was convicted of contributing to the delinquency of a minor because marijuana was found on the premises where the band was working and Krupa's band boy was only seventeen. The charge was eminently phony and was eventually dropped, but he did serve some weeks in jail and had to break up his band. Despite sensational publicity, his popularity was not affected, and after stints with old boss Goodman and old friend Tommy Dorsey, he formed a band of his own again.

Professionally, he had no more bad luck, but his first wife, to whom he was deeply devoted, died young, a child was mentally handicapped, and his health began to decline from the mid-sixties on, after he had a heart attack. About a year before his death from blood cancer, his house in Yonkers, of which he was very proud, was almost completely destroyed by fire, and his treasured scrapbooks, photos, and other memorabilia were all burned to ashes.

Experiences like the fourteen-below night out convinced Eddie Condon that just playing music he believed in wasn't enough. Between such unlikely jobs as working the Stork Club with Red McKenzie (who in addition to singing had perfected the art of what he called blue-blowing—making trumpet-like

sounds with a comb covered, not with the customary tissue paper, but with strips of newspaper, a supply of which McKenzie would keep in his breast pocket and refer to as his "reeds") and Josh Billings, a painter manqué who drummed on a suitcase strapped in wrapping paper, stroking it with whisk brooms and occasionally giving it a kick, and being the pianist in a five-piece band on a luxury cruise to Buenos Aires though he played the piano with exceedingly limited technique and only in the key of F, Condon began to talk to influential people about the real jazz. He persuaded record companies to give him a date now and then, got well-to-do people to hire him and his friends to play at private parties, and eventually organized the first public jam sessions, first in clubs, then on the concert stage, and fronted a nightclub of his own where the real stuff could be played nightly and his friends could enjoy the security of steady jobs.

Before that, however, Eddie had nearly died of pancreatitis, his life saved by a rugged constitution and a saxophone-playing intern who had befriended him and got him to a hospital and a first-class surgeon in time. Eddie was thirty-one then; this was the first of several close brushes with death, none of which deterred him from his favorite pastime—the consumption of at least a quart of hard liquor a day. In his sixties, he did compromise a little, switching from scotch to vodka, drinking a bit more milk, and for a while, taking vitamin B shots.

In early 1972, about a year and a half before his death at sixty-seven, I was sitting with Eddie in the most recent incarnation of a Greenwich Village club known as Nick's when he worked there during the years 1937-45. A trombonist who hadn't seen Eddie in years came up to say hello. "You look wonderful," he said. (That was hyperbole, but all things considered, Eddie did look remarkably well.) "How do you do it?"

Eddie fixed him with a baleful stare.

"Total neglect," he said. "Total neglect."

The first Eddie Condon's opened in December, 1945, on Third Street, just east of Washington Square, where Eddie lived. ("It takes me three minutes to walk to work and three hours to reel back," he quipped.) It was a comfortable room, and though the musicians' facilities were not exactly elegant, consisting of a windowless room off a subcellar passageway, they were completely private. And the players were always welcome upstairs between sets if they wanted to rub elbows with the customers. The latter, aside from the normal complement of squares, included such Condon fans as painter Stuart Davis, writers John Steinbeck and John O'Hara, actors Henry Fonda and Burgess Meredith, and such old chums as Bing Crosby and Johnny Mercer, when they were in town.

The opening was covered in *Time* and other notable outlets. Eddie always had good press, from the time of his first big-time venture, a 1942 Carnegie Hall concert honoring Fats Waller. In the promotion with Eddie was Ernie Anderson, an enterprising advertising man with an ear for jazz, and it was he who guided Condon's public relations for many years, sometimes a bit too effusively.

Eddie was a dream client. He was genuinely witty and very quotable. His wit was barbed but not cruel, and he had authentic style. (When asked to explain the difference between his brand of jazz and bop, he responded, "The boppers flat their fifths; we drink ours.") Moreover, he had a gift for making an instant band out of any assemblage of musicians (provided they could play straightforward jazz).

This aspect of the Condon talent was explored in a series of Saturday twilight concerts at New York's Town Hall beginning in early 1942. The first audience was so scant that Eddie addressed it as "Lady and Gentleman," but the word soon spread. When the series resumed that fall, the respected composer/critic Virgil Thomson reviewed the opening concert in the *Herald Tribune*. He particularly liked the collective improvisation by all the participants with which Condon traditionally concluded such events.

"The nine-part tuttis," wrote Thomson, "were of a grandeur, a sumptuousness of sound and a spontaneous integration of individual freedoms that makes one proud of the country that gave birth to such a high manifestation of sensibility and intelligence and happy to be present at such a full and noble expression of the musical faculties."

In 1929, when they had played the Palace, *Variety* had reviewed Condon and Company, describing them as "the poorest 7-piece orchestra on earth." In his autobiography, *We Called It Music*, Condon describes his reaction to the Thomson review: "I read it seven times, once for each member of the 'poorest 7-piece orchestra on earth.' "

The Town Hall series continued for five years. The Armed Forces Radio Service began to record the concerts and broadcast them wherever Allied soldiers and sailors were stationed. The response was overwhelming; the show won first place in a GI popularity poll. The Blue Network transcribed the concerts and augmented the transcriptions with studio recordings by the Condonites. Eddie branched out with even bigger concerts at Carnegie Hall. "Presenting 30 of the greatest living hot musicians," read the publicity; it wasn't far from accurate.

In 1947, Condon moved on to infant television. The weekly "Eddie Condon Floorshow" was the first, best, and so far only regularly scheduled jazz program on commercial television. It had a terrific house band made up of Condon stalwarts, and the guests included Louis Armstrong, Hot Lips Page, Billie Holiday, Jack Teagarden, Roy Eldridge, Sidney Bechet, Billy Butterfield, and Billy Eckstine. It was too good to last.

In 1959, the Condon club moved uptown to East Fifty-sixth Street. The Village lease had expired the year before. Uptown was different. The prices were higher, the atmosphere less relaxed. The music was still good most of the time, but the band's personnel fluctuated much more, and Eddie seldom appeared on the stand with his faithful "porkchop," as Red McKenzie had long ago dubbed the Condon guitar. And the distance from home to work and back had become much longer.

By the time the Uptown Condon's closed for good, in 1967, Eddie had once again defied death. He underwent operations for cancer in 1964 and 1965 and was given little time to live. Some well-meaning friends even organized a tribute to him; when someone inadvertently referred to the event as a "benefit," Eddie became livid. He was in the business of arranging benefits for others, not of being on the receiving end. He had a right to be angry. In any case, the premature testimonial was a flop. And Eddie fooled the doctors again; he went on living a productive life until mid-summer of 1973, when that splendid constitution finally broke down.

At the memorial service, Gene Krupa was among those who eulogized Eddie, whom he referred to by his old nickname, "Slick." He recalled how much Eddie's faith in the music and its future had meant to him and the other youngsters when the going had been tough. Less than three months later Gene himself was dead.

Eddie Condon and the men around him constituted a unique assemblage of rugged individualists.

Billy Butterfield

Only Condon could have kept them together in working order for a greater length of time than a one-night stand. I remember a front line at the old Condon's of Wild Bill Davison, cornet; Georg Brunis, trombone; and Pee Wee Russell, clarinet: three strong and completely different personalities. Neither could have been the leader of the band, but Condon's authority was undisputed. And he didn't just make sure the guys showed up on time; he set the musical policy.

Wild Bill was one of Eddie's great favorites. Fittingly born in Defiance, Ohio, Bill cut his musical eyeteeth in such jazz meccas as Cincinnati, but did work and enjoy some reputation in Chicago in the late twenties and early thirties. The death of Frank Teschemacher disrupted his plans for a big band, and he settled in Milwaukee for nearly a decade, out of the jazz limelight. When he came to New York in 1941, he immediately made a place for himself at clubs like Jimmy Ryan's on Fifty-second Street and Nick's in Greenwich Village with his rugged, damn-the-torpedoes style. He was in the house band at Condon's on opening night and remained a fixture at the club until it closed; he didn't participate in the move uptown. In 1971, he and Eddie toured together in twenty-six states with a band led by pianist Art Hodes, another old Chicago friend.

Wild Bill was born in 1906; at seventy he still plays with the fire of a young man. He, too, has had his scrapes with illness, and his appetite for spirits is almost equal to Condon's. His rasping cornet can be alternately lyrical and raunchy, and he can push any band, no matter how sluggish, into some semblance of drive.

In his spare time, Bill collects antiques and keepsakes. When he sees something he likes, it isn't safe for long. His exploits as a collector are legendary. He also likes to construct models of ships or airplanes; they are painstakingly detailed and testify to Bill's amazing steadiness of hand and eye.

Among the things Bill collects are army helmets (he is especially fond of the spiked Kaiser Wilhelm type), uniforms, and guns. Once, at one of Dick Gibson's early Colorado Jazz Parties, he was made an honorary sheriff of Aspen and presented with a badge and a six-shooter, unfortunately as loaded as its new owner. A series of mishaps ensued, resulting in the awakening, at about five A.M., of almost the entire township—an effort in which Bill's shooting was abetted by the barking of the town's many dogs.

Wild Bill Davison

Pee Wee Russell, c. 1924

It turned out to be Bill's last Jazz Party, but he always got plenty of work, so he was not too depressed on his way back to New York. Going home from the airport, he insisted on showing the taxi driver his proud new possession. New York cab-drivers are, understandably, not fond of seeing guns in the hands of their passengers, and this cabbie was no exception. Bill nevertheless insisted on showing the driver the weapon. Waving it about, he forgot that it was still loaded and accidentally fired a shot right through the windshield, only inches past the driver's head.

Convinced he had a lunatic on his hands, the driver pulled up at the nearest police station, where Bill's honorary sheriff's badge failed to impress the resident constabulary. Released on bail and taken home by his patient and understanding wife, he eventually got off with a fine and a warning. He also got his picture in the papers.

Pee Wee Russell probably never fired a gun in his life, but he got along famously with Bill. Even among the characters that made up the Condon gang, Pee Wee stood out. Born Charles Ellsworth Russell in 1906 in Maplewood, Missouri, and raised in Muskogee, Oklahoma, and St. Louis, Pee Wee was long, lean, and lanky, with the sad face of a Basset hound. Though his ancestry was primarily British, he was proud of a trace of Indian blood, insisting that his good friend Jack Teagarden, who was often taken for Indian, was "strictly a Dutchman, not Indian at all."

Pee Wee was the most deferential of men. A raised voice made him jump. But his music had great courage. It was truly original—among the most originally conceived and executed expressions in jazz, which, after all, is the most highly personal of musics—and very moving. The range of dynamics in Pee Wee's style was extreme—from a hoarse whisper or subtone moan to a piercing shriek that could slash through the loudest, brassiest ensemble.

To the uninitiated, watching Russell play was like bearing witness to a life-and-death struggle between man and instrument. Between phrases that appeared to be wrung from the clarinet under protest, Pee Wee would make faces and mutter Fieldsian asides to himself. When he received applause, he looked astonished, shook his head, and waved off the approbation.

Despite his nervousness (Pee Wee never mentioned it, nor was it noted in the far from negligible

Pee Wee Russell

amount written about him, but in a 1975 interview Bud Freeman claimed that Pee Wee suffered from St. Vitus's dance as a child, and that this was the reason for his involuntary facial and bodily movements and extreme shyness), Pee Wee knew exactly what he was doing. He was not a great technician of the clarinet like Benny Goodman (whom he much admired), but he coaxed from it the effects he wanted with considerable certainty, and his sound was the result of finely calibrated nuances of execution.

Pee Wee was also a fancier of the grape. Musicians of his generation usually started their careers early. This meant that while still in their teens they were exposed to the peculiar environment of prohibition-era night life. Small wonder that they grew up to become legendary drinkers.

Pee Wee's crisis came in 1951, when he was forty-five. It was his liver; always gaunt, he became just skin and bones. Hospitalized in San Francisco, he was photographed for *Life* with anxious old friends Jack Teagarden and Louis Armstrong at his bedside. He appeared to be dying, yet made a miraculous recovery—for once the cliché is appropriate—and enjoyed almost fourteen more years of life, in some ways the most productive and rewarding of his career.

He confounded some of his fans by forming a pianoless quartet with trombonist Marshall Brown that explored the entire jazz repertoire, up to and including John Coltrane, Ornette Coleman, and other avant-gardists. This should have been surprising only to those who never fully understood Pee Wee's music, which always had been iconoclastic and "experimental," even if most of the experiments had taken place within a fairly traditional context. (It speaks well for the musical environment fostered by Condon that it could encompass Pee Wee, though there were times when he did feel boxed in.)

He appeared at a Newport Jazz Festival in 1963 with Thelonious Monk, the man once labeled "the high priest of bebop." They played together without problems. He made the first of many visits to Europe in 1961 and toured Australia, New Zealand, and Japan with Condon and other old friends, including blues-shouter Jimmy Rushing, in 1964. The following year, he revealed a talent totally unsuspected even by his closest friends. Literally overnight, he became an accomplished painter.

Because he was comfortable enough to work in music only when it seemed worthwhile—artistically and financially—Pee Wee had time on his hands and no hobbies. This disturbed his devoted wife, Mary, who one day happened to see what was advertised as a complete painting set at Macy's. On an impulse, she bought it, brought it home, dumped it in the lap of her surprised husband, and ordered, "Here! Do something with yourself! Paint!"

Pee Wee's only prior relationship to painting had been through his friend, drummer George Wettling, who had studied seriously with Stuart Davis, dean of American abstraction. Wettling was good enough to have had a couple of gallery showings and record-album covers. Pee Wee, characteristically, didn't consult George or anyone else. Nor did he read books about painting or visit museums. He just began to paint, using no easel but resting the canvas on his lap or placing it, horizontally, on a chair. From the start, he mixed his own colors.

Pee Wee completed his first oil on November 30, 1965. Ten months later he was happily at work on his sixty-first canvas. The walls of the cozy Russell apartment were covered with his brightly colored bursts of creative energy in the new-found medium.

His style, if one had to classify it, at first glance looked like geometric abstraction, but closer inspection usually revealed representational elements. His colors were bold and beautifully harmonized, and there was a fey humor in his work that reminded one of his playing. Though friends and, after a while, art collectors he had never met began to purchase his work, he considered painting no more than "a very relaxing pastime." It distressed him when some people got the notion that he was giving up playing for painting—music was still the essence of his life.

Most pleased was Mary Russell. The two had been married for almost twenty-five years, and though she knew that her husband was much admired in jazz circles, she never really liked his playing. Since both had well-developed senses of humor, this was no great issue in their life together, but the painting was something Mary could take genuine pride in. She dubbed him "Charlie Van Goy" and organized a show at Rutgers University which the artist was too shy to attend. She had other, more ambitious plans for him when she became ill and died suddenly of cancer in June, 1967.

Pee Wee never painted again. Though friends looked after him as best they could, no one could keep him on as strict a regimen of booze as Mary had—she had made a pleasant ritual of administering his daily ration of cognac. Now, there seemed no more need to be careful. He still enjoyed playing, especially with his favorite partner of later years, Bobby Hackett of the silver-toned cornet, but gradually he seemed to slide more and more back into himself.

Pee Wee died in February, 1969, a few weeks short of sixty-three. He left behind some of the most strikingly original jazz ever played on a clarinet and about a hundred extraordinary paintings.

Bobby Hackett, born in 1915, was one of nine children of a railroad blacksmith from Providence, Rhode Island. He became part of the Condon circle when he came to New York in 1937. He played guitar as well as cornet and had an infallible ear for what jazz musicians call chord changes—the underlying harmonic structure of songs and themes.

At first he was hailed as a new Bix Beiderbecke, though his real inspiration was Louis Armstrong. However, his pretty sound, lyrical approach to ballads, and lucid and logical way of constructing his solos did recall Bix, and for a while he was reluctantly cast in this role, even re-creating famous Beiderbecke solos while featured with Horace Heidt's commercial band—a job he had taken to recover some of the losses suffered by his own short-lived big band, which included Pee Wee Russell (doubling on alto saxophone), Condon (the guitarist's only steady big-band job), and other assorted mavericks.

Hackett, a soft-spoken and gentle man who can be very stubborn when he has made up his mind about something, became one of the most widely heard of all jazz musicians when comedian Jackie Gleason featured him on some recordings he had concocted—slow, syrup-stringed renditions of romantic melodies (one album was entitled *Music, Martinis, and Memories*) enhanced by Hackett's warm, and even in this unstimulating environment, lovely and creative embellishments. The records sold enormously well, were heard on radio and piped into countless elevators and supermarkets, and led to many similar Muzak ventures for Hackett.

This was nothing new to Bobby, who years before had brought moments of real beauty to Glenn Miller's slick commercial music. When he calls the tune, however, he much prefers to surround himself with sympathetic jazz players. His music is by no means restricted to romantic lyricism. He can play a bold, singing lead to a collective ensemble or get

Edmond Hall

into the marrow of the blues—in short, he is a man for all musical seasons.

Bobby's admirers include almost every jazz trumpeter extant. Miles Davis has praised him, and he was one of Louis Armstrong's favorites. On records and in person, he often delighted Louis with his tasteful obbligato comments behind the master's vocals, or his perfect counterlines to an Armstrong trumpet lead. He has accompanied a host of singers, Frank Sinatra among them. Whoever he plays behind sounds better for it.

In recent years, Bobby has often co-led groups with trombonist Vic Dickenson, a unique stylist who was a veteran of some of the great black bands of the twenties and thirties, including Count Basie's, when he decided to concentrate on small-group work. Though he often sat in at Condon's, Vic didn't become a regular until after the club moved uptown. From then on, his sly smears and slurs often spiced Condonian ensembles. Vic's very personal blend of wit and lyricism went well with, for example, Pee Wee Russell, or with the stinging sound of another great clarinetist, Edmond Hall, originally from New Orleans but far from traditional in his approach. Ed was a Condon regular for five years in the fifties, and again later on, after a stint with Louis Armstrong's All Stars. (Vic, Ed, trombonist Benny Morton, bassists Walter Page and Leonard Gaskin, trumpeter Buck Clayton, and ex-Ellington cornetist Rex Stewart were among the black musicians who became Condon fixtures.) Vic's style also complemented Hackett's, and few musicians enjoy each other's work and personality as much as these two genuine originals.

Most veteran jazzmen, having spent much time "on the road," learn the hard way that decent food can be difficult to obtain in a strange town after the night's work is over and most ordinary mortals have long since gone to bed. Of the various ways of coping with this problem, substituting drink for food is not efficient in the long run and cultivating a taste for cardboard hamburgers and various canned junk is not much healthier.

No musician I know has found a better solution than Vic Dickenson, who always—unless it is impossible—takes lodgings where cooking facilities exist, keeps pots and pans and kitchen tools that satisfy his stringent requirements stashed with privileged friends in various cities, forages for fresh staples before the night's work begins, and is an unsurpassed master at concocting delicious-tasting

Vic Dickenson

Bud Freeman

meals from simple and honest ingredients. (You can have your haute cuisine; I'll take Vic's soulful stews and chops.) Thus fortified, the long night's work and a possible upcoming journey through the dawn hold no terrors, and temptation has no pitfalls.

Another veteran who takes good care of himself is that original Austin High Gang member and aristocrat of the tenor sax, Bud Freeman—like Dickenson born in 1906 but still in his prime. A lifelong Anglophile (he had early aspirations toward becoming a Shakespearean actor), Bud is now incongruously ensconced in Dublin, where he can indulge himself in his passion for ascots and civilized conversation. His libido, he proudly assures his friends, is unimpaired, and he finds European women much more understanding of the artist's needs than American women.

Bud's autobiography (really a collection of stories and anecdotes) is entitled *You Don't Look Like a Musician,* a comment that obviously must have pleased the author. A colleague who isn't too fond of him dubbed him "Lord Bud" and considers him a snob, but that reaction is unusual, for Bud has a sense of humor and doesn't mind being ribbed about his foibles. (Besides, he can really play his horn, and that's what counts.)

His style is his own—it belongs to none of the major schools of tenor playing described by the jazz scholars—and it has been heard for six decades. Unlike some of his unreconstructed pals, Freeman found it possible to work in the big swing bands, and his well-turned solos grace many a record by Tommy Dorsey and quite a few by Benny Goodman. His tenure in both bands was made easier by the presence of another authentic Chicagoan, Dave Tough—one of the best drummers in jazz.

While Bud has intellectual aspirations, Tough was the real thing, conversant with Tolstoy and Proust, in his youth an avid fan of H. L. Mencken's *American Mercury,* and—judging from the few fragments that have survived—a writer of style and wit. A master musician, Tough even made the transition to bebop, a music initially much resented by most of his contemporaries and friends, and propelled Woody Herman's First Herd, one of the top big bands of the mid-forties, to its greatest heights. Yet another victim of the jazz environment, he died at forty, his skull fractured in a fall on a deserted Newark street.

Bud and Davey didn't last long with Goodman, who is respected for his musicianship but not uni-

Bud Freeman with Bob Wilber

versally loved. A few years younger than most of the Chicagoans around Condon, he was a prodigy and they all knew him when. According to Bud, "When we were youngsters you couldn't have met a more loving person than Benny. He didn't have the faintest idea of the extraordinary talent he possessed. He changed a lot when he had the band. He seemed impervious to other people."

He tells a story to illustrate the point. During an engagement at the Paramount Theater, the Goodman band was required to get off stage after the show in the dark. One night a musician in the band stumbled and fell, dropping his instrument. As he lay prostrate, Benny stepped over him, picked up the clarinet, played a few scales, and turned to another bandsman, saying, "It's O.K. The clarinet is O.K."

That may seem callous, but the man who had fallen was a drinker, and Benny was no doubt aware of the fact that drinkers often fall but seldom hurt themselves badly. Also, a clarinet is a delicate and costly piece of work, a good one hard to replace, and the fallen musician himself would no doubt have thought of its welfare before his own.

Bud soon ventured out on his own as a leader, and one of his first ensembles remains among the most memorable of the many he has fronted. It was known as the Summa Cum Laude Band, a name bestowed upon it by Eddie Condon's bride-to-be, Phyllis Smith, an advertising copywriter of distinction. It was just right for a Freeman band, though it lent itself to all sorts of unflattering variants, such as "louder" and "lousy." Its members included Pee Wee, Condon, and scrappy little Max Kaminsky, who also had served time with Tommy Dorsey, and with the self-same Artie Shaw who had left him and Condon out in the fourteen-below cold.

Maxie is among the remaining guardians of the Condon legacy. In 1976, he could still be found on Sundays at Jimmy Ryan's, the sole surviving name in the jazz nightclub business dating back to the Fifty-second Street days. It is right next door to another club that carries on the tradition—the third Eddie Condon's, named in Eddie's honor by its owner, bassist Red Balaban, with official sanction from Phyllis Condon. The decor is by Johnny DeVries, who was on hand at the opening of the first Condon's and wrote the lyrics for some of Eddie's tunes (there aren't very many, but they're all good).

It's an honest saloon, and the music is in the proper tradition. Ed Hall's brother Herb is in the house band, and so is Vic Dickenson. Eddie would have liked that.

I interviewed Vic and Condon's name came up. "Eddie Condon," said Vic, "was one hell of a man."

4 More Giants of The Golden Age

No matter what one's predilections, given a more than nodding acquaintance with the music's history, the period roughly from 1935 to 1945 must be recognized as the golden age of jazz. As this period began, the music's growing pains had ended and a mature, perfectly poised style had evolved. In the words of the French critic and musician André Hodeir, a man who certainly can't be accused of bias against modernism: "Never before or since have so many great musicians existed side by side, uniting their efforts to found a marvelously rich and diversified school of jazz—and all the more rich and diversified for being both classical and romantic at the same time."

It is a characteristic of golden ages that they produce figures larger than life, and jazz is no exception. The men and women who created the music of this period came up in a unique school, a school of life as well as art. There had been little understanding or appreciation of what they were doing beyond the admiration of their peers and the gratitude of the dancers. If they were black—and most of them were—they had to function within a social caste system designed to stunt rather than further creativity. If they were white, they had to go against the grain of that system.

The year in which jazz—under the new name of "swing"—made its great popular breakthrough, a breakthrough that would eventually considerably improve the material lot of the musicians (if still far from enough for black artists) was 1935, not coincidentally the year when the classic period, the golden age of jazz began. Many of the leaders in that breakthrough more than forty years ago have fallen by the wayside—the jazz road is a hard one—but a surprising number were still active and productive in 1976. They have survived not only the rigors of the jazz life but also all the changing fads, fashions, and fancies that the music's newfound popularity soon gave rise to. In addition, of course, there were the natural developments any living art undergoes, accelerated by the communications technology of the age.

These jazz giants—and some who are gone now but who lasted a good long time—are a breed apart. They are not heroes free from the flaws of ordinary mortals. On the contrary, they seem, if anything, more essentially human than most of us. They have been in touch with every stratum of society and have observed almost everything there is to observe about human behavior. In the ancient Roman phrase, nothing human is alien to them.

Yet, in most cases they have retained their sanity, equilibrium, and perspective. They have become neither vain nor bitter and are among the rare human beings of our time who seem fulfilled. Perhaps this is because their music is at once the most individualistic and the most collaborative of arts—classic jazz is a microcosmic democracy, a functioning partnership between equals. Perhaps it is because the times through which they lived were such extraordinary ones. Perhaps it is because it takes extraordinary qualities to reach the top of a demanding profession and stay there. Whatever

Eubie Blake (at piano) and Noble Sissle in the early 1920s

Courtesy of Eubie Blake

**Eubie Blake.
Photographed in 1975,
at the age of ninety-two**

the reason, it is not romanticism in the starry eyes of the beholders that causes them to view these representatives of the classic age of jazz with awe as well as affection.

Though his career began long before the golden age and has extended far beyond it, Eubie Blake symbolizes its human qualities. In February, 1976, when he celebrated his ninety-third birthday, James Hubert Blake—composer, pianist, singer, erstwhile bandleader, and master of the art of living—was still active, enchanting audiences of all ages with his vigorous playing, astonishing memory and vivid story-telling, frank comments on social and racial matters, and liveliness and charm.

Born in Baltimore, the son of former slaves, he learned the rudiments of organ from his mother and began to sneak out of the house at night while still in his early teens to play piano at a friendly neighborhood brothel. His transgression was discovered, but he was set on an unwaveringly musical course. In 1915 he teamed up with a singer and lyric writer named Noble Sissle. A team for many years, their most notable achievement was *Shuffle Along,* the most successful and longest-running black musical show on Broadway. It was produced in 1921 and contained one of Blake's biggest hits, *I'm Just Wild About Harry.*

Another Blake evergreen is *Memories of You,* and he has written dozens of rags and other piano pieces, including waltzes. In 1946, he went into semiretirement, making occasional appearances on television or at special functions, but in 1969 he was persuaded to play at the New Orleans Jazz Festival and was such a hit that his career entered a new phase at eighty-seven. It eventually took him back to places in Europe he hadn't seen in more than fifty years and some he'd never seen before.

Between engagements, he writes new music at his comfortable house in Brooklyn, surrounded by memorabilia including honorary doctorates from Yale and the New England Conservatory (among others) and citations from ASCAP and other professional organizations. He can tell a story about each photograph or document, complaining that his memory isn't what it used to be when a name or date momentarily eludes him.

Chronologically and historically, Eubie Blake is a relic of the ragtime era and its sole important survivor. In reality, he is anything but a relic. His lively, alert mind allows us first-hand glimpses of a vanished age and makes him a living conduit of the

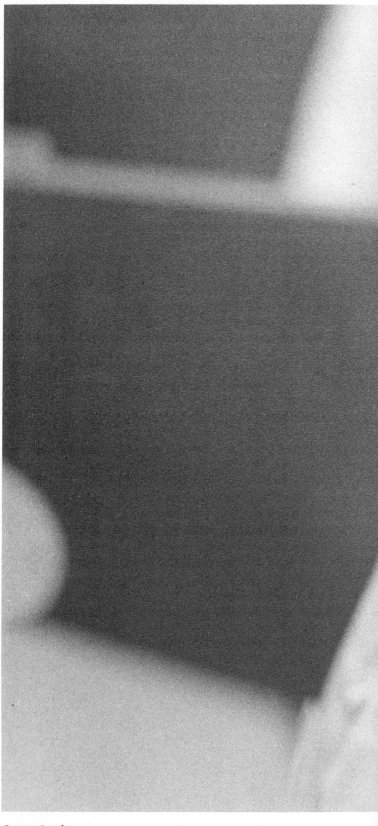

Count Basie

Count Basie

prehistory of the music called jazz, an echo from beyond its golden age.

Count Basie is the grand old man of swing. Past seventy, he still heads up his great, roaring swing machine, spending the better part of any given year on the road. And his spare, seemingly simple style and inimitable touch and time at the piano still govern the band, setting the most perfect tempos in big-band jazz—for playing *and* dancing.

The Basie band still plays for dancing. Count does concerts, too, but never to the extent Ellington did. And it is at a dance, especially when the dancers are attuned to the music, that you'll hear the Basie band at its best.

Aside from Count himself, the only other visible link with the past in the band is the guitarist, Freddie Green, who joined in March, 1937, and hasn't missed many band calls since. He is unique not just in this respect—only Ellington's Harry Carney had a longer record of unbroken service—but also as the last representative of a vanished species, the unamplified rhythm guitarist. Every big swing band had guitarists in the golden age, but changing rhythm styles did away with them. But not in Basie's band. Freddie Green's sometimes almost inaudible but always feelable strum—the incarnation of swinging 4/4 time—is so much part and parcel of the Basie conception that the band would be unthinkable without him.

Freddie is a quiet man. In the early days of the band, when Billie Holiday was its girl singer, he and Billie were sweethearts, engaged to be married. Billie didn't talk about him in her purported autobiography; considering its general tone, she did him a favor. He doesn't talk about Billie. He sits hunched over his guitar, keeping perfect time, bothered, or so it seems, only by the imperfections of his section mates—especially the drummers. For years, he suffered the presence of a flamboyant but unsteady percussionist, knowing that the man's showmanship was good for the band's popularity and doing his best to keep the time where it belonged.

He had no such problems during the days when Basie's rhythm team was known as "The All-American Rhythm Section." Basie, Freddie, bassist Walter Page, and drummer Jo Jones were together from the time the guitarist joined (the others had been aboard since 1936) until Page left in the fall of 1942, and constituted a rhythm section the equal of which the jazz world hasn't seen. (It was reunited for

Buck Clayton

a spell in the late forties.)

Page, the senior member, had led bands of his own and even been Basie's boss. He was—as far as we know—the first bassist to play four-in-a-bar, and he taught the other members of the section how to fit their parts to his. He was the governor.

Jo Jones was the firebrand. Nicknamed "The Man Who Plays Like the Wind," he was one of the first drummers to take the pulse-keeping function from the bass drum and transfer it to the cymbals. (Jo himself says Fletcher Henderson's great drummer Walter Johnson was first, but Jo popularized it and thus became one of the fathers of modern jazz drum style.) He also perfected the use of the high-hat (two facing cymbals on a rod, brought together by means of a foot pedal).

Jo was (and is) a master, and one of the visually most elegant of all drummers. His use of wire brushes is the height of subtlety, and when he plays, his face registers a gamut of expressions, from joy to pain. Unlike the taciturn Freddie Green, Jo is a talker, a philosopher of life, a man with strong and strongly expressed opinions about music and musicians. For years, he has been an informal educator of the young, and there is many a musician he has brought along on the strength of his teachings, musical and moral. He always looks out for "the kiddies," especially gifted young drummers.

Because he speaks his mind when things not to his liking are going on and has used the even more effective weapon of playing aggressively, there are some, especially among his contemporaries, who take a deep breath when Jo walks into a club or gathering. But he can still put his music where his mouth is, and when he wants to play, there's no more inspiring beat than his.

The brass and reed players that the Basie rhythm section backed up included some of the most original instrumentalists of the Swing Era. In the trumpet section, the key soloists were Buck Clayton and Harry ("Sweets") Edison, contrasting and compatible. Buck, nicknamed "Cat Eye," was described by Billie Holiday as "the most beautiful blue-eyed Negro I've ever seen" and was a ladies' man. In addition to playing a horn that could sing a tender ballad or swing the blues, Buck was responsible for many of the band's arrangements.

Before joining Basie in 1936 (passing through Kansas City on his way to a job in New York, he was persuaded to stay), Buck had crowded a lot of activity into twenty-five years of life. Born in Kansas in

Count Basie at Roseland, New York City

1912, he moved to California, played with some of the best bands there, was appointed leader of a band booked to play a ballroom in Shanghai, spent almost two years there, learning to speak several Chinese dialects, and back in Los Angeles formed his own big band, "The 14 Gentlemen from Harlem."

Since leaving Basie in 1943, Buck has mainly led his own bands of various sizes, but has also played and arranged for Benny Goodman and written for Basie, Harry James, and Ellington. He has worked in France with Mezz Mezzrow and in New York at Eddie Condon's and toured all over with his own groups.

In 1969, Buck underwent lip surgery, which affected his embouchure; shortly after he started to play again, he broke an arm in a fall, then had an operation for double hernia. This series of mishaps convinced him the time had come to give up playing, but he stays active in music as an arranger and has headed up some 1975 all-star studio sessions reminiscent of his notable "Buck Clayton Jam Sessions" from the fifties—the sort of gatherings of temperamental artists that only a man of Clayton's musical and psychological skill can keep under control. (Clayton resumed playing in 1976.)

The man behind some of Clayton's best records is also the man who brought the Basie band out of Kansas City, introduced Freddie Green to Count, and had a great effect on Basie's career—as indeed on jazz as a whole. His name appears often in our chronicle. It is John Hammond.

Hammond has great enthusiasm, great energy, strong opinions, and a strong will. He gets things done, and for more than forty years has been a prime mover in the music, which is his combined vocation and avocation. He has discovered or decisively furthered the careers of Basie, Billie Holiday, Teddy Wilson, Charlie Christian, and, in more recent times, Bob Dylan. Through his close association with Benny Goodman, he played a key role in the launching of the Swing Era. He was responsible for the rediscovery (in effect, the discovery) of boogie-woogie, the percussive, eight-to-the-bar piano style that became a national craze in the late thirties. He organized and supervised many of the best recording dates in jazz, from a 1932 Fletcher Henderson session through the classic Billie Holiday-Teddy Wilson dates to a 1975 Helen Humes album. He produced two monumental pioneering concerts at Carnegie Hall in 1938 and

1939 under the title "Spirituals to Swing"; they reflected his knowledge and understanding not only of jazz but also its root forms, black secular and religious music. Implicit in all these accomplishments is Hammond's tireless fight for recognition and dignity for black performers, and beyond that immediate goal, for racial equality, a cause he championed long before—and after—it was a fashionable liberal pursuit.

To this day, Hammond positively radiates delight in a newly discovered (or rediscovered) performer. "You simply must go hear so-and-so," he tells friends and acquaintances. "Marvelous! Just marvelous!"

Sweets Edison is the master of the musical epigram. Rooted in the blues, his playing reflects the irreverent gleam in his eye. He can take one single note or phrase and repeat it, perfectly yet surprisingly placed in the rhythmic stream, over the course of an entire chorus. His mature style consists almost entirely of pet phrases which in the hands of others would be clichés, but in his are infinitely reusable without danger of wearing out.

One of his greatest admirers is Frank Sinatra, who has often used Sweets to play discreet but insouciant obbligati for him. He is also a favorite of Norman Granz, the originator of Jazz at the Philharmonic, of whose various troupes he has been a member, on and off, since the early fifties. Sweets was never out of style, not even during the heydays of bop and cool, when so many Swing Era players were dubbed old-fashioned. Sweets has long been in demand in the Los Angeles recording studios and plays a good game of golf, almost a requirement for holding one's own on that scene.

The Basie trombone section also always sported at least two good soloists. Benny Morton and Dicky Wells, though both disciples of the great Jimmy Harrison, offered different but complementary styles: Morton mellow and melodic; Wells explosive and unpredictable, a master of blues. For a while, the wit of Vic Dickenson also graced the section, but he left when there didn't seem to be enough solo space for him.

Intramural rivalry was at its peak in the Basie sax section, among tenor players Herschel Evans and Lester Young. When the Basie band came roaring out of Kansas City in 1936, these two captured the imagination of the fans, and each had his loyal supporters. It was here that the seed of the famous "tenor battles" of the ensuing decade was planted.

Jo Jones

Benny Morton

The two-tenor tradition has been kept alive by Basie. In the fifties, the roles of Young and Evans were played by Paul Quinichette and Eddie ("Lockjaw") Davis, and Davis's distinctive style could be heard with Basie on and off through the mid-seventies.

Evans and Young, born in the same year (1909), represented opposite poles of instrumental conception and approach. Evans was an avowed disciple of Coleman Hawkins—big-toned, expansive, romantic. Young was the harbinger of a new style, his sound smoother, less vibratoed, his conception wholly original, his approach to improvisation relaxed, airy, yet the epitome of swing.

"Why don't you play alto, man? You've got an alto tone," Herschel teased Lester. Lester tapped his head. "There's things going on up there. Some of you guys are all belly."

But despite the rivalry and the teasing, said Jo Jones, the two men were almost like brothers. Herschel died of a heart condition in early 1939. Strangely, there was an occasional echo of Evans's Texas "cry" in Lester's later style.

Herschel's replacement was George ("Buddy") Tate, another Texan. An Evans admirer and a great blues man, he stayed with Basie for almost a decade, then led his own groups. For nearly twenty years he was in charge of the house band at the Celebrity Club in Harlem. His frequent tours abroad, often with old friend Buck Clayton, and his warm manner with jazz fans won him friends all over Europe, and when they came to New York, they were always welcome at the Celebrity. So, for that matter, were Buddy's home-grown fans. The Celebrity, a club that rented out to social organizations, or for family celebrations, sold no food—it was strictly bring-your-own—but there always seemed to be an extra plate for the "foreigners" from downtown.

Buddy is among the tenors who learned from both Lester Young and Coleman Hawkins, the founders of the two main schools on the instrument. Lester, though younger, died ten years before Hawkins, and his health and influence declined in his later years. Hawkins, whose style once had seemed on the verge of being eclipsed by Young, had by the time of Lester's death found new followers and was once again in ascendance. He was by all odds one of the most remarkable of the many remarkable men of jazz.

When he was called "The Father of the Tenor Sax," Hawkins would often decline the compliment, saying that others had contributed too. In part this was honesty, in part an attempt to make himself appear not quite so old, not all that historic a figure. His peers fondly called him "The Old Man" long before he began to look the part. Though short of stature, he had great presence. His impeccably

Freddie Green

Buddy Tate

tailored suits made him look taller, as did his discreetly elevated shoes, and he moved like a man who mattered. His deep voice was surprisingly strong and projected like an opera singer's. When he laughed, it cut through the babble of a crowd.

His music reflected his persona. It was impeccably crafted, with the most thorough command of the syntax of music and technique of the instrument. His sound was one of the landmarks of jazz—in itself enough to ensnare the listener. It could caress a melody and shape its lines voluptuously. His ballad playing was the essence of romanticism. On fast tunes, he was fierce, indefatigable, producing chorus upon chorus of roaring, snorting power and driving rhythm. Lester was a diver, an acrobat, a tightrope walker; Hawk was a long-distance runner, a hammer-thrower, a football player.

Jokes about his age were legion. "I was in knee pants when my mother took me to see you the first time," said Ben Webster, one of Hawk's erstwhile disciples and some eight years his junior. "That wasn't me," came the disdainful reply, "that was my father." Until he was into his sixties, Hawk was sleek, vigorous, and in full control of himself.

Though he drank his share, he never tired of insisting one had to eat in order to be able to handle whiskey. He demonstrated by devouring great quantities of food (it had to be well prepared, of course), preferably Chinese or "soul," and was himself an excellent cook, when he had the patience. A girl told me she'd sometimes fix him eight eggs for breakfast.

He would talk about how Lester Young—who was dead by then—wouldn't eat when they had toured together in Jazz at the Philharmonic. "When I got myself a sandwich," he said, "I'd get one for Lester, too. He'd thank me and take it, but when we'd get off the bus I'd look under his seat and there was the sandwich—he'd hardly touched it."

Not many years later, it was Hawk who refused to eat while continuing to drink. By then, he had let his hair and beard grow and looked like a grizzled Old Testament prophet. His beautiful suits, cut to fit a healthy figure, hung like shrouds from his bony shoulders. His fine apartment, commanding a stunning view of Central Park, was in disarray unless a friend had just cleaned it up. In the parking lot, his Chrysler Imperial (he'd been driving that model since giving up Cadillacs because they had become ostentatious; he bought a new car each year) was rusting from disuse.

Eddie ("Lockjaw") Davis

Musically, Coleman Hawkins had always refused to grow old. He had no affection or respect for age (except when he spoke of his grandmother, who had raised him and lived well into her nineties) and that was probably why, when the aging process finally began to assert itself, he deliberately accelerated it by drinking and not eating.

Still, he could play with much of the old fire when allowed the time to get back into shape. The horn was so much a part of him and making music was such a need in him that being able to play revived him. Yet he was too proud to look for work ("They can call me if they want me") and never touched the horn at home. The loyal Norman Granz was one of the few who still contacted him, but Granz wasn't very active at the time.

In his last years, Coleman Hawkins readily accepted the friendship and help of men and of some women friends, but rejected love. His distaste for the aging process made it impossible for him to admit that any woman—especially a younger one—could feel any other emotion than pity for him, and pity he didn't want. At the end, his will to live expressed itself only in his desire to play, and in those final efforts, he sounded remarkably like Lester Young had in his last days. The stylistic opposites had finally met.

When Hawkins formulated the first viable tenor saxophone style during his years with Fletcher Henderson, he influenced almost every practitioner of the instrument. Two of his most gifted disciples died young. We have mentioned Herschel Evans; the other was Leon ("Chu") Berry, whom Hawk himself valued above all others. Chu was killed by the jazz musician's greatest enemy after alcohol: the road. He was just thirty-one when the car in which he was riding with fellow members of the Cab Calloway band, on their way from a 1941 one-night stand in Brookfield, Ohio, to another in Toronto, skidded and hit a concrete bridge. The others were only slightly hurt, but Chu died four days later without having regained consciousness.

"I played a session with Chu just a few weeks before he was killed," Hawkins told me years later, "and he showed me some stuff I'd never heard before. If he had lived, he might just have become the greatest. He had genius."

Ben Webster was at first so close to Hawkins in style and sound that he was mistaken for the master. This was due in part to circumstantial evidence—Ben had taken Hawk's place in the Henderson band after a short sojourn by Lester Young, who was allowed to quit after he could no longer stand the other musicians' efforts to make him play like Hawk, and Ben was on the first Henderson records made after Hawk's departure—which doesn't make the accomplishment a lesser one. But no musician wants to be an imitator, no matter how excellent.

Webster, who started as a pianist, eventually found his own very original and distinctive style as the first important tenor sax soloist in the Duke Ellington orchestra. From 1940 to 1943—perhaps the band's peak period—Webster was a key voice in Ellington's music, and his legacy was carried on by Paul Gonsalves, a player of similar warmth and emotion. Some of the greatest Ellington works are graced by Webster solos, and one masterpiece, *Cotton Tail*, contains not only a Webster solo that became part and parcel of every tenor player's vocabulary, but also a passage for the whole sax section that is Webster's, and was his pride and joy.

Ben wore his heart on his sleeve. He was one of the most openly emotional players in jazz—an openly emotional music—and at times he lost control. He was a fine blues player, gruff and earthy, and he devised a fast style of playing that influenced a flock of tenorists in the early forties—among them Illinois Jacquet, Flip Phillips, Georgie Auld, and Charlie Ventura. *Cotton Tail* epitomizes this facet of Websterian style.

But Ben's chief strength was his ballad playing. His sound, out of Hawkins, yet very personal, the intake and expulsion of his breath becoming part of the music in a unique, against-the-rules manner, was a thing of beauty. In his later years, there was a sadness, a yearning, yet a sinewy affirmation in Ben's treatment of romantic songs, played at the slowest of tempos, yet swinging from within, that made late Webster perhaps the greatest Webster.

Ben was a big man, with the strength and temperament of a bear—good-natured and gentle until aroused, then fearless and almost impossible to immobilize. In his youth, he had worked with the traveling family band led by Lester Young's father, and saved young Lester from drowning. When Lester died, Ben was inconsolable, and when Billie Holiday, whom he also loved dearly, followed Lester only four months later, it was another blow. Three years before, Art Tatum, the musician he most admired (after Duke Ellington, who was a kind of surrogate father), had died at a mere forty-six.

Harry ("Sweets") Edison

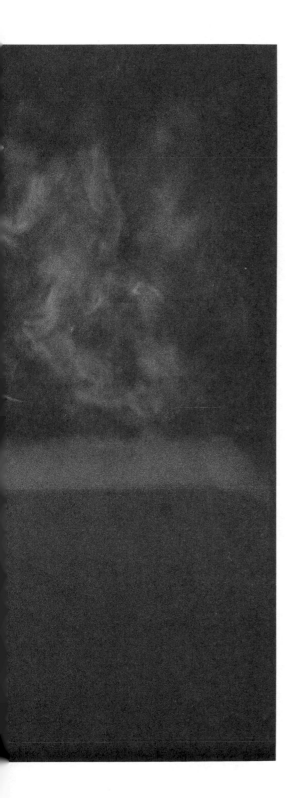

Ben was a sentimental man, and when he drank, which was too often, he would mourn for his lost heroes.

Wherever he might find himself—even in some transient hotel—Ben would place on his wall a photograph (incidentally, taken by Ole Brask) of Ellington to which was taped the caption "The Governor." And he always carried with him tapes of the music of Tatum, James P. Johnson, Fats Waller, and Ellington.

Those were lean days for Ben—his soulful music no longer seemed to be in demand, and he wasn't much of a businessman. For a while, he moved to California, mainly to look after his ailing grandmother. When he returned to New York in 1962, things got a bit better. There were young musicians interested in working with him, encouraging him, listening to his talk as well as to his horn. He worked at the Half Note in Greenwich Village, appeared in concert at the new Philharmonic Hall, and even got a gig in Harlem, where jazz of his brand—by now labeled mainstream—was seldom heard in clubs. (He happened to be working there during the time of a so-called "riot," actually a minor disturbance at 125th Street, and was overjoyed when a group of downtown friends came up to see him the following night, despite the bad press. "What are you up to?" he greeted us. "Did you come to start another riot?" Ole Brask discovered that Ben had hired two informal "bodyguards" to protect him when he came to visit Harlem.)

Ben roomed with Joe Zawinul, the Viennese pianist and composer who worked with Cannonball Adderley's group for a decade and wrote some of the group's most soulful hits. Ben had never been to Europe—one of the few musicians of his generation and fame who had somehow managed not to go—and had a country lad's fear of going where a foreign tongue was spoken.

But Joe and other friends put a bee in his bonnet, and he talked more and more of going. In December, 1964, Ben left for an engagement in Holland and never came back. His last nine years were spent first in Holland, then in Denmark. He grew very stout from too much beer and home cooking, became a fixture at the Montmartre, Copenhagen's leading jazz club—sometimes whether he was working there or not—and made a lot of fine records (in the United States, he hadn't made any between 1961 and 1964). Living abroad gave Ben a new lease on life, but he was often homesick.

Coleman Hawkins

Ben Webster

Ole Brask, who for a time acted as Ben's informal manager, once obtained a job for him in Barcelona. During the long train ride, Ben made friends with his traveling companions and before much time had passed, he was gloriously drunk. Eventually, he became boisterous and was taken off the train to a police station, where he slept it off, awakening to discover that it was the morning after his scheduled engagement and that he hadn't even gotten as far as Barcelona. He returned sober and contrite, his first thought being to somehow reimburse Brask for the train fare and lost commission.

One of Ben's buddies in his new environment was an old acquaintance from home, one of the leading Hawkins followers and tenor stars of classic jazz, Don Byas. Byas's career was sort of the reverse of

Webster's. He had played with several good bands but was known only among musicians when he was given the awesome job of taking Lester Young's place in the Basie band.

Well featured with Basie, Byas stayed for almost three years. He made his mark with a solo on *Harvard Blues* that announced a major new tenor voice with a velvety tone (one of the prettiest of all tenor sounds) and sinuous phrasing; it was one of those solos which, like Webster's *Cotton Tail*, immediately enter the repertoire of the instrument.

After Basie, Byas became a popular figure on Fifty-second Street. His ear for sophisticated harmonies made him welcome in the company of the young radicals who were forging what would become bebop. Coleman Hawkins, never afraid of a challenge, hired him and recorded with him. He recorded prolifically for the new small jazz-oriented labels that sprang up in the wake of the 1942–44 musicians' union strike against the major record companies and had a minor hit with *Laura*.

Then, in September, 1946, Byas went to Europe with a band put together by the veteran arranger Don Redman. His *Laura* was a show-stopper on the band's tour of the continent, and Byas decided to stay behind for a while when the rest of the band returned home. The "while" turned into nearly a quarter of a century—it was not until June, 1970, that Byas returned to the United States for an appearance at the Newport Jazz Festival. It was to be the culminating scene in a documentary about him produced by Dutch television. Byas had become a physical culturist in his adopted homeland (he first lived in France, then settled in Holland) and excelled at skin diving and deep-sea fishing. One of the reasons why he had resisted the temptation to return home, even for a visit, was that he was bound to run into old friends and feared this would lead him to take up drinking again.

His fears were well founded. The long absence had made his less than a household name at home—even in jazz circles. But Byas, a man with a fierce ego, expected star treatment. As the first of the American postwar expatriates in Europe, he had counseled and guided a generation of other emigrés, part-time and full-time, and though his long stay abroad had led the Europeans to take him pretty much for granted, he was still *somebody*.

His pride led him to turn down the offers for club and recording work he did get, and Byas was soon reduced to near inactivity. He sat in now and then, playing marvelously, but there was no steady work, and he started to drink again. When he drank, his stubbornness turned to mulishness. Furthermore, the prime condition he had been in (his first words when introduced to a stranger would be an invitation to hit him, "as hard as you can," in the gut; the muscles of his diaphragm were like iron) began to deteriorate. In early 1971, he went to Japan with Art Blakey's Jazz Messengers—an unlikely alliance—but he left the band after a single American engagement and hardly worked at all prior to his return to Holland that summer. Don Byas died of lung cancer about a year later in Amsterdam; he was not quite sixty years old.

Don's first instrument had been the alto sax, and his inspiration on the smaller horn was Benny Carter. Ben Webster was also a great admirer of this estimable musician, who had played alongside Coleman Hawkins in Fletcher Henderson's band for several years, then taken over leadership of McKinney's Cotton Pickers. (In both slots, he followed Don Redman, and like Redman, he was a brilliant arranger and a multi-instrumentalist. Unlike Redman, he was a major player.)

From 1933, Carter led his own bands, and a few years after, he went to Europe, where he wound up arranging for the BBC dance band, linked up again with Coleman Hawkins (the two did major missionary work among European jazzmen and left a lasting legacy), and came home in 1938 to form a big band, which he led on and off with great artistic but only middling commercial success. In 1947 he began to concentrate on Hollywood studio work, becoming one of the first black musicians to succeed in this field. At first, he had to do a lot of "ghosting," but eventually he received proper screen credits for work done and scored a number of important feature films and later a television series.

Between such chores, Carter toured with Jazz at the Philharmonic and made occasional jazz record and concert appearances, also doing a stint as visiting lecturer at Princeton University, which awarded him an honorary doctorate in 1974. In 1975, he toured the Middle East for the State Department with a Princeton sociology professor, Morroe Berger. Professor Berger lectured and Dr. Carter played.

An impeccable musician, Carter now plays alto sax almost exclusively, but for a time he also played exquisite trumpet and clarinet, with his own style on both supplemental horns. On alto, he ranks as the premier stylist of the golden age, alongside Johnny Hodges, and as an arranger he has few peers, his writing for saxophones being particularly inventive.

The honorary doctorate sits well on Benny Carter, every inch a scholar and a gentleman. His parents had wanted him to become a clergyman, and he did enroll at Wilberforce University to study theology in 1925. The college happened to have an excellent jazz band, led by Fletcher Henderson's younger brother Horace; they went on a summer tour and never made it back to school.

Among the all-stars in a band with whom Carter went to Europe in 1975 was the trumpeter Roy Eldridge, whose early inspirations had been Carter and another great saxophonist, Coleman Hawkins.

Benny Carter

Roy Eldridge

Some four years Carter's junior but a prodigy who ran away from home at fifteen to lead the juvenile band in a touring road show, joined a carnival when the show got stranded, and worked his way back home with his horn to Pittsburgh from Little Rock, Arkansas, when the carnival in turn got stranded there, Eldridge became the first great jazz trumpet stylist after Louis Armstrong.

Though his hair is gray, as becomes an elder statesman of jazz, Roy Eldridge is as feisty and full of life at sixty-five as he must have been when he ran away from home fifty years earlier. He remains one of the most exciting players in jazz, pouring himself into the music, always ready for a challenge, and when none is in the offing, challenging himself. A lower note might do just as well, but Roy will reach for the high one every time, whether the venue is a packed auditorium or a half-empty nightclub.

Few musicians in any field love playing as Roy Eldridge does. In the golden age, there were plenty of jam sessions—wherever jazz musicians would gather after regular working hours, a session would develop. In those days, when he was already a star, Roy would jam with anyone, anywhere. If there was no piano player, he would play the piano, with little technical skill but with the same driving beat that made his trumpet lines leap, or sit in on drums, which he plays well enough to have worked professionally as a drummer. (When he was with Gene Krupa's band, he would sometimes take over when the leader was tired.)

There are hardly any sessions nowadays, but if they exist, Roy will find them, or make them. Usually, he works late at his job, but when he has a night off to record, or finds himself in town on his free night, he is likely to drop in where some friendly crew is playing, unpack his horn, and make his way to the stand. The people in the house are in for a treat.

The Eldridge style at first aimed for speed and fire without much thought for the essential factor of "telling a story." It wasn't until he heard Louis Armstrong in person that he got the message—prior to that, he had taken his cues from the great saxophonists and from such fast and/or fancy trumpeters as Jabbo Smith, Rex Stewart, and Red Nichols.

With Louis's sense of structure and drama added to his speed, Roy was bound to make his mark. Featured with various good bands, he got his first innings on records with Teddy Hill, then joined Fletcher Henderson, where his sidekick became Chu Berry. By the fall of 1936, he was ready to form his own band—an eight-piecer—at Chicago's Three Deuces, where Art Tatum played piano upstairs, and Lester Young would drop in whenever Basie was in town; the three of them would make the rounds of after-hours places (where liquor was served and music made after legal closing hours) and jam or play pinochle. (Tatum was functionally blind but had peripheral vision in one eye. "He could see what he wanted to," said Roy, "and he was quite a card player.") There were, alas, no tape recorders then.

Roy's band at the Deuces had Zutty Singleton on drums and Roy's older brother, Joe, a saxophonist and arranger, on lead alto. They made records; one of them, *Heckler's Hop,* had every young (and some older) trumpeter in the country trying to learn Roy's solo. These were the years of jazz broadcasts on radio; every night, the air was humming with good sounds from ballrooms, hotels, and nightclubs all over the land. Roy had been broadcasting since his Teddy Hill days, and from then on, a young trumpeter named John Birks Gillespie tried to time the breaks in the schedules of the bands he was playing with so that he could catch Roy on the air.

Roy was billed then as "The Wizard of the Trumpet," and it seemed that there was nothing he couldn't do with the horn. When he had a big band (well, ten pieces) at the Arcadia Ballroom in New York in 1939, his repertoire included several numbers featured by Louis Armstrong. Roy, who also sang, had adopted Louis's routines, but he played them faster, higher, and longer. It was a clear challenge, but he never got his chance to lock horns with The Man.

"Joe Glaser signed both me and Hot Lips Page [another great trumpeter who might have become a challenger to Louis], but I swear he did it to keep us under wraps and away from Louis, who was having a little lip trouble then," Roy told me years later. "The one time Louis and I did get together [at the famous Metropolitan Opera House Jam Session in 1944 for *Esquire*] I was ready, but again they kept me away from him. And Louis knew I was gettin' to him, too. Just as something was about to happen, he started playing the national anthem, and that was it!"

Roy wasn't out to cut Louis, understand—he just wanted to do honest battle and prove himself. And

Roy Eldridge and Buddy Tate

the sentiments quoted above stem from a time when Louis was still alive. I hope Roy will forgive me for making them public, but they are so honest and so much Roy that they belong.

Roy is his own severest critic. It only happens once or twice a year that he plays something that really pleases him. Nowadays, the professional critics generally pay him the respect due a historical figure, a man who has played his horn for more than half a century, but it wasn't so long ago that he was still being accused of "exhibitionism," "grandstanding," "overreaching," etc. Such peevish notions arise from a misunderstanding of Roy's music. He loves to create excitement, but it isn't false or calculated or for show, but because he himself is excited. His emotions are nothing if not genuine, open, and generous. He will do his utmost to light a spark, to build a fire. There is a passion in him to make music, to create joy, and it hasn't diminished. Not even the years of working with white bands in the days when musical segregation was still the rule managed to take the edge off Roy's love for his work.

It was hard to be a pioneer. The bands Roy played with—first Gene Krupa's, then Artie Shaw's, then Krupa's again—didn't tour the South, but they did play California, and that was where the trouble usually was worst. He was getting featured billing, might even have his name outside in lights, and yet could not stay at the same hotels as his colleagues in the band. Even though his reservation had been confirmed, there would be "problems." And inside the club or ballroom, it would be all right to socialize with movie stars or other show-business folk, but not with ordinary customers. Once, he was refused admission to a place where the Shaw band was to play. "This is a white dance," he was told, though his name was outside, and he told the flunky at the door who he was.

"When I finally did get in, I played that first set, trying to keep from crying. By the time I got through the set, the tears were rolling down my cheeks. I don't know how I made it. I went up to a dressing room and stood in a corner crying and saying to myself why the hell did I come out here again when I knew what would happen. Artie came in and he was real great. He made the guy apologize and got him fired. . . . but it's not worth the glory, not worth the money, not worth anything."

At the time of this statement, Roy vowed he would never again play with a white band, but four years later he was back with Krupa. Socially, things had improved a bit, and integrated bands were no longer an exception. Without the work of Roy, the most exposed of all the pioneers, it might have taken longer. Ironically, while he was suffering the indignities of Jim Crowism, almost every trumpeter in a big band, black or white, was trying to sound a little bit like Roy Eldridge, whose nickname, "Little Jazz," fits him to perfection. He is *all* jazz, and, thanks to his own invincible energy and Norman Granz's loyalty, he is back in the limelight where he belongs.

Norman Granz is the non-musician who (aside from John Hammond and the only other possible contender, Newport Jazz Festival producer and founder of the jazz festival genre George Wein) has had the greatest influence on jazz. He started to run jam sessions in his native Los Angeles in 1943, when he was twenty-five, and organized his first Jazz at the Philharmonic concert in the following year, as a benefit for a group of young Chicanos who had been railroaded to San Quentin after the so-called "zoot suit riots." The idea of presenting a jam session on the concert stage was new, and Granz had a way with it. He knew how to preserve the natural drama inherent in the encounter between first-rate jazzmen matching wits and skills, and even when the form to some extent became for-mula, it worked. The main reason was that Granz had his own taste in jazz and that it was good, another that he was a superb organizer and a very persistent man. The first tours with Jazz at the Philharmonic were not a success, but by 1955 it was a troupe of eleven musicians and one singer, per-forming seventy-two concerts in fifty-eight Ameri-can and Canadian cities and an additional fifty con-certs in twenty-five European cities before some 400,000 persons.

Astutely, Granz had from the start recorded his concerts, in a day when "live" recording was still a rarity. He also had begun to produce records in the studio in 1944, the year in which he was responsible for the making of one of the finest jazz films, the short *Jammin' the Blues,* photographed by the fa-mous Gjon Mili, and the only film in which Lester Young can be seen. He formed his own record com-pany in 1951; in 1955, he released 112 albums, more than the combined jazz output of the two major record companies in the world.

In concert or on record, it never mattered to Granz who was in fashion and who was out. He used only musicians he liked, and that meant Lester

Norman Granz with Zoot Sims

Young, Roy Eldridge, Coleman Hawkins, and Ben Webster, at a time when their art had supposedly been eclipsed. It meant recording Art Tatum in depth, in solo and with his true peers. It meant standing by Billie Holiday (and Lester and Hawk) when they faltered. It meant recording Charlie Parker with strings because Parker wanted it and it was a good idea. It meant bringing together musicians that critics claimed were stylistically incompatible, and it meant staging exciting trumpet and drum "battles" that offended the aesthetic sensibilities of these same critics, though these extroverted doings reflected jazz's own aesthetic far better than the critics' writings.

Granz was the first promoter to insist on non-discrimination clauses in every contract, and on proper facilities and accommodations as well. He brooked no excuses, and he drove a hard financial bargain. One frustrated booker called him a "capitalist radical," a not unfitting description.

Granz sold his record business in 1961. By then, he had produced a catalogue that ran the gamut of jazz from Kid Ory to Jimmy Giuffre (his taste was rooted in the Swing Era, but he was not provincial). From 1957 on, he toured Jazz at the Philharmonic only outside the United States, and in the sixties, he more or less confined his activities to managing his two most favored artists, Ella Fitzgerald and Oscar Peterson. By 1974, he was once again producing records as lavishly as in the fifties, presenting concerts, and still following his own taste.

While Roy Eldridge was the first truly influential trumpet stylist to appear in the wake of Louis Armstrong, others, of course, had forged for themselves individual departures from the master's canon. One of the first of these was a fellow New Orleanian (well, strictly speaking he was born across the river, in Algiers). Henry ("Red") Allen was the son of a trumpeter and brass-band leader, eight years younger than Louis but raised on the same basic musical fare—right down to working on the riverboats and association with King Oliver, who brought young Red to New York in 1927. He soon went back home, but when he came North again two years later, he was ready.

Joining Luis Russell's band, made up mainly of New Orleanians and some like-minded "foreigner's," he contributed mightily to the band's successful amalgam of the New Orleans tradition and the evolving big-band idiom with his adventurous and confident solos, played with an Armstrong-like tone

but an obliqueness, rhythmic and harmonic, that was personal and new.

The Russell band backed Louis on some records and personal appearances in 1929; the encounter seemed to inspire the younger man. He spent some time with Fletcher Henderson's band—graduate school—and then joined the lesser-known but excellent Mills' Blue Rhythm Band. He made lots of records on his own, played briefly in the first regular integrated band on Fifty-second Street, co-led by Eddie Condon and clarinetist Joe Marsala, and then rejoined Russell's band, by now doing regular backup duty for Louis Armstrong. He stayed for three and one-half years, and I think it was a mistake.

There were parallels in the Armstrong and Allen personalities. Both were natural showmen; both sang and played trumpet with great exuberance. But there was—could be—only one Louis Armstrong. The prolonged daily exposure to the master was not good for Red's development. He was, of course, never featured alongside Louis—there was no room for another trumpet. But it was his job, when the band played its frequent dance dates, to "front" during the dance sets, announcing, entertaining, singing, and playing trumpet. Then it would be showtime, and Louis would come on to do his special numbers. No doubt there must have been times when some members of the audience thought Red was Louis, and there may have been times when he thought so himself. Suffice it to say that his most creative and consistent playing dates from before 1937.

After leaving the Russell band, Red led his own often excellent small groups. His work passed through a "modernistic" stage, his tone losing some of its warmth. His entertaining became strenuous, his playing oddly disjointed. He could still play brilliantly, and this was the case later on as well—during the eleven years he was featured at the Metropole, a Times Square establishment.

The Metropole was a long, narrow room with a bar running the length of it. Above the bar was a so-called bandstand, just wide enough to hold a piano, next to it two sets of drums, and a lot of musicians, stretched out single file. Behind the bandstand were huge blowups of musician's faces, and across from it, a mirrored wall. The Metropole got most of its trade off the street. It was a crowded, noisy, and not very *distingué* place.

Red was king here, and he knew how to manipulate his audience. His band worked hard; in it, usually, were musicians who had been his colleagues as far back as in the Russell and Henderson days. Because he worked so hard and made his men work as hard as he did, he made it possible for the other band (there was continuous music from eight P.M. to closing—four A.M.—and for quite a while, a trio in the afternoon, and Sunday matinees with two other full bands) to play less to the gallery. For some time, this other band was co-led by Roy Eldridge and Coleman Hawkins. Twice a night, the set changes would feature both bands in a so-called jam session, which might catch fire.

Red finally made it to Europe in 1959 in company with the ancient New Orleans trombonist Kid Ory. Perhaps because Ory was such a showboat, Red played some of his most restrained and best music with him. The European audiences loved him, and he went back several times before he was stricken by cancer in 1966. He underwent an operation, kept working, toured England in February and March of 1967, and died six weeks later.

Red Allen was a kind and decent man whose manner off the bandstand was quiet and dignified. He bought himself a new Eldorado every year and made sure it was parked where the other musicians could see it; there was something very old New Orleans about that and other of Red's ways. Sometimes, at the Metropole, he would play the most subtle trumpet and combine it with the most unsubtle showmanship. It was weird. At the Metropole, his tone also recaptured its earlier fullness and roundness. At times the tone was all there was. It was enough.

Bill Coleman, who had played alongside Red in Luis Russell's band in 1929, is a most remarkable musician. Born in 1904, he is the oldest of the post-Armstrong trumpeters to create a style for himself. With a lighter tone than fashionable at the time, he constructed rapid, dancing lines informed by an acute ear for changes. He was one of the first and most consistent of the jazz expatriates.

Born in Paris, Kentucky, he has made his home in the better-known city of that name twice, first from 1935 to 1938, then again from 1948 to the present. In the thirties, he also paid extended playing visits to India and Egypt. During his American sojourns, he worked with such excellent people as Fats Waller, Teddy Wilson, Benny Carter, and Mary Lou Williams, the first lady of jazz by any reckoning.

Henry ("Red") Allen

Henry ("Red") Allen

Aside from the New Orleans relics, who are musical primitives, Bill Coleman, who is anything but a musical primitive, must be the oldest major jazz trumpeter still active. He was appearing at festivals throughout Europe in 1975 and sounding just fine.

When Bill Coleman worked with Teddy Wilson, that estimable pianist had just reluctantly disbanded his large orchestra and scaled down to the eight pieces that eventually became six. Wilson, who probably influenced more pianists during the Swing Era than any keyboard artist before or since, had worked with various bands in the Midwest, including Speed Webb's 1930 outfit with Roy Eldridge, Vic Dickenson, and Teddy's brother Gus, a trombonist and gifted arranger who died young, and in Louis Armstrong's 1933 band.

He came to New York to work with Benny Carter and was discovered by John Hammond, who saw to it that he got a lot of recording work. Among the many musicians Teddy recorded with was Benny Goodman. At a party at singer Mildred Bailey's home, Benny and Teddy played together. The pianist's crystal-clear touch and impeccable harmonic sense (it is doubtful that Teddy has ever played a wrong change) fit Benny's conception of jazz to perfection. Joined by Benny's drummer, Gene Krupa, they made records together.

At Helen Oakley's urging, the studio trio became an in-person reality in January, 1936, at a swing matinee at the Congress Hotel in Chicago—the first organized, integrated jazz group to appear in public in America. (Of course, jazz musicians of different colors had been informally jamming together since the early twenties, and no doubt before that in New Orleans, but it had been in out-of-the-way places, for audiences of fellow musicians and night people. This was different, and a definite breakthrough.) Teddy began to travel with the band and remained

Trombonists Al Grey, Trummy Young, and Vic Dickenson

Benny Goodman and Teddy Wilson

with Goodman until the spring of 1939, leaving with Benny's blessings (and financial backing) to form his own big band.

Teddy Wilson was eminently suited for the role in which he had been cast. Handsome (he looked like a serious music student; today he looks like a slightly rumpled music professor) and soft-spoken, he had grown up and studied at Tuskegee Institute, where both his parents were teachers, and studied music in college. Later, he became the first jazz musician to teach at Juilliard.

His duties with Goodman did not prevent Teddy from recording with other people and, most importantly, under his own name. In 1935 began a series of studio sessions under his leadership (often actually organized by John Hammond) which usually featured a young singer named Billie Holiday and the best men from the bands of Henderson, Calloway, Ellington, Basie, and others who happened to be in town. The atmosphere was informal and relaxed.

Thus came into being some of the most lasting and perfect records of the golden age of jazz, three-minute masterworks in which everything is in balance—ensemble and solos, vocal and instrumental passages, tempo and mood. This is music that can be listened to again and again, music that never grows stale or dated. And much of the credit for the lucidity and balance of these records must go to Teddy Wilson.

These musical characteristics were also reflected in his big band, which lasted just one month over a year. It had Ben Webster. It had Harold Baker and Doc Cheatham, two great lyrical trumpeters. Above all, it had ensemble blend and balance that were the envy of the band establishment. But it had too much musicality and not enough showmanship. It didn't blast, nor did it croon. To the men in it, it remains the best big band they ever worked with, but it was a commercial flop.

He never talks about it, but I don't think Teddy Wilson ever quite got over the disappointment. At least, his work from here on lacks some of the inspiration, the vitality of his earlier playing, though he remains one of the best jazz pianists of his or any day. There have been years of radio staff work, periodic reunions with Goodman, and many tours abroad. Teddy keeps busy, and at times, there is a spark, a tension, something beyond the always impeccable and pianistically perfect surface.

In late 1936, Benny and Teddy, Gene Krupa,

and some of the other boys in the Goodman band went to a Los Angeles club called the Paradise, where they encountered a musical dynamo named Lionel Hampton. He was the bandleader, emcee, vocalist, drummer, and, above all, featured vibraphonist. On the latter instrument, he was the first and until then only jazz virtuoso, and his sound seemed to blend ever so well with Benny's clarinet, Teddy's piano, and Gene's drums when they sat in with the residents.

A few days later, Hampton was invited to record with the Goodman trio, making it a quartet, and in November, 1936, he accepted Benny's offer to make it a permanent unit. The quartet continued to pioneer in jazz integration, and when Krupa left, Lionel took over at the drums in the big band for a while. Like Teddy, the man now nicknamed "Hamp" had a free hand to make his own recordings, and like Teddy, he used the best available men. (Hamp recorded for Victor; Teddy for Brunswick.) His sessions, too, belong among the best from the period.

In 1940, Hamp formed his own big band (also with Benny's help) and, unlike Teddy's, it was a success. It was a driving band, a show band, reflecting the volatile personality of its leader. Hamp made an institution of the tenor battle and of *Flying Home,* the climax-ridden flag-waver that was the band's first hit and lasting signature.

And between the high notes, the grins and grunts, the sweating and eye-rolling, the "one more time" climaxes, the jumping on drums and twirling of sticks, there would be some of the magnificent vibes-playing Hamp was and is capable of. And there was always an array of interesting young soloists in the band: for years, the Hampton juggernaut was also a talent incubator with few rivals. The pay was bad, the work hard, and the leader notoriously forgetful about mentioning the soloists' names, but it was a great school for green young players, among them Illinois Jacquet, Clifford Brown, Wes Montgomery, and Charles Mingus.

In the mid-seventies, illness slowed Hamp down a bit, but he seems irrepressible. He can be irascible, and working for him is a notorious grind, but he is a musical marvel, a maker of history, and one of the most lastingly popular figures produced by jazz. He is also a devoutly religious man and an equally devout Republican—in other words, despite his flamboyance, a solid conservative. After all, he got his start as a drummer in the *Chicago Defender*

Courtesy of Dan Morgenstern

Lionel Hampton, 1940

newsboy's band and was earning a living as a musician while still in his teens.

My favorite Hampton story is not about anything extravagant. He and Tony Scott, the clarinetist, were engrossed in conversation in an all-night cafeteria after a Fifty-second Street session when a typically annoying fan kept trying to butt in. Finally, in exasperation, Hamp turned to the offender and waved him off. "Man," he said, "can't you see that me and Tony are talking some deep-mind shit?"

When Hamp left Benny Goodman in 1939, there seemed to be no way to replace him. But after a few years, when the Goodman small groups—with or without a vibraharp—had become a tradition, Red Norvo, who had broken up his big band, came aboard the Goodman sextet. (Few musicians of prominence didn't have at least a try at big bands in the Swing Era—Red's was pretty damn good and lasted quite a while.) Up to then, Red had played the xylophone—the wooden precursor of the vibraphone—which he single-handledly transformed from a vaudeville novelty to a musical instrument. His graceful, melodic, and somewhat introspective style was quite a contrast to Hamp's extroversion, even when translated to the more sonorous vibes. But Red had a puckish sense of humor, and he swung.

Not long after his first stay with Benny, Red joined Woody Herman's roaring First Herd, led some groups of his own, including a marvelous chamber-style trio with Tal Farlow on guitar and Charles Mingus on bass—Red was among the Swing Era musicians who adapted to bop—and then went on doing occasional stints with Goodman and touring with all-star groups.

With his full red beard, Norvo looks like a retired sea captain. When the setting is compatible, he still does justice to his title from the days when he and tempestuous-tempered and sweet-voiced Mildred Bailey were married and known as "Mr. and Mrs. Swing."

Teddy Wilson and Lionel Hampton were not the only black musicians Benny Goodman hired. When Fletcher Henderson temporarily gave up bandleading in 1939, he became Benny's band and sextet pianist, and later that year, the remarkable young guitarist Charlie Christian, yet another John Hammond discovery, joined the sextet and made the electric guitar the last word in jazz. In 1940, Benny lured trumpeter Cootie Williams away from Duke

Ellington (for which some Ellington fanatics never forgave him, though Duke did) and made him a regular bandsman as well as featured sextet member. There were several short stints by great drummers, among them Jo Jones and Sid Catlett.

Trummy Young lasted six months. He had been the trombone star and sometime vocalist with the famous Jimmie Lunceford band, spent some time with Charlie Barnet, and had been on the CBS radio staff before joining Benny. A bit later, Trummy settled in Honolulu (though born in Savannah, he looks Hawaiian) and remained until 1952, when he joined Louis Armstrong's All Stars for twelve years. He was Louis's good right arm during those years, leaving only because his wife insisted he return home to Hawaii. He has been there ever since, working contentedly but hiding one of the seminal jazz trombone styles and coming out only occasionally for exclusive get-togethers like Dick Gibson's annual Colorado Jazz Party, where he delights his peers with his still robust and flexible playing and charms the fans with his genuine friendliness.

Another Goodman alumnus who has been a prime mover at the Colorado Jazz Party, and who in the seventies was playing with Goodman once again, is bassist Slam Stewart.

Stewart is one of the great musical humorists in jazz. He bows his bass with much dexterity and simultaneously hums the note he bows one octave higher. Bowing came naturally to Slam; he played violin from the age of six, attended Boston Conservatory, and took up bass at twenty. He met the madcap guitarist, singer, dancer, and multi-instrumentalist Slim Gaillard in 1937. They formed a duo, Slim & Slam, and scored a hit with *Flat Foot Floogie*, a nonsense ditty. Slam subsequently joined Art Tatum's trio, played with Goodman, formed his own group, and became a fixture on Fifty-second Street, recording with bands of every description, including Dizzy Gillespie and Charlie Parker. In addition to his effective solo work, Stewart is a superb rhythm-section player.

The man who hired so many great jazz players (to the list of Goodman's black stars-to-be must be added such ofay luminaries as Bunny Berigan, Harry James, Dave Tough, Bud Freeman, Jess Stacy, Johnny Guarnieri, Vido Musso, Stan Getz, and many more) remains an enigma. He launched many successful careers, not only with exposure but also with financial aid and business advice (in addi-

Red Norvo

tion to Wilson's and Hampton's bands, he helped to start Gene Krupa's and Harry James's).

Stories of Goodman's indifference and seeming callousness abound, yet there are musicians who credit him with much more than being a great clarinetist and successful bandleader. Because of his great success, Benny has been singled out for criticism from a racial angle. His title "King of Swing," it is claimed, more justly belonged to Count Basie, Jimmie Lunceford, or even Duke Ellington (who, of course, preceded, outlasted, and transcended the Swing Era). He has even been accused of exploiting black talent because he hired black arrangers and instrumentalists—a peculiar kind of logic when one recalls the risks he took when the static was coming from the opposite direction.

Maybe the swing crown should have been placed on some other head, but it is well to remember that such popular accolades are bestowed not on the basis of artistic or moral principles but as a result of plain and simple popularity. And there can be no question that it was the Goodman phenomenon that launched the Swing Era, and that it was Goodman's perseverance and dedication to high musical standards, and yes, jazz principles, that made the launching possible.

His detractors have even taken to belittling his musical abilities. A famous jazz critic, who for some years tried hard to make a name for himself in other potentially greener fields but seems compelled to return to the music to keep his name alive, even stooped so low as to designate Benny as an untalented studio hack who would never have amounted to anything in jazz if he hadn't "ripped off" black talent.

The fact is that Benny Goodman was an extraordinarily gifted jazz clarinetist long before he formed a band that used arrangements by Fletcher Henderson and other first-rate black and white arrangers. The evidence is on the records and is quite indisputable, matters of taste notwithstanding. And once he had achieved success as a bandleader, Benny did his best to keep the spirit of improvised jazz alive in his small groups. His influence as a clarinetist on almost everyone who took up the instrument in his wake also speaks for itself.

Goodman grew up in Chicago, the son of a Russian Jewish immigrant tailor. The family was large (Benny was one of nine siblings) and poor. Benny and several of his brothers got their instruments and first instruction from Hull House, a charitable in-stitution. Benny was gifted enough to receive free private tuition from Franz Schoepp, clarinetist with the Chicago Symphony; among the fellow students he encountered there was a black clarinetist seven years his senior, Buster Bailey, who was to go on to the big time with King Oliver, Fletcher Henderson, and the wonderful John Kirby band—"The Biggest Little Band in the Land." Buster and Benny sometimes played duets and formed a mutual admiration society that lasted until Buster's death in 1967. Benny was at the funeral.

Benny joined the musicians' union at thirteen; he had been playing unofficial "gigs" before then, but now he started to bring home substantial help toward the upkeep of the large household. His companions on these early jobs, disdainful of the kid in short pants until he picked up his horn, included most of the Austin High Gang; fellow Hull House student Art Hodes, born in Russia but brought to Chicago as an infant, who played the blues like a black man; and, on a Great Lakes "riverboat" excursion, Bix Beiderbecke himself.

Benny's early model was Jimmie Noone, the New Orleans clarinet master, and there are traces of the Noone style in mature Goodman. The clarinet is an elegant instrument, and Goodman got that elegance from Noone and from the French Creole classical clarinet tradition, which is where Noone got it from in the first place. But Benny added to that elegance the guttiness of the white Chicago school, which reflected the influence of Noone's New Orleans antipode, Johnny Dodds.

Benny joined drummer Ben Pollack's band at seventeen, in 1926. Pollack had been with the New Orleans Rhythm Kings. He wanted a dance band that could also play jazz, and he had Jimmy McPartland, Bud Freeman, a serious and not very swinging trombonist/arranger named Glenn Miller, and a not too serious but very swinging trombonist from Texas named Jack Teagarden in his band during Benny's three-year tenure.

Then came years of studio and radio work in New York, lucrative but often arid, though there were jazz holidays, in and out of the studio. And in 1934 came the first Goodman big band, a failure sustained by a national radio show. It was a flop at the Roosevelt Hotel, home of Guy Lombardo, where the waiters held their ears, the customers complained, and the management asked for waltzes and gave two weeks' notice. Benny stuck by his guns. The band's 1935 cross-country tour was a relative disaster until they hit California, where the air time of their radio show was just right for young dancers to be tuned in, and the Palomar Ballroom in Los Angeles, where the full house knew the "hot" numbers in the band's book and cheered when Benny and the men let out all the stops.

There followed a record seven months at the Congress Hotel in Chicago, and the Swing Era was under way. Bands that succeeded with a "hot" (jazz) rather than "sweet" (traditional dance music) policy did so in Goodman's wake.

A lot of credit goes to that first Goodman band, the Henderson arrangements, Gene Krupa's drumming, and the precision of the sections, but there are some who feel that Benny's 1940–42 band, with Cootie Williams, Eddie Sauter's tricky arrangements (some by Henderson as well), Mel Powell's or Johnny Guarnieri's piano, Dave Tough on drums, and Benny in inspired form was a more swinging, musically interesting group.

Benny gave up regular bandleading in the late forties, after a flirtation with bebop, but continued to assemble bands for special occasions. More often, he was to be found at the helm of small groups. In 1962, he became the first American jazzman to tour Russia, received by the head of state of the country from which his parents had fled.

Benny Goodman has become an institution, still capable of drawing crowds anywhere, and, more significantly, sometimes still capable of inspired clarinet flights. He is a difficult and complicated man, whose seeming indifference to his fellows may be an absentmindedness that rivals the archetypal professor's (a true Goodman story: Benny, after a night's work, steps into a cab parked outside the club, leans back, and says nothing. After a while, the cabby asks, "Where to, mister?" Whereupon Benny opens the door, prepares to step to the curb, and asks, "What do I owe you?").

Those who can cope with Goodman's peculiarities find him a generous employer. He seems to have few intimate friends but is close to his family. Long ago he married the former Lady Alice Duckworth, John Hammond's sister. Jazz owes Goodman more than some are prepared to admit. Pee Wee Russell got fidgety when unkind Benny Goodman stories were trotted out. He would end the round with the decisive comment, "Ben is a hell of a clarinet player!"

Mary Lou Williams speaks well of Benny. She wrote for his band in the thirties and again in the forties and for a while played piano in his sextet. Benny was among the regular visitors to her Harlem apartment when it was a favorite meeting place for musicians in the early forties.

Mary Lou is, in the words of Duke Ellington, "perpetually contemporary." She began her professional career while still in junior high school and took over leadership of her first husband's band in 1927, when he got an offer to join a better outfit. She was all of seventeen then. Eventually, she joined her husband and substituted for the band's pianist, who was often late. She also began to arrange for the band, which she soon joined full-time. The band was Andy Kirk's Twelve Little Clouds of Joy, one of the best groups to emerge from Kansas City. It enjoyed considerable popularity during the thirties and recorded prolifically. Its musical tone was set by Mary Lou Williams; one of the band's records was a tribute to her: *The Lady Who Swings the Band.*

As a pianist, Mary Lou was advanced when she made her first solo recording in 1930; almost a half century later, her style is still undated and fresh. She left full-time music for three years when she became deeply involved in religious studies and charitable works, but the experience had tangible musical results. When she resumed her regular career, she composed the jazz mass *Black Christ of the Andes,* dedicated to St. Martin de Porres, the first black saint. Later came *Mary Lou's Mass,* the first jazz work to be performed in St. Patrick's Cathedral as part of a regular service. It also formed the basis for one of Alvin Ailey's most charming ballets.

Mary Lou Williams plays for several months of each year at the Cookery, a pleasant Greenwich Village restaurant operated by Barney Josephson, former owner of Café Society (Downtown and Uptown), among New York's most fabled jazz spots in the golden age. Otherwise, she keeps busy touring, recording, writing, helping others, and staying young.

Mary Lou's first inspiration on the piano was Earl Hines, of whom we have spoken at some length in relation to Louis Armstrong. His collaborations with Louis from the late twenties have become candidates for immortality; if, as one expects, jazz survives, they will most certainly remain landmarks of the music. Not much less impressive are Hines's piano solos from the same period. In 1973, he re-recorded some of these pieces, and the results were

**Benny Goodman and (left to right)
George Benson, Jo Jones, and Milt Hinton**

Slam Stewart

just as remarkable—perhaps even more so. They were eloquent testimony to the fact that Earl Hines, father of modern jazz piano, was as creative and fertile in his fifth decade of professional music-making as he had been in his first.

In between, "Fatha" Hines (the nickname was bestowed on him by a radio announcer in the early thirties, when he was anything but fatherly) has enjoyed a career that included a long stretch of big-band leading (from 1928 to 1947). Though it ranked with the best, his band's permanent location for many years at the Grand Terrace Ballroom in Chicago prevented it from making the impact in New York that was required for ultimate success. Nonetheless, Hines racked up an impressive record as a talent spotter: singers Ivie Anderson and Herb Jeffries (both of whom found fame with Duke Ellington) and Billy Eckstine and Sarah Vaughan (both of whom he launched on hugely successful solo careers); instrumentalists Budd Johnson, Trummy Young, Ray Nance, Freddie Webster, Dizzy Gillespie, Charlie Parker, Bennie Green, Wardell Gray, and many more.

In 1948, he rejoined his old chum Louis Armstrong, making the Armstrong All Stars truly so. Though he stayed for nearly three years, the association was not a happy one. Too long accustomed to being a leader, and prodigiously equipped with talent and stage presence, Hines did not function well in the shadow of Louis, who could upstage anyone, even Hines, by just being there.

Back to leading his own small groups, one of which included such excellent younger players as trombonist Bennie Green, clarinetist Aaron Sachs, bassist Tommy Potter, and drummer Osie Johnson, he did a long stint leading a semitraditional group at a club in San Francisco. Except for an occasional impressive record, Hines seemed a forgotten man. In the early sixties he toured with a gloomy conglomeration featuring an organist and several girl singers and offering but a smidgin of the Hines piano magic. In 1963, a friend and I hit upon the idea of presenting Hines in concert as a pianist, period. With the help of critic Stanley Dance, a long-time Hines confidant, his reluctant services were procured. Hines refused to believe that any-

Osie Johnson

Mary Lou Williams

Earl Hines

Budd Johnson

one would care to hear him play solo piano, insisted on a rhythm section, and implored us also to engage the saxophonist Budd Johnson, his former sideman and musical director, as an added attraction.

We were pleased to do so, for Johnson was one of our favorites as well. His main instrument is the tenor sax, but he is accomplished on all the reeds. He is also a gifted arranger. Born in 1910, he was featured with Louis Armstrong in 1933 and began his association with Hines in the following year. He was among the few established musicians to sympathize with the aspirations of the bebop movement, in which he played an important role, working with Dizzy Gillespie on Fifty-second Street, helping Billy Eckstine to organize his big band, arranging for Gene Krupa, Woody Herman, and Buddy Rich, and guiding and counseling many other bands, large and small.

The concert, a double-header presented at the Little Theater on Broadway, was a smash, drawing critical acclaim in the *New York Times* and the *New Yorker* (with a profile hard on the heels of the review). The concert was recorded, and another record date took place the following day. A new career was launched for Hines, and since then he has been recording prolifically, mostly as a soloist or in a trio setting, and working consistently here and abroad with a larger group including a horn player and a girl singer. These added ingredients satisfy the need for show-business trimmings without which so many survivors of the golden age seem slightly lost. But Hines knows by now that people indeed want to hear his piano playing, which is as full of surprises and life as ever.

As for Budd Johnson, his reunion with Hines at the concert led to further collaborations, including a tour of Russia in 1966. In his sixties, he is as vigorous and creative a musician as ever; his contributions to jazz history have yet to be fully recognized.

A firm believer in decorum on and off the bandstand, a man who through all his productive life has practiced moderation in all things, Earl Hines stands at the opposite temperamental pole from Hezekiah Leroy Gordon Smith, better known as "Stuff" Smith, the mad genius of the jazz fiddle. Stuff (he acquired the nickname because he had a faulty memory for the names of his colleagues and would routinely address them as "Hey, Stuff!") arrived on New York's Fifty-second Street in 1936. Prior to that memorable moment, he had been tutored by his father, who made him his first violin (he

**Stuff Smith and Jonah Jones
at the Onyx Club, 1936**

was seven), won a musical scholarship to Johnson C. Smith University in North Carolina, but ran away with a touring show instead, joined Alphonso Trent's band (a brilliant outfit that never came East but was famous in Texas), worked in a road band led by Jelly Roll Morton, and settled in Buffalo, where he eventually formed the group he brought to New York.

It included trumpeter Jonah Jones, who, like Stuff, sang and clowned in the Armstrong manner, which helped bring the customers into the Onyx Club. Stuff was in residence here for more than a year, amazing the customers with his electrically amplified fiddling (he pioneered in the use of this device). Among them was Fritz Kreisler, who didn't think it was possible to do what Stuff patently did.

The band, by now with the great Cozy Cole on drums, moved on to Hollywood, where Stuff encountered union problems. A non-conformist and non-humanitarian, he blithely cheated his sidemen out of part of their wages. When they found out and demanded to collect, he would show them his knife, which had an extra long and extra sharp blade.

A bout with pneumonia put an end to Stuff's try at leading a big band in 1942, but the trio he brought to Fifty-second Street for the following two years was a fascinating group. Violin, piano, and bass could outswing groups three times the size, drums and all. Stuff, pound for pound, was probably the most demonically swinging musician in the annals of jazz.

In the fifties, Stuff dropped from sight, but the redoubtable Norman Granz found him, recorded him in several settings (including a date with Dizzy Gillespie, a great Stuff fan who had used him on records a few years earlier), and took him to Europe on tour. While there, Stuff collapsed and was rushed to a Dutch hospital in critical condition. He seemed to have more ailments than the doctors could diagnose. His entire supply of blood was replenished and parts of his stomach and liver were removed. He recovered in record time, returning home as swinging and ornery as ever.

There were sporadic appearances in New York and California, but Stuff liked what he had seen in Europe. In 1965, he teamed up with the Danish jazz baron Timme Rosenkrantz, a lifelong jazz enthusiast who never seemed to have any money, yet managed to visit New York with regularity and always made his way back home somehow.

Timme was one of the world's most dedicated jazz lovers. His father had been a noted writer of historical novels, and he was descended from one of Denmark's oldest noble families. Timme made his living, such as it was, writing humorous stories and books, which were genuinely funny but perhaps a bit too Danish in their humor to translate well—and Danish publishers' royalties don't go very far. Occasionally, he organized record dates (the first was issued under the name of Timme Rosenkrantz and his Barrelhouse Barons), and for a short while he operated a jazz record store in Harlem. In 1945 (he spent the war years in New York, having been conveniently trapped there by the German invasion of his homeland) he produced a famous Town Hall jazz concert featuring Don Byas, Stuff Smith, Teddy Wilson, Red Norvo, Bill Coleman, and others, which was recorded and has been in print almost continuously. He also founded the first Danish jazz magazine (it was short-lived) and took excellent photographs of his favorite musicians.

Timme always seemed to know where the action was. He met and heard Art Tatum long before that genius of the keyboard had been discovered. He knew his way around Harlem better than even John Hammond, who didn't "hang out" in the intense way Timme did—the baron's affection for alcoholic beverages ran a close second to his love for jazz. In later years, Timme would still return to New York whenever he could raise the fare, though he missed the vanished Harlem and Fifty-second Street jazz scenes. On his final visit, he was taping interviews for his radio show and trying to book talent for his newly opened (and, of course, financially unsuccessful) jazz club in Copenhagen, but he collapsed in his furnished room and died in a hospital without having regained consciousness. That was in the summer of 1969. Timme was fifty-eight years old.

Timme became Stuff's manager. The enterprise was not destined to fill his pockets, but he had a lot of fun as well as considerable problems. Stuff was now headquartered in Copenhagen, winning over local fans already conditioned to the charms of the jazz violin by the work of Svend Asmussen, the stellar Danish practitioner. From this base, Stuff made frequent tours of the continent. During a visit to Belgium, he was again stricken. He was taken to Paris, where there were specialists deemed capable of dealing with his problem, diagnosed as a liver ailment. The astonished surgeons found his liver to be the approximate size of a pea, declared him a

"medical museum," and listed him in critical condition after the operation.

Stuff was up and about the next day, entertaining the nurses with his fantastic fiddling and naughty advances. He checked himself out a few days later to fill the remainder of his Brussels engagement, claiming he couldn't afford to lose the pay. It was that fabulous constitution's last stand. In September, 1967, during a job in Munich, Stuff dropped dead. He was buried near Copenhagen by his young Danish wife. He was fifty-eight.

No one is quite certain of the age of another fabulous fiddler, the first great jazz violinist of them all. Joe Venuti used to claim he was born in 1904, on an ocean liner on its way from Italy to New York. Later, researchers established that he was born in Lecco, near Milan, in 1899, but he does not refute rumors that he might be considerably older.

Whatever his age, Venuti is a marvel. He hit New York in the early twenties, having begun his career in Philadelphia, where he befriended the somewhat younger Salvatore Massaro, a guitarist later known professionally as Eddie Lang. The two became inseparable, making delightful duet and quartet recordings, backing innumerable singers on records and stage, and working in some of the best bands of the day—Jean Goldkette, Paul Whiteman, and Roger Wolfe Kahn, the son of banker Otto Kahn, who wanted to lead the best dance band money could buy.

Lang was a quiet sort, though great at poker, but Venuti was flamboyant and a champion practical joker. He dumped passed-out Bix Beiderbecke in a bathtub, filled it with Jell-O and water, and hung around to watch Bix awake to find himself encased in purple gelatin. He led a band at a splendid society ball, draped in an elegant suit of tails, with his back to the audience, his fly open, and his tool, which he occasionally waved with his nonbaton hand, exposed for the musicians to see, the while throwing kisses and smiles over his shoulder to the unsuspecting dancers, some of whom wondered why the musicians seemed so effusively happy.

One of his prize stunts was to call the first few dozen bassists in the New York union book and ask them to be at the corner of Fiftieth Street and Broadway at a given hour in the early evening. He then rented a hotel room with a good view of the corner and proceeded to enjoy the sight of bewildered bass players bumping into each other with their cumbersome instruments. The union made

Joe Venuti

Joe Venuti

him pay each man for a night's work, but Venuti claimed the spectacle had been worth every cent and more.

The Depression put an end to such costly horse-play, so Venuti confined himself to such things as sending one-armed trumpeter Wingy Manone a single cuff link for Christmas. The death of Lang at thirty in 1933 of complications following a tonsilec-tomy (the guitarist had meanwhile become Bing Crosby's accompanist) put a temporary damper on Venuti's spirits. He had had a close call himself in 1929, sustaining near-fatal injuries in a car crash while touring with Whiteman.

Like almost every name musician, Venuti led a big band in the thirties, with indifferent musical results. Later, he worked in the Hollywood studios, appeared on Crosby's radio show, toured with small combos, and eventually settled in Seattle. Rarely recorded and nearly a forgotten figure, he was pre-sented in New York in 1967 by Dick Gibson, the jazz enthusiast who had featured him at several of his memorable annual jazz parties in Colorado and found that he was still a vital and exciting per-former.

A smash at Newport in 1968, Venuti toured Europe the following year, began to record regu-larly again, and has pursued a busy career since, briefly interrupted by illness in 1970. In 1975, Venuti and Earl Hines recorded together—just the two of them. Feeling each other out at first like two sly old foxes, they decided to forget about egos and just make music, and soon the sparks were flying. Watching these two "old men" go at it, their joy in their work apparent not only in the music but also in the joking and laughter between "takes" and the joint listening that followed the session, was to bear witness to the indestructible life force of jazz, as incorporated in two of the last great survivors of its golden age.

5 Some Modern Masters

"I must admit it," said Dizzy Gillespie to the audience at New York's Philharmonic Hall, which had just greeted him with a tumultuous ovation. "I'm the elder statesman of bebop!" The occasion was a 1975 concert in Dizzy's honor at which the trumpeter, on the threshold of fifty-eight, was the most energetic and creative celebrant. Waxing serious for a moment after his jocular acknowledgment of the applause, he noted that "our music has arrived. It's accepted; it's part of history."

John Birks Gillespie could be justly proud, for it was he and Charlie Parker—more than any others—who brought about what has been described as the first jazz revolution: the advent of the style with the odd name of bebop. In retrospect, bebop appears as a quite logical and reasonable evolutionary step from what had gone before, but at the time—the years from 1945 to 1950 or so—it was either heresy or revealed truth, depending on where you stood.

Dizzy was uniquely suited to be the standard-bearer of bop. A brilliant showman as well as a

Dizzy Gillespie

brilliant instrumentalist, he was, despite his penchant for zany antics, anything but what his nickname implied. Even when he had earned it—as the youngest member of Teddy Hill's big band, for such stunts as getting up while another trumpeter was taking a solo and miming him; appearing on the bandstand wearing an overcoat, hat, and gloves; or turning his chair around and playing with his back to the audience—he was the one who encouraged the other men in the band to borrow money from him during a European tour in order to avoid wasting his own. "Dizzy as a fox," as leader Hill put it.

He graduated to Cab Calloway's band, for which he also wrote some interesting arrangements, but was still a cutup. His firing from the band, however, was precipitated by a false accusation. A spitball was thrown from the trumpet section onto the stage during a show, coming to rest right in the center of the spotlight as trombonist Tyree Glenn soloed. It was thrown by Jonah Jones, but Calloway blamed bad boy Dizzy. Bassist Milt Hinton tells what happened next:

"Cab bawled the daylights out of Dizzy [who] resented being blamed for something that wasn't his fault, but he wouldn't tell on Jonah and Jonah had already gone out into the street. An argument ensued; Cab made a pass at Dizzy, and Dizzy came at him with a knife. I grabbed Diz's hand, but he was stronger. Cab was nicked in the scuffle before they were separated."

Calloway didn't realize he had been cut (on the behind, in fact) until he changed his clothes and saw the blood. He promptly fired Dizzy, who calmly packed up his horn and went home to New York. Fortunately, the fateful event had taken place no further away than Hartford, Connecticut. When the band returned from the tour, Dizzy was on hand to greet them. He gave Cab a big smile, and Cab couldn't resist smiling back.

Dizzy went on to Earl Hines's band, and here he and Charlie Parker, whom he had met briefly years before in Kansas City, finally got together. The attraction was strong, for both men, in their different ways, had been moving toward the same goal, a breaking up of the traditional rhythmic and harmonic patterns in jazz. Parker was an intuitive musician—a force of nature—while Dizzy was more analytical in his approach. In musical terms he knew exactly what was going on at all times.

When Hines's featured singer, Billy Eckstine, decided to form his own band in 1944, Parker and

Courtesy of Dan Morgenstern

Charlie Parker

Gillespie were the first he asked to come aboard. The Eckstine band became the incubator of bop and the terror of club owners and ballroom operators, who loved Eckstine's silken baritone but didn't know what to make of the band's wild music and wilder manners.

Parker didn't last long with the band. Once, at a club in St. Louis, the owner admonished him for having taken a drink with a customer, pointing out that he didn't want black musicians to drink from the same glasses his white clientele were using. Parker calmly proceeded to break every glass in sight, explaining he couldn't be sure they hadn't all been contaminated. Further violence was only narrowly avoided.

Dizzy didn't stay in the band long either, preferring the freedom of jobbing around New York, mainly on Fifty-second Street—Swing Street—which was a beehive of musical activity during the last years of the war. But a booking agent—the same who had persuaded Eckstine to leave Hines—thought he was ready for his own big band. Their first tour took the band through the South, where people still wanted to hear the blues, not ultra-modern jazz, which favored tempos too fast for comfortable dancing. The band flopped.

Meanwhile, Parker (beginning to become known as "Bird," a nickname of obscure origin, apparently shortened from "Yardbird," a synonym for chicken, of which Parker had been inordinately fond as a youth—so much so that when a car in which he was riding ran over one, he insisted the driver back up so he could retrieve the unfortunate bird and have it for dinner) had made some recordings with Dizzy that were to have an effect on jazz musicians similar to that of the Armstrong Hot Five twenty years earlier.

After Dizzy broke up his big band, Bird became part of a sextet he took to Los Angeles. California was not ready for bop, and some local citizens didn't like the idea that two of the men in the band were white. Bird didn't care for Dizzy's clowning on the stand (or perhaps resented the fact that the trumpeter was the leader of the group). Most local musicians were crazy about the new sounds, but the owner of the club was not. When the band got its notice, Bird stayed behind, cashing in his return plane ticket. He needed ready cash; he had become a full-fledged junkie, helplessly addicted to heroin.

Dizzy never fell victim to this unfortunate addiction, but though he spoke out against it vigorously,

Bird helped to popularize it among jazz players. This side effect of bop didn't endear the music to those already hostile toward it.

Bop, though often irreverent and never staid, was the first jazz played publicly for art's sake rather than entertainment. A music born in the after-hours jamming and experimenting jazzmen had always indulged in, it was a product of new attitudes, partly social and political, partly aesthetic, toward life in general and music in particular.

The war was to some extent responsible; it brought about new awareness of and sensitivity to racial injustice. Jazz was slowly but surely becoming recognized as an art form and building an audience of dedicated listeners who didn't feel the need to be entertained by extra-musical means. And concomitantly, a new phenomenon, the jazz critic, was telling the musicians that they were artists—something they had known all along but hadn't really expected to be officially told.

And then the upheavals wrought by the draft in the band business brought into the limelight, suddenly and without psychological preparation, dozens and dozens of very young musicians whose musical precociousness was not matched by emotional and psychological maturity. Charlie Parker himself—introduced to drugs through exposure to Kansas City's wide-open night life at fifteen or less—was the archetype of this new breed of jazzman, though the war had nothing to do with his premature indoctrination.

Take the case of Stan Getz, a greatly gifted youngster from a poor Jewish home. A truant officer yanked him off his first professional big-band job; he was fifteen. At sixteen he was on the road with Jack Teagarden's band; the trombonist had become his legal guardian to make it official. A string of big-band jobs followed; there was no more home life for young Stan, a teenager who had become a featured soloist with big-time bands and was making lots of money.

Small wonder he became "hooked"; big wonder that he made it through that nightmare and sustained a career that at one point saw him the most popular jazz instrumentalist of them all, via his famous recording of *Desafinado,* the song that launched the bossa-nova fad.

Others were not so lucky; Dizzy Gillespie's most promising follower, Fats Navarro, just a few years Getz's senior, was dead at twenty-six, a victim of lung disease aggravated by heroin addiction. His

nickname had become a cruel irony; his weight was down from over two hundred pounds to barely half of that by the end.

Bud Powell, who translated bop to the piano keyboard, adding his admiration for Art Tatum and his own dazzling imagination, left school at fifteen to become a professional; Cootie Williams was his legal guardian. When he was eighteen, Bud got drunk in Philadelphia. He was arrested for "disorderly conduct"; the cops beat him severely over the head.

Bud had always been a bit strange, but not long after the incident in Philadelphia he had to be hospitalized and spent ten months in a mental institution. After that, he had what is politely called a "drinking problem"; it was never solved. Committed once again for nearly a year, he was given shock treatment, then a popular pastime for psychiatrists. Though he continued to play, sometimes still brilliantly, until his death at forty-one in 1966, he was never again a fully functional human being. "People think Bud is crazy or lost," said a close friend, "but he's really in a state of grace." Bud Powell named one of his most striking piano pieces *Un Poco Loco*.

What made things even worse for the immature youngsters thrown into a life that posed problems even for older, more stable people was that soon after the war the times for making a good living from jazz were over. The postwar economic slump, the advent of television, changing public tastes (singers were on top now), the growing expenses of keeping a band on the road—all these factors combined to kill the band business, or at least to reduce it to a mere handful of steadily employed jazz-flavored large ensembles.

Fifty-second Street, too, was waning. Strippers gradually displaced jazz musicians in the remaining clubs; eventually, almost one whole side of the famous block was razed to make room for the expansion of Rockefeller Center. Soon, Jimmy Ryan's was the only jazz spot left where once every other door had led to music.

Bop made its new home further west, on Broadway. First came the Royal Roost, a chicken restaurant converted to jazz. It was here that Miles Davis, a young trumpeter from St. Louis, made his first mark as a leader, in 1949, after having earned his spurs with Charlie Parker's group. The band Miles put together was short-lived, but it made some highly influential records. A unique nine-piece group, it featured, among other stars-to-be, Max Roach on drums, John Lewis at the piano, Lee Konitz on alto sax, and Gerry Mulligan on the infrequently heard and cumbersome baritone sax. There were also a French horn and a tuba.

The arrangements reflected the influence of a man named Gil Evans, who had been writing for Claude Thornhill's band, in which Konitz and Mulligan had also played. The music was quite different from the often intense and high-strung sounds of bop; after a while, it was labeled "cool." When the recordings by the Davis band were brought out again some years later, it was under the title "The Birth of the Cool."

Davis had moved on by then; so had his cohorts. Max Roach, perhaps the most musically sophisticated of jazz percussionists, had also made his reputation with Parker. He linked up with a phenomenal young trumpeter, Clifford Brown, to form the Brown-Roach Quintet, a group that represented the final flowering of bop. It came to an abrupt end in June, 1956, when Brown, who was all of twenty-six, was killed in a car that was taking him to the group's next job, along with Bud Powell's pianist brother Richie, and Richie's wife, who was driving. It was raining, it was early morning, and the car skidded out of control.

It took Roach years to get over the blow, but he continued to lead his own excellent groups, experimenting with an increasingly important melodic role for the drums. He became one of the first jazz artists to articulate the ideas of black cultural self-determination. His "Freedom Now" suite was a controversial and effective work combining his music with words by his then wife, singer Abbey Lincoln. (A featured soloist on the 1961 recording was veteran Coleman Hawkins.)

In the early seventies, Roach was appointed professor of music at the University of Massachusetts. The role suits him well. He takes time out to work with a fascinating all-percussion group, or to appear with old comrades-in-arms such as Gillespie, whose tribute concert he graced. (Another guest was Stan Getz.)

Lee Konitz, at the time of the Miles Davis band, had been working with a group led by the iconoclastic Chicago-born pianist Lennie Tristano, who had his own approach to jazz. It coincided with bop in time and converged on it in terms of harmonic sophistication, but was really a thing unto itself. A recording made by Tristano in 1949 was a precursor of the kind of "free" improvisation that became a jazz trend nearly twenty years later, but the impact of his music was mainly due to the fascinating, interwoven lines played by his saxophonists—Konitz on alto and Warne Marsh on tenor.

Tristano, teacher and guru as well as strong musical leader, had Konitz under his spell for a long time, though the saxophonist made occasional forays on his own. Always an original, he became one of the most committed improvisers in music, taking risks, making old songs seem new again, exploring, discovering. Increasingly he is finding people who want to listen, both here and abroad.

John Lewis had been the pianist in Dizzy Gillespie's second big band—the one that made it. A serious, studious man who majored in anthropology in college and once considered an academic career, he worked with Lester Young and others while pursuing formal musical studies in New York after having left Gillespie and spent a few months in France.

Lewis had made some interesting quartet recordings with a colleague from Dizzy's band, the vibraphonist Milt Jackson. In 1954, they decided to make the quartet a working unit. The other members were bassist Percy Heath and drummer Kenny Clarke—the latter the father of bop drumming, who had taken Jo Jones's innovations a few steps further and created the perfect rhythmic underpinning for the music of Parker and Gillespie.

The group took the name Modern Jazz Quartet; it was a cooperative, with Lewis as musical director. Clarke left after a year; his replacement, Connie Kay, stayed until the quartet disbanded in 1974. That was the only personnel change. No other group in jazz history achieved such longevity and stability.

The Modern Jazz Quartet, a kind of chamber group, was among the first jazz units to specialize in concert work, though they continued to play nightclubs; it was necessary. The quartet also emphasized a style of dress and demeanor appropriate to the concert hall, for which they were mocked by some who felt it was incongruous for a jazz group to appear in elegantly tailored suits of tails and adopt the stage manners of classical musicians. That Lewis also experimented with the adaptation of such classical forms as the fugue to jazz uses was further cause for criticism from the same quarters—self-appointed guardians of the jazz essence. For others, often equally misguided, the

Modern Jazz Quartet was proof of the coming of age of jazz, which seemed to them to be shedding its embarrassing street manners and colloquial speech.

Both sides were wrong. The quartet remained true to the jazz tradition, which Lewis was concerned with expanding, not abandoning. For every fugue in the group's repertoire there were two blues. And in Milt Jackson, the group had one of the real masters of modern blues playing, as well as a ballad player of great warmth.

Lewis became one of jazz's major composers, working in large orchestral idioms as well as writing for the quartet. When the Modern Jazz Quartet finally disbanded, perhaps because it had become too venerable an institution—though there was nothing calcified about its music even at the end—Lewis accepted a professorship at City College of New York, thus realizing his early ambition for a role in academia without having to give up his music. With his benign, slightly preoccupied mein and the bulging briefcase he rarely seems to be without, John Lewis looked the part of a professor long before he became one.

As for Milt Jackson, who had always pursued his ambitions for group leadership during the quartet's regular sabbaticals, he set out on his own, assured of a large and loyal following. For even those who had found the quartet's music a bit cold never accused Milt, fondly known as "Bags," of lacking the requisite passion.

In any case, Bags was now also free to pursue his avocation for cooking and baking, though there was no reason to assume that he would at this stage of the game attempt to upset his old record of having polished off twenty-six pancakes in one sitting, set in the very early days of the Modern Jazz Quartet.

For a brief while, Milt was featured with Woody Herman's band, a notable presence on the musical scene of the late forties. Herman had been around, and he would stay around.

Woody Herman has been leading a big band longer than any living jazz musician except Count Basie, who had a slight head start. Woody was twenty-three when he was elected leader of a cooperative band formed by members of Isham Jones's orchestra in 1936, after Jones had decided to disband. The personable young clarinetist, saxaphonist, and singer was already a show-business veteran.

He began his career in childhood, singing and dancing in vaudeville. The Herman outfit, known

Woody Herman

as "The Band That Plays the Blues," eventually established itself just a notch below the top swing bands. (At first, the going was often rough. At a Houston hotel, the manager sent Woody a note during opening night. "You will kindly stop playing and singing those nigger blues," it read.)

Woody broke through in 1944 at the helm of a band that had sparkling scores by young arrangers influenced by Duke Ellington (Ralph Burns) and bebop (Neal Hefti). It had two great soloists in Bill Harris (trombone) and Flip Phillips (tenor sax), and, for a while, a third in trumpeter Sonny Berman, victim of a heroin overdose at twenty-two. It had a driving rhythm section with Chubby Jackson on bass and the Chicago veteran Davey Tough on drums. It became known as the First Herd.

The Second Herd, formed in 1947, was an even better band. Its famous saxophone section included Stan Getz, Zoot Sims, Herbie Steward, and the marvelous baritonist Serge Chaloff (1923-1957). Steward's replacement was Al Cohn. By way of Jimmy Giuffre's *Four Brothers,* it established a new sound for saxophone sections. In addition to Milt Jackson, such notable black artists as Gene Ammons, Ernie Royal, and Oscar Pettiford passed through its ranks.

Since then, there have been so many Herds that Woody himself has lost count. What they all have in common is a commitment to the spirit of jazz. The bandsmen grow ever younger, it appears, while Woody, who long ago took to calling himself "Old Man Herman," seems ageless. His playing, notably on soprano sax, is still fresh. The grind of forty years on the big-band road has not worn thin his patience.

"No name bandleader has ever been better liked by the men who worked for him," Leonard Feather wrote many years ago. It is still true.

Serge Chaloff's chief rival in the days of the Second Herd was Gerry Mulligan, an illustrious alumnus of the Miles Davis Birth of the Cool band. In 1952, he formed a quartet in California that became one of the decade's most popular jazz groups. With only bass and drums (the latter played softly and subtly by Chico Hamilton) backing his own pleasantly dry-sounding baritone sax and the understated trumpet of young Chet Baker, a Mulligan discovery, the quartet achieved great clarity of line. Its records caught on quickly, and though it lasted only a year in its original form, it made the fortunes of both Mulligan and Baker.

Mulligan, who had established himself as a gifted arranger and composer before his playing came equally to the fore, retained the essential idea of the quartet for some time, then formed one of the few innovative big bands of the sixties, teamed up for a while with Dave Brubeck, and after a period of relative inactivity seemed ready in the mid-seventies to reemerge as a major figure in the music.

Success was not a serious problem for Mulligan, a highly intelligent, cultured man who had sowed most of his wild oats before it arrived. For the younger Baker, who unlike Mulligan had not been reared in the mainstream of jazz activity, the sudden popularity was hard to handle. His fugitive-sounding trumpet, which owed much to Miles Davis's early manner, and his light, boyish singing voice found great favor with young audiences of the day, and Baker became a somewhat unwilling cult figure of the beat generation.

Along with this went drug abuse, and it hit Baker harder than most—most who survived, that is to say. From 1955 on, he spent much time in Europe, where for a while there was more tolerance for his kind of affliction. But in 1960 he was jailed in Italy, where he had made his home, and eventually deported. Having exhausted his welcome in most of western Europe, he came home, playing better than ever, and for a while seemed to have found his equilibrium.

But his luck ran out again—there are always people on the fringes of the music world poised to pounce on reformed sinners and push them back. This time, Baker sank almost to the bottom, what was left of his reputation exploited in occasional silly commercial recording ventures (*Chet Baker and the Mariachi Brass* and such), but otherwise relegated to obscure jobs. On his way home from such a gig early one morning in San Francisco, he was set upon, robbed of his instruments and money, and badly beaten—almost all his front teeth were knocked out.

It seemed to be the end of a once promising career, but instead became the beginning of a decisive comeback. Baker enrolled in a methadone program, got his teeth repaired, and made his way to New York, where he went to work unspectacularly but regularly, playing as well as ever. He made some good records, was reunited with Mulligan, and even eulogized by Rex Reed—which shouldn't be held against him.

When Baker first appeared, he was under the

Gerry Mulligan

Chet Baker

spell of Miles Davis, but Davis himself, that most mercurial of musicians, had already moved on to something different from his "cool" stage. Born in 1926 into a middle-class environment in a suburb of St. Louis (his father was a dentist), Davis has always relished playing the role of rebel. He came to New York at nineteen, in the spring of 1945, to study at the Juilliard School of Music, but soon found himself in the best possible jazz graduate school—Charlie Parker's quintet. Some felt he wasn't ready, but Parker obviously thought otherwise. And he was right, for young Davis, while no virtuoso, already had rare musical sensibility and his own voice.

Then came the Birth of the Cool band (Davis's first collaboration with Gil Evans, who was to play an important role in his career later on), an invitation to play the Paris Jazz Festival in 1949 with his own quintet, and a period of drug problems typical of the times. In 1955, Davis was ready. He formed a group that included tenor saxophonist John Coltrane and a fine rhythm section and infused it with his strong musical personality. He had developed into a compelling soloist in a style of extraordinary simplicity and lucidity, based on nuance and understatement, very melodic and expressed with a haunting sound that became one of the most recognizable in jazz.

In 1957 he began a series of recordings with Gil Evans, who crafted for him challenging and complimentary settings scored for unusual combinations of brasses and woodwinds that brought new colors to jazz ensemble writing. One of these ventures was a suite culled from the music for Gershwin's *Porgy and Bess;* another, *Sketches of Spain,* was based on both folk and classical music from the Spanish tradition.

Evans, Canadian-born and California-bred, fifteen years Davis's senior, had led his own dance orchestra in the thirties. When it was taken over by Singer Skinnay Ennis, he continued as its arranger, but it was through his work for Claude Thornhill's band from 1941 on, and especially his adaptations of early bebop pieces for this band, that he made his jazz reputation.

Evans is self-taught as an arranger and didn't seriously play any instrument until he took up piano (at forty!) in 1952. Both as a musician and as a human being, he exerted great influence on a number of seminal jazzmen who gathered at his "salon" at the turn of the forties.

Gerry Mulligan has described the setting: "Gil lived in a room in a basement on 55th Street, near 5th Avenue. Actually it was behind a Chinese laundry and had all the pipes for the building as well as a sink, a bed, a piano, a hot-plate, and no heat." Most of the participants in the Birth of the Cool band, which had its beginnings as a workshop idea, gathered there, as well as other gifted musicians, some of whom were destined to make it, others not. As far as getting the band together was concerned, according to Mulligan it was Miles Davis "who cracked the whip." Evans was not much of a disciplinarian, and still isn't, but generations of musicians have gravitated toward him to learn more about their art and craft.

Evans is a perfectionist. His output is relatively small, but immensely important. His most fertile periods were the Thornhill years; the years 1957 to 1960, beginning with the Miles collaborations and leading to several albums of his own and a brief spell with a regular big band; and from the early seventies on, when he again had a band with an existence beyond the recording studio, if not with ideal regularity.

Because he is a perfectionist, Evans tends to be impractical when it comes to business matters. Promoters who have tried to work with him have been driven to despair when confronted with rehearsal schedules way beyond available means. But somehow Evans usually completes what he starts. His work of recent vintage has once again extended the horizons of big-band music, incorporating concepts of free improvisation, multiple layers of rhythm, the use of synthesizers and other electronic devices, etc., in a most imaginative manner. Gil Evans ought to be declared a natural resource and subsidized to do what he wants, as Ellington should have been.

Miles Davis is also a perfectionist, but he works within a small-group format, which is more flexible and manageable from the economic standpoint. Furthermore, he has a charismatic personality that, with the aid of considerable publicity, has caught the fancy of the jazz public and enabled him to enjoy great creative freedom as well as reap the rewards of popularity that usually come only to those who compromise their art or are natural entertainers.

It was the quintet with Coltrane (for a while enlarged to a sextet by the presence of Cannonball Adderley, the alto saxophonist who went on to lead

some of the most popular jazz groups of the recent past until his untimely death at forty-six in 1975) that brought Miles to the plateau of popularity he has since inhabited. His success also served to launch Coltrane, perhaps the most influential jazzman of the sixties, and an astonishing number of other gifted musicians who passed through Davis-led groups. In fact, Davis is a master talent-spotter. Herbie Hancock, Chick Corea, Wayne Shorter, Keith Jarrett, Airto, John McLaughlin, and Tony Williams are just a few of his famous alumni.

No doubt Davis's long association with Columbia Records and its publicity machine has stood him in good stead. On the other hand, nobody has ever told Miles what to do with his music. Critics who think his recent direction, which has brought him closer to rock and soul music than to their idea of what jazz should be, is the result of record-company persuasion demonstrate their ignorance.

Miles is his own man; his need to be up-to-date, to change, to move on, is not dictated by outside pressure but by inner needs. It is his good fortune that he also has the creative resources to accommodate this need. This expresses itself not only in his music, but in his sometimes outrageous but always effective style of dress, his fancy taste in cars and interior decoration, and the delight he takes in shocking people.

Withal, the real Miles Davis is a vulnerable man whose public persona has been carefully developed to hide the fact that he is well-bred and sensitive, can be kind and generous to a fault, and seems to insult people only to test their love and loyalty. That he doesn't suffer fools gladly is beside the point.

He may not play *My Funny Valentine* anymore, disparaging those who still want to hear it, but the pain and yearning he put into that song are still there. Pain, after all, is part of his lot. For years, he has had a pin in one hip and is in constant discomfort from this condition. Later, he broke both ankles in a car accident when he smashed his silver Lamborghini into a traffic island; the fractures seem not to have healed properly. He suffers from bleeding ulcers. And his impatience and roughness with friends and strangers is to a considerable extent the result of his inability to speak in much above a harsh whisper: years ago, he had an operation on his vocal cords and was cautioned not to strain them too soon; in a fit of anger, he forgot himself, shouted, and lost most of his voice.

Another modern master who sometimes frightens people off is Charles Mingus, the bassist, composer, and bandleader who has created one of the most personal bodies of music in jazz. Mingus wears his heart on his sleeve; he holds nothing back. Unlike Miles, he has at times subjected fellow musicians to physical as well as verbal abuse, but such excesses appear to be behind him now; though the volcano still smolders, it no longer erupts.

Mingus's autobiography, *Beneath the Underdog*, is full of hyperbole and frustrating to those who want jazz anecdotes and musical analysis, yet very much worth reading. It reveals Mingus's way of looking at life as basically an adversary proceeding, which goes far in explaining some of his less-appealing behavior. It also reveals his openness and honesty—tall tales notwithstanding. And it contains a gem of a description of Mingus's departure from the band of one of his musical and personal heroes, Duke Ellington.

At intermission during an engagement at the Apollo Theatre, Mingus (who writes of himself in the third person) and trombonist Juan Tizol, a veteran band member, have an argument:

> You leave the rehearsal room, proceed toward the stage with your bass and take your place and at the moment Duke brings down the baton for "A-Train" and the curtain of the Apollo goes up, a yelling, whopping Tizol rushes out and lunges at you with a bolo knife. The rest you remember mostly from Duke's own words in his dressing room as he changes after the show.
>
> "Now Charles," he says, looking amused, putting Cartier links into the cuffs of his beautiful hand-made shirt, "you could have forewarned me—you left me out of the act entirely! At least you could have let me cue in a few chords as you ran through that Nijinsky routine. I congratulate you on your performance, but why didn't you and Juan inform me about the adagio you planned so that we could score it? I must say I never saw a large man so agile—I never saw *anybody* make such tremendous leaps! The gambado over the piano carrying your bass was colossal. When you exited after that I thought, 'That man's really afraid of Juan's knife and at the speed he's going he's probably home in bed by now.' But no, back you came through the same door with your bass still intact. For a moment I was hopeful you'd decided to sit down and play but instead you slashed Juan's chair in two with a fire axe! Really, Charles, that's destructive. Everybody knows Juan has a knife but nobody

Gil Evans

ever took it seriously—he likes to pull it out and show it to people, you understand. So I'm afraid, Charles—I've never fired anybody—you'll have to quit my band. I don't need any new problems. Juan's an old problem, I can cope with that, but you seem to have a whole bag of new tricks. I must ask you to be kind enough to give me your notice, Mingus."

Many years later, Ellington, Mingus, and Max Roach made a fascinating recording together, but the session almost fell apart. Mingus began to pack up his bass and leave in the middle of things. Duke, ever the master psychologist, asked what was wrong, and Mingus, professing his love for Duke, explained that he couldn't play with Roach. Duke ventured that it couldn't be that serious, right in the middle of a date, but Mingus went out toward the elevator. Duke followed him there.

> And after he had rolled off a few more beefs, and when he was in the elevator about to push the button, I said, quietly and slowly:
>
> "Mingus, my man, United Artists [the company for which the record in question was being made] gave you a full-page ad in the Christmas *Billboard*. It was beautiful."
>
> "Yeah."
>
> "You know," I continued, "if Columbia Records had spent that kind of money on promoting me, I would still be with them today."
>
> He picked up the bass, came back into the studio, and we recorded very happily from then on until the album was completed.

Long before the word became fashionable in jazz circles, Mingus called his bands "workshops." No musician who has worked with Mingus has failed to benefit from the experience. Good musicians invariably improve, and he has the ability to coax quite adequate performances from players who never before or after reach the same level.

Mingus's heroes are Ellington, Art Tatum, and Charlie Parker. His compositions are strongly influenced by Duke but have their own flavor. As a bass virtuoso, and he is that indeed, Mingus is unique. He can make the instrument as expressive as a jazz horn, though there are times when he seems to be wrestling with it rather than playing it. Mingus's music has an intensely physical quality and is as openly emotional as anything in jazz.

Like Mingus, Thelonious Monk has created his own music, and like Mingus's, it is closely related to

bop but not the *ding an sich*. Even among so strongly individualistic personalities as the makers of modern jazz, Monk stands out in terms of egocentricity. He does not seem to be wholly of this world and has never followed its customs more than superficially.

He even keeps his own time; for years, he might sleep for a couple of days, then stay up for the next three, and so on. When he married his childhood sweetheart, he insisted she move into his small apartment, and when they had a son, he still refused to move. As possessions accumulated—and he was loathe to throw anything away—they were stacked horizontally. The family lived there until the building had to be vacated.

Monk's creed is "play yourself," and he follows it to the utmost. He never compromised; others had to fit in with him, not vice versa. Mainly self-taught (he had some piano lessons at eleven), his technique is "wrong"—he plays in a percussive manner, fingers almost unbending—but it works splendidly for him. In his early years of playing, however, he demonstrated considerable facility in a more conventional vein.

This can be ascertained from the private recordings made during the time he was a member of the house band at Minton's Playhouse, a Harlem nightclub that became one of the focal points of the budding bop evolution in the early forties. Here, the music would generally start when it stopped elsewhere; Minton's was an after-hours spot. This was perfect for Monk, who often slept on the premises, not going home for days on end. Before that, he had toured with a faith healer ("she healed; I played") and worked in obscure Harlem clubs. Born in North Carolina in 1917, he grew up in New York's Hell's Kitchen.

Coleman Hawkins, who admired him, was the only musician brave enough to hire him for a "downtown" job; this was in 1944, on Fifty-second Street, and also resulted in Monk's first formal record date. His style was nearly formed by then; what followed was refinement of a basic approach to music rooted in crystallized simplicity, a paring down to essentials as ruthless as the most far-reaching abstract techniques employed in the plastic arts.

For years, he worked only sporadically; hiring him was a calculated risk. On a dance date at a ballroom, he found the piano's pedal nonfunctional; since it was in his way, he simply bent down and

Charles Mingus

Sonny Stitt

ripped off the pedal assembly, then disdainfully tossed it aside. The manager was not pleased.

In 1947, Blue Note Records, one of the pioneer jazz labels, gave him his first own record date. The results were most intriguing and caused much critical comment, pro and con. There were further dates for Blue Note, and they produced a fascinating body of music, long since accepted as the work of a master, yet little employment was generated from this, though it led to a growing reputation for Monk.

He already had the respect and admiration of his peers. Yet, when he and Miles Davis recorded together in 1954, the trumpeter requested that he "lay out" (that is, refrain from playing) while he was taking his solos; Monk's way of accompanying forces the soloist to play Monk's way. Monk also had trouble obtaining the then necessary cabaret card.

From the mid-fifties on, however, Monk found it easier to obtain fairly steady employment. In the main, this was due to the special relationship that evolved between Monk and the Termini Brothers, owners of the Five Spot, a jazz club on the Bowery which for a while became the main venue for uncompromising new jazz. Neither management nor customers complained when Monk's time sense told him not to show up for work before the night was half over, and he would repay the courtesy by playing sets that lasted considerably longer than the conventional fifty minutes.

In 1964, Monk was accorded the singular recognition of a cover story in *Time* (the only prior jazz subjects had been Louis Armstrong and Dave Brubeck), and this led to further expansion of his work schedule. He had previously made a couple of playing visits to Europe; now international tours became annual events, under the aegis of George Wein, producer of the Newport Jazz Festival and himself a pianist and Monk fan.

Monk thus became established, after years of "playing himself" exclusively, as an important part of the international jazz hierarchy. He even learned, under the tutelage of his devoted wife, who always traveled with him, to show up on time for concerts and recording sessions. But Nellie Monk had to bring along the pots and pans to cook her husband's favorite dishes, such as rice and beans, no matter where they might find themselves.

Like so many great jazzmen, Monk has a kind of natural showmanship that never fails to delight audiences. He is a conservative dresser, favoring traditionally cut suits, but loves odd headgear and will wear anything from a fancy fur hat to a Chinese skullcap, indoors and out. When the spirit moves him, he gets up from the piano bench and performs a dance (he is a large man with a bearish gait) that consists of lurching, leaping steps, angular in a way reminiscent of his music's rhythms.

Monk never makes any announcements and is taciturn in the extreme and a notoriously difficult interview. However, what he says is as concentrated and meaningful as what he plays. He was officially neither surprised nor pleased at his belated acceptance as a performer, but implicitly proud of his refusal to compromise, as the following reflects: "All you're supposed to do is lay down the sounds and let the people pick up on them. Nothing more to it than that."

When asked his opinion of a famous pianist (who had put Monk down as a musical primitive who doesn't know how to play the piano) during a "Blindfold Test," a record quiz conducted for years by veteran critic Leonard Feather, he got up and inquired: "Where's the bathroom?"

Practical criticism!

Monk's health has not been good in recent years, but after a lengthy absence from performing, he made a triumphant appearance at the 1975 Newport-in-New-York Festival, and followed up with a splendid Carnegie Hall concert early in 1976.

One of Monk's earliest admirers was the drummer on his first own record date, Art Blakey. A compact dynamo of energy, Blakey had played with the Billy Eckstine band; prior to that, with Fletcher Henderson. Blakey, Max Roach, and Kenny Clarke form the founding triumvirate of modern jazz drumming. The other two are skilled and highly sophisticated artists, but Blakey is an elemental force. An early convert to Islam (the real thing, not some local sect), Blakey has long been interested in African and other ethnic drum styles, and his playing, though it swings in a definitively jazz manner, reflects this. Since 1955, he has led his Jazz Messengers, and the alumni of the group constitute a Who's Who of formidable jazz names. These have included trumpeters Clifford Brown and Lee Morgan, both cut off in their prime, and the robust Freddie Hubbard; tenor saxophonist Wayne Shorter; and pianist Keith Jarrett.

Blakey is a hard taskmaster, setting the same driving pace for others that he demands from himself, but he is also a skilled presenter and flowery master of ceremonies, who, unlike many other modern leaders, makes sure that his sidemen's names are clearly and frequently mentioned in the course of any public performance. His musical allegiance has always been to a bop-rooted and relatively straightforward conception of jazz. When he briefly deviated from this course, it was with disappointing results, and soon he was able to find young and younger musicians able and willing to continue the Messenger tradition.

In the company of peers, Blakey rises to the occasion. He was the tireless spark plug for a group justly called the Stars of Jazz, assembled in 1972–73 by George Wein for international touring. His cohorts were Dizzy Gillespie, the trombonist Kai Winding, the alto and tenor saxophonist Sonny Stitt, Monk, and bassist Al McKibbon. Blakey saw to it that the pace didn't flag.

A drummer with some of Blakey's elemental energy but a unique ability to play polyrhythmically, yet always keeping the basic pulse going, though he might shift it from bass drum to snare to cymbal and back again within the stretch of a few minutes, is Elvin Jones, youngest of four brothers, three of whom are outstanding jazz players (pianist Hank and cornetist-bandleader-composer/arranger Thad Jones are the others). With his uncommonly long and limber limbs in perfect independence, Elvin in action is a sight to behold, and he always makes music, not noise. For years, he was the core of John Coltrane's support in the quartet led by the saxophonist—quite likely the most influential jazz group of the sixties.

A drummer who showed himself capable of stepping into Elvin's shoes with the Coltrane group on several occasions is Roy Haynes, who must be ranked with the great masters of modern jazz percussions. The dapper Haynes, who was once selected by *Esquire* magazine as one of the best-dressed men of the year, is so imaginative and resourceful a soloist that he sometimes makes the listener think the drums are a melodic instrument.

Prior to the advent of Coltrane, the leading tenor saxophonist in modern jazz had been Sonny Rollins. He is that again today, and not just because Coltrane suddenly left the position vacant. Rollins had remained in contention well before Coltrane's death. Indeed, it was Rollins who first vacated the number-one spot. That was in 1959, when, after returning from a European tour, he decided that he needed time to think and meditate, and for more

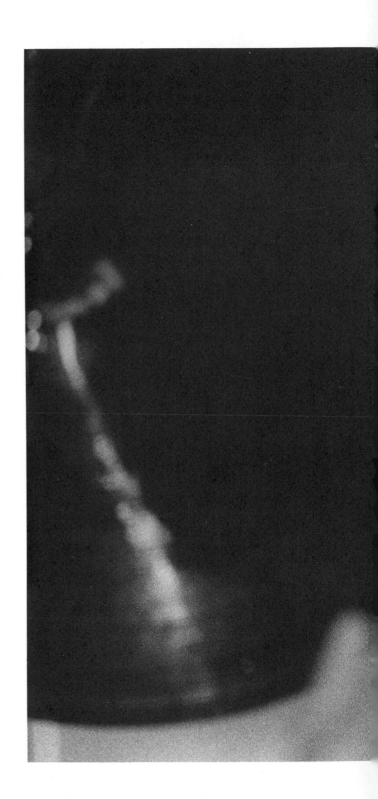

Art Blakey

than two years withdrew completely from active musical life.

New York-born, Rollins as a young man worked and recorded with Bud Powell, Miles Davis, and Thelonious Monk, among others. It was as a member of the Clifford Brown-Max Roach Quintet that Rollins really came into his own. His somewhat acerbic tone, virile and expressive mode, and at times sarcastic musical humor are characteristics of a most individual style and sound, and Rollins is one of the music's great improvisers, capable of sustaining interest with minimal or no accompaniment over long stretches of time.

Early in his career, Rollins had a brush with the scourge of modern jazz, but it was brief and left no lasting ill effects. He has long been a devotee of Yoga and body-building exercises; his style demands impressive physical command of the instrument. It also depends on inspiration, and while a Rollins performance is never boring, it can range from invigorating to ecstasy-inducing. Few experiences in contemporary jazz listening can compare with catching Rollins on a good night; he'll lift you up to the heights.

This was evident when he returned from his first self-imposed sabbatical, and again when he came back from a somewhat shorter retreat that included visits to Japanese and Indian shrines (but never with any of the bland, self-serving public utterances that often accompany such pilgrimages) in the early seventies. Upon his second return, Sonny found, to his surprise, that he had become a legend among young jazz listeners. It was they who joined seasoned fans on line outside the Village Vanguard, standing in the rain but feeling amply rewarded once they got in and heard Sonny preach his inspired sermons on standard jazz texts.

If Sonny has a direct ancestor, other than Coleman Hawkins, he would be the tenorman who also influenced John Coltrane profoundly and was the first to develop what might be called an authentic bebop tenor style. This is Dexter Gordon—"Long, Tall Dexter," as one of his early records has it—one of Copenhagen's most popular adopted sons since 1962, and unfortunately an infrequent visitor to his homeland.

Born in Los Angeles in 1923, Gordon was the son of a doctor whose patients included Duke Ellington and who died suddenly of a heart attack when Dexter was seventeen. The boy had been playing clarinet since he was thirteen and promptly left school when his father died, joining Lionel

Joe ("Flip") Phillips

Hampton's new band. Here, his section mate was Illinois Jacquet, and they were featured in a friendly battle on a piece called *Pork Chops,* which unfortunately was never recorded.

Dexter next played with Louis Armstrong and then in Billy Eckstine's fabulous band, which made him ready for New York and work with Charlie Parker. He had by now evolved the style that would become so influential, an amalgam of Lester Young's sinuous and Coleman Hawkins's robust approaches, with the added spice of Charlie Parker's rhythmic and harmonic discoveries and Dexter's own imaginative delivery.

Once again, the bane of modern jazzmen made its appearance, and the fifties were rather dim days for Dexter. He occasionally surfaced to make a record, showing he could still play with the old authority and swing, but never stayed long enough to reestablish himself. In 1960, he emerged for good. Since then, he has regained his rightful place among the masters, backed up by a string of impressive recordings. His relaxed ways and charming manners fit well with his new environment; he is a perfect honorary Dane.

Copenhagen was also hospitable to Stan Getz, who lived there for several years in the late fifties and early sixties. The tenor saxophonist had made his breakthrough at twenty, with his lovely solo on Woody Herman's 1947 recording of *Early Autumn.* It established him as one of the supreme melodists in jazz, and an influential stylist in his own right, not just a gifted Lester Young disciple.

The stay in Copenhagen was not his first in Scandinavia; in 1955, he was cured in Sweden of the illness that afflicted so many jazzmen of his generation. In the year he returned home, 1961, he recorded one of the finest works of his career, *Focus,* an extended piece for string ensemble, rhythm section, and improvising jazz soloist by Eddie Sauter, the composer/arranger who had made his mark with the bands of Red Norvo and Benny Goodman and with his own and Bill Finegan's Sauter-Finegan Orchestra.

Though the 1960s brought radical changes in jazz, Getz, popularly identified with cool jazz, scored his greatest success in 1962. Like most jazz recordings that become hits in the popular field, *Desafinado* was a fluke. Getz recorded this Brazilian samba tune with the guitarist Charlie Byrd, who had brought it and some other gently flowing melodies back from a South American tour. Rhythmically

Roy Haynes

and melodically, it suited Getz's conception perfectly, and the record's success made him one of the most popular instrumentalists of the decade and launched the bossa-nova fad—the term is Brazilian for "new wrinkle" and denotes a combination of samba and jazz elements.

Getz's artistry transcended the bossa-nova fad, and he did not let success compromise his musical integrity. His playing became even more assured. He surrounded himself with gifted younger musicians—the vibraharpist Gary Burton and pianist-composer Chick Corea among them—and has remained in the forefront of jazz. He has learned to control his volatile temper (once, at Chicago's London House, a nightclub where the clatter and chatter of the diners could become maddening to musicians and listeners alike, he placed one foot, not gently, on the well-stocked table of some particularly offensive ringsiders) and has matured and mellowed both as a man and a musician.

Denmark has also been a haven for other American jazzmen in exile, temporary or permanent: Stuff Smith, Ben Webster, Lee Konitz, and two of the most radical modernists, Albert Ayler and Cecil Taylor. Ayler was a visible jazz presence for a mere eight years, from the time he made his first record in Stockholm in 1962 until his death by drowning in 1970, at the age of thirty-four. Born in Cleveland, he spent his apprentice years in the rhythm-and-blues field, touring with the great blues harmonica player Little Walter at sixteen. He was in Paris and Copenhagen in 1960, but didn't make much of an impression. It was only when he sat in with Cecil Taylor at the Montmartre Club in Copenhagen in 1962 that people began to take notice of his playing, which seemed strange even in an avant-garde context.

Ayler was a primitive. His sound was rough and highly vocalized, his themes (and he played almost exclusively his own) short, fragmented, and reminiscent of bugle calls, field hollers, marches, and bagpipe music. Vehement and dramatic, veering between the poles of declamatory bathos and hortatory screams and cries, his music brought to mind a Salvation Army band on LSD.

When he wasn't playing, Ayler seemed an amiable sort, though not very talkative and seemingly dominated by his younger brother, who played trumpet in the group, had a history of mental instability, and usually acted as spokesman for Albert. By the time he made his way to significant American appearances in 1964, experimental and venturesome modern jazz had gained a small but devoted audience; Ayler managed to cause controversy within it. To those cool or hostile to all new music, he seemed a madman or a fraud, or merely comical proof of the suspicion that this stuff was all nonsense anyway.

In one of his infrequent utterances about his art, Ayler stated that it "was not about notes but about music," meaning, presumably, the whole rather than its parts. Ayler was rather more representative of a rhythm-and-blues musician freed from formal restraints than of the jazz tradition itself. His music, if one was prepared to accept it on its own terms, could be quite moving and even exhilarating, but it was too eccentric to have much significant or lasting influence.

Ayler's death has never been satisfactorily explained. His decomposing body was found in the East River an estimated three weeks after he had jumped, fallen, or been pushed into its waters. He was living in Brooklyn at the time; whatever work he was able to obtain in music almost solely came from European tours.

Cecil Taylor, with whom Ayler guested in Copenhagen, is far from a musical primitive. A thoroughly schooled musician who spent four years at New England Conservatory, he at first found little acceptance for his unusual style of playing within jazz circles. I remember that musicians distinctly his inferiors from the standpoint of instrumental command would walk disdainfully off the stand when Taylor sat in at jam sessions in New York in the early fifties; I also remember that when he did get to play, the results could be of almost frightening intensity. From a pianistic perspective, he was already an incredible musician.

Around 1956, Taylor formed his own quartet, which included soprano saxophonist Steve Lacy, and made his first records, one for a small label that soon went out of business, the other a performance at the Newport Jazz Festival, which that year was being recorded in its entirety by Norman Granz. I hadn't heard Taylor in four years or so and was amazed at the cohesion of the group and the clarity of Taylor's own playing.

The next few years brought some more interesting records (one with John Coltrane), but Taylor still met with great difficulties in gaining acceptance for his music. The Five Spot was hospitable, and Taylor would drain himself of all he had in him

Cecil Taylor

when playing there, but it was in Europe, specifically in Copenhagen, that the first real signs of recognition came, such as an invitation to perform at the 1969 Copenhagen Jazz Festival.

For some years, Taylor taught jazz, first at the University of Wisconsin, then at Amherst, developing a loyal and devoted following among his students, organizing large student ensembles that performed his compositions, and doing less well in his relations with administration and faculty.

An intense, high-strung, and keenly intelligent man, Taylor has consciously fought to free his music from modern European influences, but it seems inseparable from such roots, though it has a genuine base in jazz as well and is none the worse for it. In recent years, Taylor has broken through to a wider audience, drawing packed houses at the new Five Spot in 1975.

He now seems more at peace with himself, though his music remains charged with energy. His skills as a pianist, honed by years of intensive music-making, are phenomenal—he can articulate individual notes in flurries of such high velocity that the music seems a blur, and his control is the envy of any virtuoso. But he also communicates on a more directly emotional level, and while he probably will never reach a mass audience, seems assured of a quite sizable following, considering the demanding nature of his music. At least one may safely say that no contemporary "serious" composer of comparable complexity can claim so many ears for his music.

Just as Taylor was beginning to be heard around the East, a Texas saxophonist who had settled in Los Angeles was struggling to stay in music. He had to support himself as an elevator operator, and as they had done to Taylor, musicians would walk off the stand when he tried to participate in jam sessions. Eventually, he did find a group of young musicians hospitable to his unorthodox ways. Some of them would later become his sidemen, but at this point, a few nights of sitting in for coffee and cakes was all they could provide Ornette Coleman with, and the management and customers did not share their appreciation of his style.

Despairing of ever getting a proper hearing for his playing, Coleman decided he might get some of the pieces he had written recorded by other musicians. With this in mind, he approached Les Koenig, the owner of a small, independent record company. He performed some of his compositions for Koenig, who was so taken by the serious young

Ornette Coleman

man's playing that he promptly decided to record him. The resulting record, though in retrospect Coleman's most conventional, caused considerable controversy. The year was 1958; John Coltrane was still with Miles Davis, who had just begun to explore the potentials of modal playing, and the jazz world was far from ready for Coleman's departure from such norms as the tempered scale, European harmony, and conventional bar-line structure.

But this first controversy was as nothing compared to the debate unleashed by Coleman's arrival in New York in 1959, at the helm of a quartet so close-knit it seemed to consist of mutually attuned telepaths. The venue for this debut was, appropriately enough, the Five Spot, and Coleman had acquired advance publicity from such supporters as John Lewis (whose Modern Jazz Quartet colleague, Milt Jackson, thought Coleman's music nonsensical) and Gunther Schuller, the composer and conductor who had made a jazz name for himself with his theory and practice of "third stream" music—a merging of jazz and Western classical traditions.

While no one—musician or critic—could quite figure out what Coleman was up to (he is an intuitive, self-taught player and composer whose explanations of his methods only seem to confuse the issue), there could be no doubt that his music had its own logic and cohesion. Charles Mingus put it well: "He plays right wrong."

Right or wrong, Ornette Coleman became one of the most influential musicians in recent jazz history. It was he who opened the doors for a decade of radical experimentation and searching, for what would alternatively be labeled "avant-garde jazz," "the new thing," and finally and most fittingly, "free jazz." The last was in fact the title of a Coleman album from 1960, containing nearly forty minutes of continuous improvisation, themeless, unrehearsed, and remarkable.

Always going his own way, Coleman subsequently wrote a string quartet, a piece for woodwind ensemble, and a work for full symphony orchestra, *The Skies of America*. He received a Guggenheim fellowship in composition and studied with Gunther Schuller. Yet he remained a maverick and found it almost as difficult to come to terms with recognition as it had been to survive neglect.

Those who initially had called him a charlatan eventually had to accept his sincerity, if not his artistry, and he continued to challenge them. When

Don Cherry

Bill Evans with his son, Evan

they had managed to admit grudgingly that his saxophone playing had some claims to jazz legitimacy, he took a leave of absence from the scene and returned also playing trumpet and violin, his approach to both instruments entirely unorthodox. Or he upset his jazz followers by writing in "classical" idioms alien to them, though this music was as much a reflection of his methods as his jazz works.

Though his influence has been great, it was often indirect, and he continues to be a loner. Generously, he opened his Lower East Side home, called "Artist's House," to other musicians and performers, only to find that they suspected his motives. His relations with the business end of the music world have always been complicated by his naiveté, which, however, is combined with a certain cunning.

But in the end he is right, of course, when he explains that he feels a promoter should ask him what he wants to do rather than how much money he wants—even if that same promoter has shown considerable good faith by financing a performance of his symphonic work. Though he would not put it in such terms, Coleman feels it is intrinsically wrong to treat music as a commodity. But it is characteristic that he also feels he is the one to have discovered that this is a problem. That he has managed to do as well as he has speaks not only for him but also for "the system," with all its faults.

Among the members of the 1959 Coleman quartet that set New York and the jazz world on its ear was a frighteningly skinny trumpeter whose use of a miniature instrument seemed appropriate—a full-sized horn might just have been too much for Don Cherry to handle. Cherry was among the musicians who had been first to accept Ornette in Los Angeles and had played on his first record. Their collaboration seemed almost symbiotic, and for quite some time Cherry was the only horn player to understand Coleman's language. Nevertheless, his playing had technical shortcomings, more apparent in solo than ensemble work. He gradually overcame these, as he also overcame the problem of drug addiction that at one time afflicted all but the harassed leader of the Coleman quartet.

Cherry still looks alarmingly thin, but he is now a guru of sorts who preaches and practices clean, "organic" living, has made his home in Sweden for a number of years, and, like Coleman, has added a number of other instruments to his arsenal. He has a knack for bringing coherence to a brand of music that often seems to lack organizing principles, perhaps because his communal feeling is genuine.

Aside from his first recording, Coleman never used a piano in his bands. The piano, of course, is an instrument bound to the tempered scale. It is fitting that the musician who exerted the greatest influence on the jazz of the sixties in a direction counter to the dissolution of traditional rules should be a pianist.

Bill Evans is that rarity among musicians, a true intellectual, but while his music is lucid and crystal clear, it is also full of feeling. In fact, Evans is an intensely lyrical player. His control of his materials, which continue to be those of the mainstream of jazz, which is to say song-form melodies—including some exquisite tunes of his own, such as *Waltz for Debby*—is astonishing, and he has developed a harmonic language as personal, in its own way, as Thelonious Monk's. It is this aspect of his playing, in particular, that has influenced so many musicians, even when the roads they took led in other directions.

For years, Evans's stance at the piano—back arched to the point where his head would become invisible, hidden beneath his hunched shoulders and almost level with the keyboard—was the very image of the introspective artist totally absorbed in his work. But he has straightened his posture and has filled out physically, so that his big, strong hands no longer seem to have been grafted onto a more delicate bone structure. His music has a new strength. All this reflects the solving of an old, persistent personal problem. And, at forty-six, he has become a father for the first time.

Let us complete this roundup of modern masters with three pianists who are stylistically unclassifiable and among the handful of jazz artists of the last twenty-five years to have achieved great and lasting popular acceptance.

Dave Brubeck, born in 1920, is the eldest. He studied with Darius Milhaud and briefly with Arnold Schönberg, and first made a slight stir in jazz circles with an experimental octet based in San Francisco. But when he broke through in the early fifties, it was with the conventional quartet instrumentation of alto saxophone, piano, bass, and drums.

In the fifties, Brubeck became a household name, especially on college campuses. With his popular saxophonist, Paul Desmond, who worked with him for almost twenty years, Brubeck captured the ears of listeners otherwise immune to the charms of jazz. He did it with, among other things, an approach to improvisation which, despite its seeming complexity, was easy to follow. His music also communicated because he seemed to enjoy making it—his large, shaggy-maned head swinging back and forth like a pendulum, feet tapping vehemently as he built his solos to pounding climaxes. He seemed to personify the involved creator. Brubeck's pleasant and open personality helped, too; he genuinely liked people and didn't become impatient with questions from the uninitiated, as more sophisticated musicians often did.

The urbane, witty Desmond, with his elegant, sinuous style, made an unlikely yet perfect companion to Brubeck. Jazz critics often used praise of Desmond to damn Brubeck, which wasn't fair to either man; the more generous among them made mention of Brubeck's gifts as a composer, which are not inconsiderable.

Nevertheless, Brubeck's main contribution is probably that he initiated a lot of people into jazz. His own work, which includes a full-fledged mass, is a bit simplistic. Of Brubeck's four sons, three are musicians, and in the early seventies he often performed with them. "Two Generations of Brubecks" was a wholesome spectacle indeed, and many parents who had been Brubeck fans twenty years before took their offspring to see it.

In 1975, Brubeck reformed his classic quartet, with Desmond, for a twenty-fifth anniversary tour—his popularity abroad had been as great as in his homeland, and the quartet had been one of the first jazz groups to make successful world tours. It was a question frequently encountered from well-meaning airline personnel on their extensive travels that led Desmond to tentatively title his planned memoirs "How Many Are There in Your Quartet?"

At the time of the Brubeck Quartet reunion, Oscar Peterson was concentrating, for the first time in his career, on solo playing, a format well suited to his prodigious technique. One of the few Canadian-born jazzmen of international stature (Gil Evans and Maynard Ferguson are others), Peterson played trumpet at the age of five, but had to quit when he contracted tuberculosis; he switched to piano and received thorough classical training. At fourteen, he won a prize and was offered a regular spot on a Montreal radio show; at nineteen, he became a member of one of Canada's most popular bands.

The breakthrough came five years later, in 1949, when impressario Norman Granz brought him to New York for a Carnegie Hall appearance with *Jazz at the Philharmonic.* In the following year, Peterson began to record for Granz and tour with the Philharmonic troupe. He formed a trio (modeled on that of his chief inspiration, Nat King Cole—Oscar can do an astonishingly close vocal impression of Cole as well) with the great bassist Ray Brown, and guitarist Irving Ashby, later replaced by the formidable Barney Kessel, and then, for the longest stay, by the equally formidable Herb Ellis.

The guitar was later exchanged for drums—a more conventional trio setting. Throughout these years, Peterson also appeared on a variety of Granz-produced recordings, accompanying almost every artist in the Granz stable. In this role, Peterson's driving beat, harmonic acuity, and very quick ear stood him in good stead and often inspired the soloists he supported. Granz also recorded Peterson copiously with his trio, and his output dwarfs that of most jazz practitioners.

Eventually, a distinctive Peterson style emerged from his eclecticism, with the influence of Art Tatum to the fore. Peterson's command of the instrument continued to grow, and while his virtuosic impulses at times still overwhelm the music, even a listener drawn to less flamboyant playing cannot deny that he is in the presence of a master.

Like Brubeck and Peterson, Erroll Garner was among the first jazz performers to specialize in concert work (for a while, he was even booked by Sol Hurok). Unlike them, he had no classical training. In fact, Garner doesn't read music. Prior to linking up with enlightened management—in the person of his singularly dedicated manager of more than two decades, Martha Glaser—the self-taught erstwhile prodigy from Pittsburgh had paid plenty of jazz dues, for a while working two jobs simultaneously on Fifty-second Street.

Garner, though by no means anachronistic in his music, is a kind of throwback to an earlier day of jazz. He arrived at his own unique and instantly recognizable style early, and never saw any need to change it. It is a style essentially melodic, whether he is embellishing a romantic ballad with voluptuous harmonies and cascading arpeggios, or enlivening a rhythmic tune with the lilting beat of his lag-along left hand, strumming chords a bit in the manner of a guitar.

Dave Brubeck

Oscar Peterson

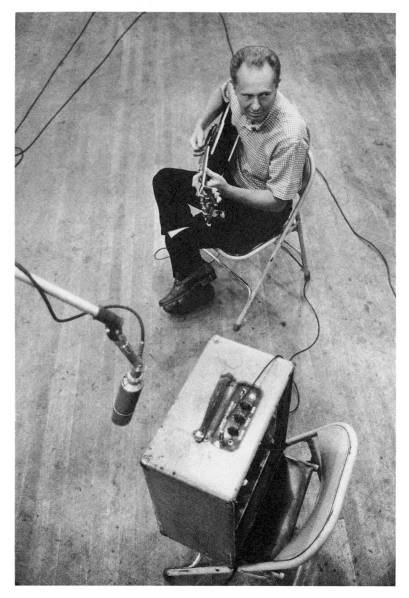

Herb Ellis

Garner's music is filled with puckish humor, and he is the only musician I know who can make an audience laugh without saying a word—purely by musical means, and not through obvious musical jokes but with real musical wit. Like Brubeck, Garner makes his audiences feel that they can follow what he does when he is improvising; unlike Brubeck, he leads them into a world of subtle and airy delights.

A short, compact man of elfish mien, who expends terrific energy when he performs, Garner is a very private person despite his popularity. If you are lucky, you may be in a club some night when he drops by to sit in with someone he likes to play with—his old friend and fellow Pittsburgher Roy Eldridge, for instance—and then the sparks will fly. Though he has been working with his own accompanying trio for years, Garner is still one of the greatest pianists to have in a band, large or small. And he loves to play. There are no barriers between him and his audience, only total communication. And it is in this happy sense that Erroll is a throwback to an earlier, less complicated phase of jazz than the era called, for lack of a better term, modern.

By the mid-1970s, that era had definitely ended, replaced by a musical atmosphere in which all manner of styles and forms coexist peacefully. Diversity seems the order of the day, and for the first time in many years, young musicians are taking an active interest in the history of the music. Whether this will pave the way for marvelous things to come or is an indication that the great, creative days of jazz are coming to an end, only time will tell.

6

The Singers

All music derives from song, the voice being the first instrument of them all, and jazz is no exception. Jazz singing is a very special art, with a tradition all its own.

As we have seen, one of the key characteristics of early instrumental jazz was the players' attempts to vocalize their sounds. King Oliver muted his trumpet with various devices, including the lowly bathroom plunger—to this day an essential piece of equipment in any jazz trumpeter's arsenal. Growls, flutters, various "freak" effects were coloristic devices widely used by black musicians and imitated by their white emulators. Tommy Ladnier, the New Orleans trumpeter, was billed as "The Talking Cornet" when he toured Europe in the twenties.

The voices of black people are different from those of whites. There is no counterpart to the bel canto tradition in Africa, a continent where some languages use changes in inflection as we use words, subtle modifications of the same basic sound carrying a variety of meanings. African song is rough by genteel Western standards—which is not to say that there haven't been great black singers in that tradition.

Deprived of musical instruments, the slaves who were brought to America at first subsisted on a musical diet entirely of song, accompanied by such rhythmic sounds as could be made through or while working. Eventually, they fashioned drums and other percussion devices, then banjos and other impromptu stringed instruments, but singing was still the thing.

It was of two basic kinds—work song and religious song. It was the latter that first made the white world aware of the musical genius of the black race, but we know now that the famous spirituals were presented to white audiences in versions shorn of most of their expressive power. What is known today as gospel singing is the real thing. After emancipation, the third important kind of black song appeared—the blues. This basic, simple form lends itself to infinite variation, and it has conquered the world in the guises of jazz, rock, and soul.

In jazz singing as well as in instrumental jazz, Louis Armstrong looms large. It was he who introduced black vocal technique and sound to a wider audience. At first, his singing was considered comical, or at least odd, but as his popularity increased and he began to sing the popular romantic songs of the day, many white people—notably musicians—realized what an expressive instrument this seemingly rough and untutored voice really was.

Aside from his sound, his rhythm, phrasing, and feeling had an impact on popular singing well beyond the confines of jazz. If one compares the style of early Bing Crosby to that of other pop singers of the twenties one realizes that two things—jazz and the microphone—revolutionized this branch of the vocal art.

Crosby wasn't a jazz singer, but he was in close contact with the jazz world through the great players who passed through the ranks of the Paul Whiteman band. He could scat very nicely, and his grasp of rhythmic jazz essentials and relaxed phrasing are miles apart from the stilted, now laughable singing style of the average white dance band vocalist of the period—and some blacks as well.

On the other hand, Crosby is miles removed from the authentic blues at the root of Armstrong's singing. In the twenties, white people didn't hear much country blues, if any. The first blues to be recorded was of the more polite, vaudeville and minstrel-influenced style popular with urban blacks. Only after a few years of this did the greatest of female blues singers, Ma Rainey and Bessie Smith, get to make records.

Ma Rainey was known as "The Mother of the Blues" and claimed to have introduced the style to the black professional entertainment world. She certainly was one of the first to do so, and no doubt contributed to the basic stylization of the blues form. For years, it was taken for granted that the somewhat younger Bessie Smith had been Ma's protégé and toured with her troupe; research has shown this to be wrong. Though the two singers knew and admired each other, their first contact came much later, after Bessie was already well established.

Bessie Smith was a remarkable artist and a remarkable woman. She needed no microphone to fill the largest hall with her marvelous voice, and every word she sang was clearly enunciated, albeit with natural, unaffected diction. And she had a stage personality to match the power of her voice.

"Bessie Smith was a fabulous deal to watch," guitarist Danny Barker recalled. "She was a large, pretty woman and she dominated the stage. You didn't turn your head when she went on. You just watched Bessie. If you had any church background, like people who came from the South as I did, you would recognize a similarity between what she was doing and what those preachers and evangelists from there did, and how they moved people. She could bring about mass hypnotism."

Another musician who worked with Bessie, Sy Oliver, recalled that she once said, prior to a show, "I'm going to walk me one today." He didn't know what she meant until he noticed, after Bessie had sung a few numbers, that a man in the audience had risen from his seat and was moving slowly down the theater aisle toward the stage, as if in a trance. He remained transfixed in front of the singer until her song had ended, at which point he came out of his hypnotized state, looked around him in confusion, and eventually returned to his seat, accompanied by laughter from the audience. Bessie could do this at will.

Barker put his finger on something when he mentioned the church. Though the blues was scorned by respectable religious blacks (many an aspiring jazz musician was forbidden to practice the blues or play blues or jazz records in his parents' home), it was the secular counterpart of the music heard especially in

Ma Rainey's Georgia Jazz Band, c.
1924–25. Left to right: "Gabriel,"
Albert Wynn, Dave Nelson, Ma, Ed
Pollack, Thomas A. Dorsey

Baptist and "sanctified" churches. Mahalia Jackson, perhaps the greatest and certainly the most famous of all gospel singers, was admittedly inspired by Bessie Smith, though she never sang a blues in her life. And there is much similarity in the musical approach of the two great singers, as well as in their voices.

Bessie began to make records in 1923, and through the next ten years recorded 160 songs, most of them blues, but also such things as the famous *Nobody Knows You When You're Down and Out*. Most of these, like most of all blues, dealt with various aspects of love—treated with a directness, sexual frankness, and humor far removed from the romantic treacle of Tin Pan Alley songs—but there were also other subjects, such as in *Poor Man's Blues* and her own *Back Water Blues,* inspired by observation of the effects of a Mississippi flood, and one of Bessie's masterpieces. No matter what she dealt with, Bessie brought it to life.

The best musicians available backed her up on records, among them Louis Armstrong himself. The relationship between blues singer and accompanying instrumentalist is a very special one, illuminating the instrumental quality of the singing and the vocal quality of the playing, horn responding to voice in an unbroken pattern of musical continuity.

Bessie's career had its ups and downs, but at the time of her death in an automobile accident while on tour in the Deep South, she was ready to make a comeback. She had, however, appeared in New York as late as the year before her death in September, 1937, and the stories about her professional decline are no more true than the much publicized fiction blaming her death on racial discrimination—it is claimed that she bled to death because the white hospital to which the ambulance took her first would not admit her. This account, built up by frequent repetition and given added resonance by allusions to it in Edward Albee's play *The Death of Bessie Smith,* has been proven false but nevertheless survives. There are enough true horrors in the annals of blues and jazz, and Bessie Smith's death was tragic enough in itself.

What actually happened was this. The car in which Bessie was riding had hit the back of a slow-moving truck. The impact was on Bessie's side and she was severely injured. The first car to arrive at the scene of the early morning accident was driven by a young white doctor on a fishing trip with a friend. The doctor applied first aid while his friend went to call an ambulance. When no ambulance had appeared after some time, the pair decided to take the badly injured singer to the hospital in their car. While they were clearing the back seat, another car approached at high speed; they just managed to jump aside before it hit the doctor's car, propelling it into what was left of the vehicle in which Bessie had been riding, and barely missing Bessie and the doctor's friend. The people in the third car, a young white couple who had been drinking, were not severely hurt, and as the doctor was examining them, an ambulance finally arrived, as well as several law officers. Bessie was carried to the ambulance, and as it took off for Clarksdale, Mississippi, the nearest town, another ambulance arrived to take the injured couple—one had been called by the truck driver involved in the original accident, the other by the doctor's friend. The doctor, interviewed in detail by Bessie Smith's biographer Chris Albertson, judges that even by today's medical standards, Bessie would have had just a fifty-fifty chance of survival. Given the 1937 situation, and a rural Mississippi hospital, she had almost no chance and died of internal injuries in the Afro-American Hospital in Clarksdale at 11:30 A.M. The ambulance driver confirmed twenty years later that he had taken her straight there; it was a black ambulance and it would not have made sense to him to drive to a white hospital.

By the time of Bessie's death, her repertory had been amended to include the popular songs that had become the mainstay of the jazz repertoire. Ethel Waters, a singer who had begun her career with blues and had applied blues tactics to pop songs, was among those who paved the way for this change, and Louis Armstrong, of course, had a hand in it.

The singer who perhaps brought this special art to its greatest heights was inspired by Bessie and Louis. Her name was Billie Holiday, and she was able to infuse the often cheap and platitudinous lyrics of popular songs with such honest feeling that she lifted them into the realm of true art. She had a small voice and no musical training, though her father was a jazz guitarist who had played with Fletcher Henderson and other good bands, and someone aptly described her as "the girl who sings as if her shoes don't fit." There was no one like her.

Before she wrote her autobiography in collaboration with a journalist with a taste for the sensational (her life was quite lurid enough on its own terms),

Bessie Smith, c. 1925

Photograph by Timme Rosenkrantz. Collection of Duncan Schiedt

Ben Webster, Billie Holiday, unidentified guitarist, and Johnny Russell in Harlem, 1935

she gave this account of her start as a singer:

> Mother and I were starving. . . . We lived on 145th Street near Seventh Avenue. One day we were so hungry we could barely breathe. I started out the door. It was cold as all hell and I walked from 145th to 133rd, down Seventh Avenue, going in every joint trying to find work. Finally, I got so desperate I stopped in the Log Cabin Club run by Jerry Preston. . . . I asked Preston for a job, told him I was a dancer. He said to dance. I tried it. He said I stunk. I told him I could sing. He said sing. Over in the corner was an old guy playing the piano. He struck *Travelin' All Alone* and I sang. The customers stopped drinking. They turned around and watched. The pianist, Dick Wilson, swung into *Body and Soul*. You should have seen those people—all of them started crying. Preston came over, shook his head, and said, "Kid, you win." That's how I got my start. First thing I did was get a sandwich. I gulped it down. Believe me, the crowd gave me eighteen dollars in tips. I ran out the door, bought a whole chicken, ran up Seventh Avenue to my home. Mother and I ate that night— and we've been eating pretty well since.

It was at Jerry Preston's that John Hammond first heard Billie and arranged for her to record with Benny Goodman. That was in 1933; she was eighteen. Nothing happened with the first records, but when Hammond brought her into a studio again some eighteen months later, it was a different story. That initial session, with Teddy Wilson leading an all-star group including Roy Eldridge, Ben Webster, and Goodman, set the pattern for dozens and dozens to come, among which not one is less than good and some, notably those with Lester Young in the band, are among the rarest jewels in the treasury of recorded jazz. Soon, some of the sessions were under her own name, and she would sing two choruses and the instrumentalists would do one instead of vice versa. And by 1940, there might not be any instrumental interlude at all, or only a half chorus. Billie Holiday had become a song stylist rather than, as she put it, "somebody's damn vocalist."

Before she made her breakthrough as a single attraction, at Café Society Downtown and on Fifty-second Street, she paid her dues as a band singer, first with Count Basie (again Hammond's doing) for nearly a year, then with Artie Shaw as the first black girl singer featured with a white band. The things she had to cope with were similar to those that would face Roy Eldridge a few years later—maybe worse, because she was a woman and more vulnerable. She stood it for eight months.

At Café Society, she discovered that she could do material like *Strange Fruit*, a bone-chilling song about lynching, and also added more blues to her repertoire, including the wonderful *Fine and Mellow,* her own concoction. In 1940, after an argument with her mother, she and lyricist Arthur Herzog came up with *God Bless the Child*, an unusual "message" song that became a hit with young audiences in the late sixties.

By then, Billie had been dead for almost ten years, a victim of heroin, the unreasonable attitude of society toward addiction, especially if the addict was black and famous, and her own self-destructive nature. She served a year and a day in prison in 1947–48, having been busted in Philadelphia, always one of the worst towns for black performers to get into trouble with the law. After that, she was unable to work in a New York nightclub because of the so-called cabaret card, without which you couldn't work in a place that served alcohol and which was impossible to obtain if you had served time in prison, especially for a narcotics violation. But she did a triumphant comeback concert at Carnegie Hall and appeared on Broadway and in movie theaters. In late 1948, she was tried and acquitted in San Francisco on another narcotics charge; Jake Erlich was her lawyer.

By the early fifties, her voice had begun to show the consequences of years of heavy drinking and smoking, but strangely enough this cracked, croaking instrument was capable of producing incredibly moving music. Norman Granz recorded her frequently, once again with great jazzmen backing her; in person, she still worked with just a trio. Her fans were, in their own way, as fanatic as Judy Garland's, and she had a similar morbid appeal. Unlike Miss Garland, however, she got no television shows or film roles. She made just one appearance in a major film, *New Orleans,* with Louis Armstrong in 1947. Though her part was that of a maid, she made it seem glamorous. She was a woman of striking presence and beauty. In 1957, there was a television spot in a remarkable show, "The Sound of Jazz," which stands as the best program on the subject ever done. It reunited her with Lester Young.

In March, 1959, Billie attended Lester's funeral. She wanted to sing, but Mrs. Young would not allow it. The funeral was to be respectable, and Billie Holiday was a notorious woman—that seemed to be the rationale. Instead, trombonist Tyree Glenn played *Holy City*. Outside the funeral home, musician friends tried to console her. "They wouldn't let me sing. Those m—s wouldn't let me sing," was all she said between the tears, over and over again.

On May 25, 1959, Billie made her last public appearance, at a New York benefit concert. She was so emaciated that the audience was stunned when she came into view. Jo Jones helped her on and off stage. Soon thereafter, she was hospitalized and at first seemed to be making progress. Then a "friend" smuggled in some dope for her, and she was arrested on what became her deathbed. "They even took my damn comic books," she told a musician allowed to visit.

Billie Holiday died on July 17, 1959, aged forty-four. Joe Glaser saw to it that she had a big sendoff.

"I don't think I'm singing," she said once. "I feel like I'm playing a horn. I try to improvise like Les Young, like Louis Armstrong, or someone else I admire. What comes out is what I feel."

And Carmen McRae, quite a singer in her own right, said: "The only time Billie is at ease and at rest with herself is when she sings."

Three years younger than Billie and quite unlike her in temperament and style, Ella Fitzgerald has enjoyed a career that in comparison seems like a fairy tale. Discovered while singing at an amateur show at Harlem's Lincoln Theater in 1934, Ella joined Chick Webb's band at Benny Carter's recommendation. She was sixteen, and Webb became her guardian.

Webb, a tiny hunchback who was a dynamo of a drummer, had a good band and was very popular at the Savoy Ballroom in Harlem, where the band was resident, but it was Ella's singing that catapulted the band to fame by way of a rather silly novelty number, *A Tisket, A Tasket,* in which Ella sang her own lyrics in a most engaging manner.

The Fitzgerald voice, true and clear as a bell, had considerable range for a popular singer, and she had perfect intonation. Her rhythmic sense was sure, and there was a joyous, infectious quality to her work, especially on fast pieces. She developed a style of scat singing—a kind of wordless vocalizing introduced by Louis Armstrong in 1925 but no doubt around before then—that brought her great popularity at the dawn of the bebop era.

She had taken over nominal leadership of the Webb band when the gallant little drummer died of tuberculosis of the spine in June, 1939. Then, she embarked on a successful career as a solo attraction and recording star. From 1946, she also frequently worked with Norman Granz's Jazz at the Philharmonic, visiting Europe and Japan with the touring unit.

Though she was the acknowledged favorite of most of her peers by the mid-forties, it wasn't until Granz was able to take over as her personal manager that her career moved into high gear. Through Granz, she began to play such choice locations as the best Las Vegas hotels, and she appeared in several feature films, notably *Pete Kelly's Blues*. Granz also recorded her in different settings than the people at Decca, a label for which she had worked for twenty years. Instead of novelties, she was now featured in the best of Ellington, Gershwin, Rodgers and Hart, Cole Porter, etc.

Soon the "First Lady of Song," as Ella was known, moved into a realm inhabited by only a few jazz artists, on a plane with the Sinatras and Crosbys. She has been there ever since, surmounting eye trouble that necessitated several operations in the early seventies, but having no other apparent problems.

Such a position would make most performers feel quite secure, but not Ella. A negative comment in a review, no matter how unimportant the publication or how slight the criticism, is capable of reducing her to tears, and though she seems the most seasoned of performers, she still suffers from nervousness before each appearance. Less endearing is her attitude toward possible competition. When Roy Eldridge was featured in her accompanying group she seldom gave him solos to play, and if he got a big hand, she would cut out the offending solo spot forthwith. Such childish (rather than childlike) traits are part of Ella's total personality, and those who know her well accept them in good grace.

Though she has become increasingly convincing in serious songs, Ella's forte is happy, unproblematic vehicles that allow her voice and improvisatory talent free reign. She swings like few other singers ever have and communicates a *joie de vivre* that is most infectious. She, too, can sing "like a horn," but in a playful manner quite different from Billie Holiday.

The most important female singer to appear in the wake of these two remarkable ladies is Sarah Vaughan. Equipped with the greatest voice—in the

Billie Holiday

traditional meaning of that term—of any jazz singer, she was born in Newark in 1924 and received her early training in that city's Mount Zion Baptist Church. She also studied piano. Like Ella, she was discovered at an amateur contest, this one at Harlem's famous Apollo Theatre in 1943. It was Billy Eckstine who heard her and recommended her to his old boss, Earl Hines. She made her debut with the Hines band at the Apollo, doubling on second piano when Hines fronted the band. The following year she joined Eckstine's wild bebop band for a year or so, and from then on has appeared as a soloist.

She was the first singer of note to catch on to the musical sophistication of the boppers, recording with Charlie Parker and Dizzy Gillespie. Her uncanny harmonic sense enabled her to fashion horn-like improvisations and embellishments related to the tonal universe of modern jazz. At the same time, the rich, voluptuous sound of her voice and her flair for melody assured her of a popular following, and for a time it even seemed she had been lost to jazz as her recordings became more and more commercial in character.

Even at its most commercial, however, Sarah Vaughan's artistry was undeniable, and eventually she returned to a jazz-oriented format. In addition, an earlier tendency toward coyness was transcended, without loss of the playful element that made her earlier work so enjoyable.

When she made her first appearance as a solo attraction (at Café Society Downtown), Sarah was a shy, awkward girl with a gap between her front teeth and dowdy dresses. In the band playing opposite her was trumpeter George Treadwell. A romance quickly developed, and when she became Mrs. Treadwell a transformation began to take place. Before long, Sarah Vaughan was glamour incarnate, with a radiant, charming stage personality, capable of transporting her fans into ecstacy with just a few bars of her greatest hits, such as *Misty* or *Tenderly*. Her later marital liaisons were not successful, but in 1975 she married again, and friends say they have never seen her happier.

Like Ella Fitzgerald, Sarah Vaughan is essentially a private person; she has never been involved in notoriety and has no hobbies or peculiarities. She might have become a great gospel or classical singer, but it is doubtful that her imagination and inventiveness could have unfolded elsewhere as fully as it has in jazz.

Before we take leave of the golden age, mention should be made of Mildred Bailey (1907-1951), the first woman singer to be regularly featured with a big band. The band was Paul Whiteman's, in which her brother, Al Rinker, was a member of the Rhythm Boys (Bing Crosby was another), and the year was 1929.

Mildred had a sweet, pure voice, rather high yet pleasant, and a special lilt in her phrasing. A large woman, she had a ferocious temper (during her marriage to Red Norvo, when they were known professionally as Mr. and Mrs. Swing, she became involved in an argument with her husband that resulted in a number of valuable objects, including an expensive fur piece, being thrown into a fireplace by her own hand) but a generous nature. She was most famous for her rendition of Hoagy Carmichael's *Rockin' Chair,* and, like Billie Holiday, made records with first-rate jazz musicians, supervised by John Hammond.

If Mildred Bailey was the only white singer of the golden age in a class with Billie and Ella, Anita O'Day is the only modern jazz singer to occupy a similar position. She made her reputation with Gene Krupa's band, which she joined in 1941 at the age of twenty-one. Unlike most band singers, who were quite content to function as sex symbols, Anita wanted to make it on the strength of her musicianship alone and appeared in tailored suits instead of décolleté evening gowns, giving rise to mistaken notions concerning her sexual orientation.

Her husky, febrile voice had a *jazz* sound, and her rhythmic sense was superior to many an instrumentalist's. While she scored with novelty numbers that teamed her with Roy Eldridge (like so many jazz trumpeters an Armstrong-inspired singer), notably the hit *Let Me Off Uptown,* she was just as impressive on warm ballads. And she could sing the blues. Joining Stan Kenton in 1944 for a year, she set the style for future Kenton singers—both her replacements, June Christy and later Chris Connor, were cast in the O'Day mold, though neither was her equal.

Unpredictable and unconventional, Anita intermittently suffered from the same affliction as Billie Holiday, but in the late fifties her career enjoyed a resurgence. Her appearance at Newport in 1958, with a new, elegant image (white picture hat, matching long gloves, slinky blue dress), was captured in the film made at the festival that year, *Jazz on a Summer's Day,* and brought her a new crop of

fans. She also made some excellent recordings for Norman Granz.

In relative obscurity again some ten years later, Anita reemerged once more, and while perhaps not as prominent as she deserves to be, is still at the forefront of her profession. Whether up or down, Anita O'Day has always been an uncompromising jazz singer, perhaps eccentric, but undeniably original and musical.

If the rising art of jazz singing, styled to the medium of popular songwriting (which not coincidentally reached its zenith in the twenties and thirties) eclipsed the blues as the favorite vocal medium of urban black audiences, that did not mean that the blues disappeared. In fact, about the time urban blues went into temporary decline, record companies discovered its rural counterpart, as dominated by male singers as urban style had been by females. Much more basic, accompanied mostly by guitar (often played by the singer himself) or piano, almost never by a horn, and tied to a specific region

(the Mississippi delta, Texas, Tennessee), country blues proliferated in the thirties. The cornerstone had been laid by Blind Lemon Jefferson in the preceding decade.

Blind Lemon was born in Texas in 1897 and died in Chicago during the winter of 1929–30. Few of the circumstances of his life are known, but between April, 1926, and September, 1929, he recorded some eighty blues songs that are among the most powerful and fascinating in the idiom and paved the way for all the male blues singers to follow, from Leroy Carr to B.B. King. He has been described by contemporaries as everything from a gross lecher and drunk who was paid off for record dates in whiskey and the services of prostitutes, to a kindly, generous, God-fearing man who wouldn't play his guitar on a Sunday for any amount of money. Among those who crossed his path were Leadbelly and Josh White.

Slowly but surely, the country blues made its way into the mainstream of American music, first

Anita O'Day

Mildred Bailey, c. 1935

through the folklorists—specifically the Lomaxes, father John and son Alan, who made field trips and recordings for the Library of Congress—then through the left-wing intelligentsia which had already discovered white American folk music via Woody Guthrie and Pete Seeger. The main cog in this movement was Leadbelly, the astonishing, intimidating ex-convict twice pardoned from the chain gang through the power of his singing and guitar playing. Discovered by the Lomaxes and brought to New York by them, he was a walking repository of folk tradition, black and also white.

In his wake came Josh White, who had begun his singing and recording career as a gospel performer, but also had been associated with Blind Lemon Jefferson and with the great Leroy Carr—the man who more than any other was responsible for the eventual transition of the blues from a folk form to popular music. Born in South Carolina, the son of a preacher, White was a handsome, muscular man and a guitarist of ferocious power. He had a smooth yet burnished voice and, though self-taught, an ear for formal harmonic idioms that made his blues and folk songs palatable to sophisticated listeners who couldn't quite digest the raw power of Leadbelly.

It was at Barney Josephson's Café Society Downtown that White found his form and his audience. Josephson made him wear open-neck shirts. "He was a terror with the girls," the club owner recalled, "and when they saw that neck—all muscles and tendons—they wanted to bite it." His repertoire ranged from chain-gang songs and social protest material (much of the latter composed by himself, including a blues dedicated to "Comrade Stalin") to gentle love songs (*I Gave My Love a Cherry; Black Is the Color*). His version of *One Meat Ball* became a hit. In the fifties, when McCarthyism made things uncomfortable for performers with past left-wing ties, White spent much time in England, where he became very popular, and also visited other European countries. He died at the age of fifty-four in 1969; his son, Josh White, Jr., who sings and plays in a style much influenced by his father, has forged a successful acting career for himself.

Two rural bluesmen who came to New York in the early forties and teamed up a few years later have become the most durable blues duo in the business, enjoying great popularity on the folk-music circuit and touring throughout the world.

Blind Lemon Jefferson, 1927

Josh White

Sonny Terry

Sonny Terry, the elder of the two, suffered severe eye injuries as a child and is functionally blind. A good singer, he is most famous for his amazing harmonica playing. He coaxes from the little instrument a variety of strange sounds, haunting or humorous, and is able to accompany his own singing in such a way that his vocal hollering and harmonica whooping seem to blend into a single jet stream of sound.

Sonny tells a nice story about his audition for *Finian's Rainbow,* in the original Broadway production of which he had a featured spot. He sang his blues and played his harmonica to everyone's liking and was asked if he could do his number the same way every night.

"No, man," he replied. "I sing and play what I feel." Told that this was too bad, since his spot involved a problem of timing and cues, Sonny remained adamant; he had to do it his own way.

Had he any idea how much he would be paid to perform, he was asked. He did not, but that had nothing to do with it, he responded. The producer mentioned a figure—a lot more than Sonny had ever been paid for anything.

"I jumped," he recalls, and said, " 'Yes, man, I can do that number *exactly* the same way every night, don't you worry!' "

Sonny's partner, Brownie McGhee, plays guitar and sings in a manner influenced by the legendary Blind Boy Fuller, with whom Terry coincidentally made his first recordings—McGhee's first professional work was done under the pseudonym of Blind Boy Fuller No. 2. The two complement each other well. Together they appeared in *Cat on a Hot Tin Roof,* both on Broadway and on the road, and have made many records. Though their art is au-

thentic, they managed to break through to audiences not otherwise open to blues, not least because of their uncontrived showmanship.

Eventually, the rise of rock 'n' roll prepared the ground for much broader acceptance of the blues, which was rock's basic source, and had itself undergone many transformations in the forties and fifties. As far as jazz is concerned, the thirties was perhaps the decade least influenced by the blues. Yet, there was a strong blues current in the music of the Swing Era, most explicitly that which came out of Kansas City.

Two singers associated with that city, Jimmy Rushing and Joe Turner, came to the fore through the good offices of John Hammond. Rushing was the singer with Count Basie's band and had in fact been associated with Basie since 1928, when both were in Walter Page's Blue Devils and together joined Bennie Moten's orchestra.

Rushing's voice was a true tenor, light in coloration, slightly nasal but attractively so. Though famous for and thoroughly at home in the blues, he also sang popular tunes and considered himself a jazz rather than a blues man. However, he was inextricably associated with the blues, and his periodic protests were not to be taken too seriously. Jimmy had started his singing career before the microphone age, and his voice had enough penetrating power to make itself heard over the Basie horns in full cry.

A rotund man fondly known as "Mister Five by Five" (in later years he was, in fact, almost as wide as he was tall), Rushing excelled at happy, rhythmic blues like *Sent for You Yesterday,* but also could be very moving in a more serious vein, as in *Jimmy's Blues,* with its famous closing lines:

Sonny Terry

Brownie McGhee

Jimmy Rushing

Jimmy Rushing

Anybody ask you
Who was it sang this song
Tell 'em little Jimmy Rushing
He's been here and gone.*

Jimmy had wonderful, clear diction and among the many blues he made famous with Basie was the unusual *Harvard Blues,* the lyrics to which had been dreamed up by George Frazier, one of the first American jazz critics, later arbiter of taste for *Esquire,* and still later, iconoclastic columnist for Boston newspapers. The lament of an undergraduate, it contained these lines, taken almost verbatim from university regulations: "I can't keep dogs/Or women in my room." Rushing sang Frazier's blues with the utmost authenticity, but the reviewer who assumed that the singer had no notion whereof he was singing did Rushing an injustice. An intelligent, literate man, he knew very well what Frazier's various Harvardian allusions meant, which made his deadpan rendition all the more praiseworthy.

Rushing left Basie in 1950, led his own little band for a couple of years, and then embarked upon the solo career that made him one of the most popular attractions at jazz festivals, concerts, and clubs throughout the world. By sheer force of voice and gesture, he could make the most lead-footed band swing, and he was a hard man to follow on any bill. Occasionally, he still appeared with Basie and also did guest spots with the big bands of Benny Goodman and Harry James.

In 1969, his good friend Gordon Parks gave Rushing a featured role in the film *The Learning Tree,* and the singer gave an excellent performance as the genial, lecherous proprietor of an Oklahoma road- and whorehouse. During the last few years of his life, illness curtailed his activities, but until three weeks before his death at sixty-eight in 1972, he appeared on weekends at the Half Note, then still a cozy club on the waterfront in downtown Manhattan. A family-run place, it reminded him of the restaurant he had helped his family operate in Oklahoma City forty years before.

The other great singer to emerge from Kansas City, Joe Turner, was strictly a blues man. When he did an occasional pop tune, such as *Pennies from Heaven,* his modal inflections made it sound like blues.

Joe's father was killed in a car crash when the boy was fifteen. Big and tall, he began to work as a singer and bartender in various Kansas City clubs;

the city's night life was going strong. He soon teamed up with pianist Pete Johnson; they worked together for years. John Hammond heard them, brought them to New York for his 1938 Spirituals to Swing concert, and got them jobs at Café Society Downtown. But they got homesick and went back to Kansas City.

However, the benign corruption of Boss Pendergast was coming to an end, so the pair reluctantly returned to New York, where they made a record of their great duet, *Roll 'Em Pete,* to this day a staple in many a bluesman's repertoire. Eventually, they settled in Los Angeles. Here, Joe was featured in Duke Ellington's revue *Jump for Joy* and then hit the road with Pete and the other great boogie-woogie pianists. In 1945, Joe and Pete opened their own club, the Blue Room, in Los Angeles, but Pete, whose health was not good, moved to Buffalo in 1950.

Then Joe got lucky. He had several hit records, including *The Chains of Love* and *Shake, Rattle, and Roll,* toured Europe, appeared at Newport and in films, and today lives comfortably in California,

making occasional trips to Europe and recording for Norman Granz.

Joe Turner is a blues shouter, his voice surprisingly high for so big a man, his way with a melodic line almost oriental in its nondiatonic effect. Like Rushing, he has a powerful beat capable of swinging any group of musicians. Oddly enough, one of his most affecting performances was made with a band led by the most harmonically and technically sophisticated of all jazz pianists, Art Tatum. This is *Wee Baby Blues,* with its wonderful opening lines:

> It was early one mornin'
> And I was on my way to school,
> Yeah, that was the mornin'
> When I broke my mother's rule.*

Turner's hit records were part of the phenomenon called rhythm-and-blues, r&b for short, which was the urban black pop music the blues had transformed itself into by the mid-forties. It influenced—indeed made possible—the coming of rock.

Among the beneficial side effects of the rock

phenomenon was the discovery by many young white Americans of authentic blues, but at the same time the inroads rock made with black audiences adversely affected the careers of such blues artists as Lightnin' Hopkins, whose work now began to be considered old-fashioned. So, as these bluesmen lost their black audience, they gained a new white following. By the seventies, as more and more blacks were rediscovering their roots, the surviving bluesmen once again found favor among their own people, though commercial soul music dominated the black mass audience.

In the mid-thirties, Sam ("Lightnin'") Hopkins settled in Houston (he was born in Centerville, Texas, in 1912) and has made his home there since. He began to sing and play guitar and piano as a child, but didn't turn professional until the forties, making his first records in 1946. Though he achieved considerable popularity and has made many records and toured extensively in the United States and Europe, Hopkins's work has retained an amazing spontaneity in words and music. Almost all his blues are based on personal experience (as op-

posed to the work of such men as Rushing and Turner, who made up few original lyrics, and when they did, almost always adapted them from traditional sources). He is a storyteller in music, fascinatingly real yet a skilled entertainer, a representative of the very earliest blues, which were the personal stories of the singer.

Still another kind of jazz singing evolved during the bop era. Pure bebop singing, of which Dizzy Gillespie is the foremost representative, was an adaptation of scat in which the nonsense syllables were redesigned to fit the new rhythmic patterns. (One of the greatest scat singers, by the way, was Cab Calloway, in whose band young Dizzy Gillespie worked for several years.) The dominant ballad style of the day was Billy Eckstine's. It was a pop rather than jazz phenomenon; if you wanted to hear good jazz singing, you turned to the ladies.

Bop did make a contribution to male vocal styles, however. This was a logical outgrowth of the period's interest in improvised inventions rather than conventional song melody. A dancer named Eddie Jefferson first came upon the idea of fashion-

Eddie Jefferson

Annie Ross

ing words to the solos recorded by great jazzmen. (He credits his partner, Irv Taylor, with originating the thought, but admits that he himself was the more prolific adapter.) For years, Eddie practiced his art only for his own amusement and that of his friends and to help recall the solos he liked best. But when an acquaintance borrowed his lyrics to James Moody's solo on *I'm in the Mood for Love*, recorded them as his own, and the record became a minor hit, Jefferson decided to throw his hat in the ring.

He began to make records, too; among the first was a setting of Coleman Hawkins's famous *Body and Soul* solo, which had been Jefferson's original venture in the genre. He then joined James Moody's band, appropriately enough, and since then has made occasional records (a 1975 one includes an adaptation of Miles Davis's *Bitches Brew!*) and occasional festival and club appearances. Jefferson is an engaging performer, and his lyrics follow the twists and turns of instrumentally conceived melodic lines with exceptional wit and inventiveness.

Among the first to follow in the wake of Jefferson and his initially better-known acolyte, King Pleasure (a mysterious individual whose real name is Clarence Beeks), was Annie Ross, a singing actress born Annabelle Short in Surrey, England, but raised in Los Angeles from age three, by her aunt, Ella Logan, an excellent rhythm singer herself.

Annie Ross appeared in several *Our Gang* film shorts and was Judy Garland's sister in *Presenting Lily Mars;* she returned to England in 1947 and played the lead in the London production of *Burlesque*. Miss Logan was fond of jazz, and Annie got some jobs singing with jazz groups in England and France. Back in the United States, she studied with Luther Henderson, who had been Lena Horne's accompanist.

In 1952, Annie Ross recorded her settings of two pieces by tenor saxophonist Wardell Gray, *Twisted* and *Farmer's Market;* her lyrics were zany and funny and her delivery just right; the record was a minor hit among jazz fans. Annie subsequently returned to Europe, sang with Lionel Hampton's band, teamed up with Blossom Dearie, the talented singer-pianist-composer-arranger, starred in the revue *Cranks,* returned to New York with it when it came to Broadway, and in early 1958 joined singers Jon Hendricks and Dave Lambert in a recording experiment, *Sing a Song of Basie,* setting famous instrumental recordings by the famous band to group and individual vocalizing. The album was a success and led to personal appearances by the group (dubbed Lambert, Hendricks & Ross), which suddenly became the most popular vocal group in jazz.

Annie remained with L,H&R until 1962, when she decided to settle in England. She opened her own club in London, later was a big hit in *Threepenny Opera,* and then retired from active performing.

Her partners in L,H&R had both labored hard in the musical vineyards before success came. Dave Lambert, the senior member of the trio, studied drums for a year when he was ten; this was his only formal musical background. Born in Boston in 1917, he played summer jobs as a drummer in his early twenties and also worked as a tree surgeon for the CCC. A paratrooper in the war, he was discharged in 1943, joined Johnny Long's band as vocalist, and later sang with Gene Krupa's band, along with Buddy Stewart; together, they made *What's This,* the first bop vocal record, in 1945.

Lambert led a vocal quartet in a Broadway show, recorded with his own group, the Lambert Singers, and made vocal arrangements for various singers and bands. His Greenwich Village basement apartment became a haven for singers and musicians. Lambert was hospitality incarnate. The place was famous for its vocal jam sessions, where singers including Tony Bennett and other stars-to-be would match musical wits and trade eight-and-four-bar phrases just like jazz instrumentalists.

One of the singers who popped in at Lambert's was born in Newark, Ohio, and raised in Toledo, one of seventeen children and fifteen survivors. Jon Hendricks sang on radio as a child; after high school he joined a brother-in-law's band as vocalist. Following army service during World War II, he studied at the University of Toledo, meanwhile teaching himself to play drums. He worked as a drummer and singer for several years, then came to New York to try his luck as a songwriter, meeting with slim success. He recorded a vocal adaptation of Woody Herman's *Four Brothers* for an obscure label that soon went out of business and was heard in a supporting role on a King Pleasure record.

When he met Lambert, the two decided to record a new version of *Four Brothers,* using multitracking techniques, and from this came the idea for *Sing a Song of Basie,* and, suddenly, success. (The lyrics

Dave Lambert, Jon Hendricks, and Annie Ross

Benny Carter and Helen Humes

Maxine Sullivan

for the group were by Hendricks.)

For several years, L,H&R was indeed, as one of their albums proclaimed, "the hottest new group in jazz." *Time* called Hendricks "the James Joyce of jazz," hyperbole spawned by Hendricks's cleverness with words, fitted ingeniously to the convolutions of instrumental solo or ensemble lines and often executed at a speed Eddie Jefferson or King Pleasure would not have attempted.

But clever and well done as they were, the works of the hip threesome were, after all, basically novelties, and when the newness wore off, there was no place for them to go. Annie Ross quit while the going was still good; she was replaced by Yolande Bavan, a Ceylonese singer and actress. As Lambert, Hendricks, and Bavan the group continued until 1964, when it was decided that the time had come to call it quits.

Hendricks embarked upon a solo career. Eventually he settled in London, then returned to the United States in the early seventies, settled in San Francisco, for a while reviewed jazz for a daily paper, and in 1975 made a record in much the same mold as his earlier work.

Dave Lambert enjoyed the company of his many friends for a while. He loved to make things with his hands: wood carvings for children he knew, carpentry work for friends. He helped put on benefits for Synanon and did other good works.

It was as a good samaritan that Dave Lambert met his end on the night of October 3, 1966. He stopped on the Connecticut Turnpike to help a fellow motorist who was having trouble changing a tire, was struck by a car that failed to see the warning light, and was killed instantly.

Two fine singers from the thirties enjoyed comebacks in the sixties and seventies: Maxine Sullivan and Helen Humes.

Diminutive, genteel Maxine, born in 1911 near Pittsburgh, first did radio work in her hometown and was heard singing at the Benjamin Harrison Literary Club by Ina Ray Hutton's pianist (Miss Hutton led one of the best all-girl swing bands), who introduced her to pianist-arranger Claude Thornhill. Thornhill engineered her recording debut in 1937, with his arrangements played by an all-star jazz group. Among them was a tasteful swing setting of the old Scottish ballad *Loch Lomond*. It was a hit. Maxine got a job on Fifty-second Street singing at the Onyx Club with bassist John Kirby's little band; she and Kirby were married soon after.

Loch Lomond typecast Maxine; despite her ability to do all sorts of material, she was made to record a string of folk songs adapted to swing. But she got into movies and was seen opposite Louis Armstrong in *Going Places* as well as in a minor showboat epic called *St. Louis Blues.* Years later she appeared in *Take a Giant Step.*

She visited England in 1948 and 1954, in the late fifties decided to study nursing, and also took up the valve trombone. She was now married to pianist Cliff Jackson (her marriage to Kirby had ended in 1941), and she kept busy running their apartment house in the Bronx, where the tenants were all fellow musicians. From time to time, Maxine would make appearances in clubs or at festivals, her light, cool voice as pleasing as ever, her style still a model of relaxation and poise.

From 1969, she began to team up with the recently formed World's Greatest Jazz Band, recorded with an offshoot of the band, appeared at Newport, and in 1975 was beginning efforts to turn her house into a jazz museum in memory of Cliff Jackson.

Helen Humes, a native of Louisville, made her recording debut in 1927 at the age of fourteen, singing some surprisingly mature blues. She completed her schooling, however, before doing a long stint as singer with Vernon Andrade's band and working at the Cotton Club in Cincinnati, where John Hammond heard her and recommended her to Count Basie as Billie Holiday's replacement in 1938. Her well-placed, true soprano, somewhat reminiscent of Mildred Bailey's in color, and her relaxed beat and good jazz phrasing went well with Basie. Like her male counterpart, Jimmy Rushing, Helen was a jazz stylist who also could sing good blues.

She left Basie in 1941, appeared at the Village Vanguard, and toured a lot before settling in California, where in 1945 she scored a considerable hit with a novelty called *Be-baba-leba* and a funny, then risqué blues, *Million Dollar Secret,* the point of which was that old men make the best husbands. This turned her career in the direction of r&b for a while, but she had returned to jazz by the time she toured Australia with Red Norvo's band in 1956, doing so well that she was asked to stay and become an Australian citizen—not a commonplace occurrence down under. She did move there in 1964, things having gotten rather slow at home, but soon returned to Louisville to look after her mother. For

Helen Humes

a time she worked in a munitions factory, though she did come to New York for a Newport festival appearance in 1974 and visited Europe the same year.

It was in 1975, however, that Barney Josephson was persuaded by John Hammond and Stanley Dance (the latter also the man who had brought her to Newport in 1974) to hire Helen Humes for an extended stay at the Cookery. Here, her infectious style (I once described her as singing with a smile in her voice), vivacious personality, and good choice of material made her a definitive hit. There were rave reviews in the *New Yorker,* the *New York Times,* and the *Village Voice,* and Hammond produced an album with her for Columbia.

Helen Humes was invited back to the Cookery for 1976. At sixty-two, she was once again in demand, another convincing demonstration of the theorem that in jazz, good things not only last but get better.

The styles of Helen Humes, Maxine Sullivan, and indeed all the singers discussed here remained unaffected by one of the most far-reaching developments in popular singing since the advent of Louis Armstrong. This was the coming of Ray Charles, the man who dared to mix gospel and the blues—religious and secular music. To the chagrin of the religious sector and the disapproval of many older jazzmen, Charles adapted the rhythms and inflections of gospel music to pop materials, stirring the mixture well with jazz spices for good measure.

Born in Albany, Georgia, in 1932, Charles lost his sight at six and was sent to a school for the blind in Florida, where he received sound musical training. He left at fifteen to play piano and saxophone with local bands and in 1949 formed his own trio, patterned on his then idol, Nat King Cole. He settled far west in Seattle, where he made his first records. They were not successful, but Charles made a decent living appearing on local television.

In 1954 he formed a small band with a different style, which he developed carefully over the next few years. His singing and piano playing by now showed a profound gospel influence. He turned out a steady stream of hits, including *I Got a Woman, Hallelujah I Love Her So,* and *What'd I Say,* first for the black·audience, then reaching the white public as well.

In 1960 he changed recording affiliation, began to record with strings, and had a big hit with his version of an old pop standard, *Georgia on My Mind.* He subsequently even made forays into the country-and-western repertoire; they were hugely successful. Since 1960, Charles has been appearing with a big band, vocal group, and show, touring frequently and meeting with continued success, but his great period of influence was 1954-60.

A highly emotional performer, Charles brought to popular singing some of the special fervor and urgency hitherto associated with gospel music. In purely musical terms, he also appropriated the melismatic techniques of gospel song—that is, elaborate embellishment of the melodic line. It was often very effective, but could also verge on the contrived—it is one thing to become ecstatic about heavenly matters, quite another to go into fits about some imagined love affair. But when mixed with Charles's strong feeling for jazz and his terrific beat, the gospel/blues hybrid worked well indeed, as in the responsorial *What'd I Say.*

There is no doubt that Charles effected a revolution in popular music, for the barriers of restraint already broken by rock were now demolished by the introduction of the spiritual into secular music. Since Charles, gospel techniques are routinely applied by black singers to whatever materials they tackle.

Mahalia Jackson was among those most strongly opposed to Charles's tactics, and she was joined by religious-minded jazz musicians. Eventually, the struggle proved quite hopeless, and even Miss Jackson herself began to include non-gospel songs in her repertoire, though her material was always of a spiritual nature.

Despite her avowed Bessie Smith influence, Mahalia never sang jazz or blues. She did, however, allow Columbia Records to join her with Duke Ellington's orchestra in performing *Come Sunday* from *Black, Brown, and Beige,* Ellington's paean to black America, and she appeared frequently at Newport, and in the film *Jazz on a Summer's Day,* made there in 1958.

Mahalia first recorded in 1937, but it wasn't until the late forties that white audiences got an inkling of the art of this magnificent singer. In 1952, she made her first European tour, visiting Denmark, where her recording of *Silent Night* had become a great hit. By the mid-fifties she was a worldwide celebrity. When asked why she wouldn't sing blues, though her art was so obviously blues-inflected, she would answer: "Blues are the songs of despair, but gospel songs are the songs of hope." To many others, how-

Mahalia Jackson

ever, the blues function as an expression of at least resilience and survival if not hope. But it was only in the hands of Bessie Smith that blues acquired that special majesty with which Mahalia imbued her "songs of hope."

Mahalia Jackson died in 1972. The distinct categories of music in which she believed had already become blurred, and the process is continuing. There are still pure blues and pure gospel singing, but most younger practitioners blend them, adding jazz and even country-and-western elements.

This amalgam, which has become known as "soul" singing, has produced some gifted artists. No less an authority than Lennie Tristano, the jazz pianist, composer, and sage, has claimed that Diana Ross is the greatest jazz singer since Billie Holiday. Though Miss Ross a few years later did portray Billie in a film supposedly based on the great lady's career and did an admirable and uncharacteristic job of copying the Holiday style, few would go along with Tristano's judgment.

Perhaps young singers will once again turn to such models as Sarah Vaughan and Ella Fitzgerald, Louis Armstrong and Jimmy Rushing, but until then, or until some entirely new approach evolves, jazz singing as a distinct form will remain in the hands of surviving veteran performers.

Autographing after concert

7 Keepers of the Flame

The music called jazz has undergone many changes in its relatively brief but surprisingly rich history. Yet all of it—from old New Orleans to new free jazz—belongs to one musical family.

There is a jazz tradition, and its essence has to do with what Thelonious Monk, a man of few but pointed words, had in mind when he said that "jazz and freedom go hand in hand." There are many ways of approaching this tradition. Some forge special links with the past, recasting aspects of it in new and personal molds. Others reach forward, searching for new modes of expression, new combinations of sound and meaning. And some find fulfillment in opening up the past and present to the future, in teaching and instructing the musicians and listeners of tomorrow. Still others have no conscious ideology but just make their own music according to their own inner light. All these, in their different ways, are keepers of the jazz flame.

The big-band tradition is an important part of the jazz legacy, kept alive in the main by veterans of the Swing Era and the unique Duke Ellington until

Mel Lewis and Thad Jones

Thad Jones and Mel Lewis came along. These Dioscuri of jazz first met in the mid-fifties, when Thad was playing trumpet and arranging for Count Basie, and Mel was drumming for Stan Kenton. Their friendship ripened when they played together in Gerry Mulligan's orchestra, and in 1965, they decided to form a big band of their own. By this time, both men were members of the elite corps of New York studio musicians, and the band's personnel was initially drawn from the ranks of colleagues who, like the co-leaders, loved big-band jazz but had little opportunity to play it.

From the very first rehearsal, it was evident that something special had been born. Before long, the band was playing every Monday night at the Village Vanguard, New York's oldest jazz club, whose owner, Max Gordon, had become one of its greatest fans. In February, 1976, the Thad Jones-Mel Lewis Jazz Orchestra celebrated its tenth anniversary of Monday nights at the Vanguard. During that decade, the band toured Russia for the State Department (with Lithuanian-born Max Gordon as their special guest), made frequent visits to Japan, Europe, and most major American cities, recorded a number of outstanding albums, and created some of the freshest and most original big-band music of the time. Two key members, saxophonists Pepper Adams and Jerry Dodgion, have been aboard from the start, many young players have learned much from playing with the band, and many seasoned veterans have found new joy in making music through their association with Thad and Mel.

Thad Jones is the most masterly composer and arranger still working in the big-band tradition and a wholly original instrumentalist (a role in which, perhaps wisely, he does not feature himself much with the band). Jones insists, with good reason, that Lewis is the ideal big-band drummer. The cement of talent and friendship has held together a great band for more than a decade.

The once fertile field of studio music which nurtured the Thad Jones-Mel Lewis band in its formative years began to dry up in the early seventies. The introduction of electronic instruments and novel recording techniques shrank the numbers of musicians required to perform the commercial jingles, backgrounds for vocalists, etc., that were the meal tickets of the studio players, and economic instability and changing tastes in music further reduced opportunities for work.

Still, the best and hardiest survived, among them

Ruby Braff

the veteran bassist Milt Hinton, who entered the studio scene in 1954. By then, he had been a professional since the late twenties. Born in 1910 in Vicksburg, Mississippi, but brought to Chicago as a child, he began his career in the days when New Orleans musicians still ruled the jazz roost of Chicago and it was hard for "foreigners" to gain admittance to the inner circle. Milt managed. He played in Erskine Tate's theater orchestra, in the small group of Eddie South, the "Dark Angel of the Violin," and with drummer Zutty Singleton before joining Cab Calloway's band in 1936. He stayed for fifteen years, including the band's greatest days, when Chu Berry, Dizzy Gillespie, Jonah Jones, Tyree Glenn, Danny Barker, and Cozy Cole were in the ranks. Then, after two months with Count Basie and seven with Louis Armstrong, Milt joined the CBS network staff in New York. His playing and recording affiliations in the ensuing decades constitute an encyclopedia of jazz.

Milt's nickname is "Judge," which has reference to sagacity and tolerance rather than severity, though he does not suffer fools gladly. He always seems to be working, yet has time for his hobby, jazz history. He has compiled a formidable collection of jazz memorabilia, including many photographs taken by himself, and interviews taped in the den of his comfortable suburban home with important musical figures, among them many now dead. He has also taught jazz at Hunter College and found the time to serve as co-chairman of the jazz panel of the National Endowment for the Arts. Withal, he still loves to play the bass, as is plain for all to see when he is in action.

In the year Milt Hinton left the road and entered the studios, a young Boston-born-and-bred trumpeter came to New York to try his luck. Ruby Braff was twenty-seven in 1954, and almost all jazz trumpeters of his age were disciples of the Dizzy Gillespie school. Braff, however, followed Louis Armstrong and thus was considered something of an anomaly.

However, he had a forceful enough personality, musical and otherwise, to make himself heard. For a time, he was a protégé of John Hammond, but his greatest booster throughout his career has been George Wein, the stalwart producer of the Newport Jazz Festival and its many worldwide offshoots.

Wein began his career in music as a pianist, and later, as he became an entrepreneur and club owner, he continued to play. He hired Braff to play

in the house band at his Boston club, Storyville, and the trumpeter made his recording debut on Wein's label of the same name. Over the years, Braff has participated in many editions of the Newport All Stars, Wein-led groups that perform at his festivals and elsewhere.

Nevertheless, Braff has clearly made his way in jazz on the strength of his own talent and convictions, shaping his own distinctive style within the aesthetic framework of his choice. His use of dynamics and his explorations of the bottom range of the trumpet are especially original, and there is no longer anything anomalous about his music, if indeed there ever was. Only in America, with its essentially ahistorical progress orientation, did it seem odd for a young jazzman of Braff's generation to prefer a style not of the latest vintage. In Europe, Braff's music was received without surprise.

Ruby can be quite irascible, and his musical alliances have seldom lasted long. (Wein, the exception, always forgives and forgets, as he does with every musician whose work he admires; it is one of the reasons for his success as a promoter.) One of Ruby's most rewarding partnerships was with guitarist George Barnes. Their quartet, in which the co-leaders were supported by rhythm guitar and bass, brought forth some of the most lyrical and melodic chamber jazz of recent times.

Braff and Barnes didn't last, but Al Cohn and Zoot Sims might be called the jazz inseparables. Their first encounter took place in 1948, when Al joined Woody Herman's reed section, of which Zoot was already a member. They teamed up formally for the first time in 1955.

Both were born in 1925, Zoot in October in Inglewood, California, Al in November in New York City. Both started on clarinet and switched to tenor saxophone. Both were inspired by Lester Young. Both turned professional in their teens and served time with various big bands until their paths crossed in Herman's Second Herd. Both settled in New York after leaving the band in 1949, often playing together on record dates or casual engagements or at informal sessions.

The two-tenor-plus-rhythm-section format was so well received when Al and Zoot introduced it that a series of excellent records as well as intermittent in-person appearances followed. In the sixties, the Half Note Club on New York's waterfront was a haven for Al and Zoot whenever they were able to get together, and in later years Dick Gibson's Col-

orado Jazz Party and the third Eddie Condon's served a similar function. It doesn't matter how much time elapses between such encounters; as soon as the two men mount the bandstand, communion reigns.

Withal, they are distinct personalities, musically and otherwise. Cohn is a gifted and prolific arranger, whose assignments have included scoring for Broadway musicals. This work tends to keep him close to New York (he commutes from the Poconos), while Zoot roams the world as a freelance player. Each man has found his own voice, with Lester Young as the common point of departure. The irrepressible Zoot is the driving force of any group he plays with, large or small. He loves to jam and will sit in with anything, from a traditional New Orleans band to an avant-garde ensemble. His playing is the incarnation of the jazz spirit and a definition of swinging. Al's work as a writer has kept him away from the horn for lengthy periods, but it never takes him long to warm up to a playing occasion. He is an impassioned player, his sound a bit darker than Zoot's, and his ballad playing at its best has a cantorial depth of feeling.

Some years ago, Zoot took up the soprano saxophone, adding a new flavor to his collaborations with his old friend. Together and separately, Al Cohn and Zoot Sims consistently represent the best in unpretentious, free-swinging jazz. They have never suffered an identity crisis.

Bob Wilber and Kenny Davern have not been collaborators for very long—two years or so at this writing—but the rapport between them bodes well for a lasting relationship. Both are masters of two instruments, the clarinet and the soprano saxophone, and they share a respect for and understanding of the jazz tradition uncommon in any musical generation and particularly in theirs.

Wilber, born in 1928, is seven years Davern's senior. He came of musical age early, leading his own jazz group in high school. The Scarsdale Wildcats became the nucleus of the Bob Wilber Wildcats, the first American revivalist group of consequence in the East. The very first was Lu Watters's San Francisco band, which copied King Oliver and Jelly Roll Morton in single-minded and somewhat plodding fashion. The Wildcats were more venturesome.

Wilber studied with Sidney Bechet, and his youthful work came amazingly close to the master. He later went to Juilliard and the Eastman School

Bob Wilber

of Music, rounding out his formal training. At twenty, he led a band that included veteran black musicians who had worked with Oliver and Morton, but the music was not a copy of any old model, though Wilber himself still sounded like Bechet. At twenty-four, he studied with Lennie Tristano, a master of the modern school, then took up tenor saxophone (he had been doubling on clarinet from the start) and formed a swing-oriented cooperative group, The Six, going on to work with Benny Goodman, Bobby Hackett, Eddie Condon, and Max Kaminsky.

When he eventually returned to the soprano sax, the Bechet influence was no longer predominant—this was quite coincidentally pointed up by Wilber's playing a curved model soprano rather than the more common straight type favored by Bechet. His work now had a Johnny Hodges-like flow and grace, and he became interested in the small-group music of Ellington. After spending some years with the World's Greatest Jazz Band, a nine-piece group with the exaggerated name founded by Yank Lawson and Bob Haggart, he formed his own Soprano Summit, with Kenny Davern as co-leader.

Davern had also gone through a revivalist phase, emulating the New Orleans clarinetist George Lewis. This was preceded by some big-band section work on saxophones. At nineteen, he was with Jack Teagarden, then worked with various Dixieland-oriented groups. He put together an excellent band of his own, working at Nick's in Greenwich Village, then a bastion of watered-down "Nicksieland" music; predictably, the band got fired for refusing to play the requisite repertory of war-horses. That was in 1961; by then, Davern had formed a warm and lasting friendship with Pee Wee Russell, who had a strong influence on the young man's approach to music. Davern occasionally played experimental jazz with, among others, the unique trombonist Roswell Rudd, a contemporary who had also started out as a traditionalist. He also worked often with the pianist Dick Wellstood, a remarkable player who got his start with Wilber's Wildcats. Davern took up the soprano saxophone, which eventually became his primary instrument.

Davern and Wilber complement and stimulate each other, the reserved Wilber prodded by the bold Davern. Their little band is unique. It draws its large repertory from the rich but neglected tradition of the clarinet and soprano saxophone, reintroducing lovely pieces of music that haven't been

Kenny Davern

performed in decades. In addition, it plays original compositions, mostly by Wilber, a judicious selection of jazz standards, and Fats Waller specialties and other drolleries contributed by the group's guitarist and singer, Marty Grosz—the son of the great German satirical painter George Grosz. In the jazz climate of the seventies, more hospitable to diversity than that of any previous decade, Soprano Summit has a chance to survive. The growing interest in jazz history among high-school and college students will help; Soprano Summit is very well equipped to illuminate the subject.

Among the many prominent jazz practitioners who have taken up various forms of teaching, pianist Marian McPartland has shown particular aptitude and enthusiasm for the task. Her work with young children has met with equal success in both fashionable Long Island and inner city Washington.

She was Marian Page, a British pianist working for USO, when she met and married cornetist Jimmy McPartland during the final months of the war in Europe. The couple came to the United States in 1946 and formed a band that played in Jimmy's modified Chicago style. Marian had her own musical ideas, however, and in 1951 she formed a trio, playing in a boppish vein. The following year she began an engagement at the Hickory House, one of the last surviving music spots on Fifty-second Street. It lasted eight years.

At first, her work suffered from a fault common to European jazz players of that day—uncertain time. She had a tendency to rush tempos, and her beat was watery. But she worked hard and had a succession of fine rhythm players backing her up, among them the splendid drummer Joe Morello, who came to prominence with her.

Bright and personable, she also cultivated other talents, composing the score for a prize-winning documentary film, doing her own jazz radio program, and writing articles and reviews for the jazz press. Her playing continued to develop. She has become a consummate pianist with a full-bodied, expansive approach to the instrument, a self-assured performer, and a genuine musical personality.

Marian McPartland has never lost the well-bred aura of English gentility, but she is a very hip lady. She has her own record company, with a small but distinguished catalogue. She still writes about jazz and teaches its essentials to delighted children. She has been profiled in the *New Yorker* and plays at the chic Hotel Carlyle on upper Madison Avenue. It has become pointless to mention sex or country of origin when discussing the music of Marian McPartland.

Marian may have many strings to her bow, but when it comes to multiple activities, she is no match for fellow pianist Billy Taylor, who somehow has been able to keep his musical career well afloat in spite of all his extracurricular activities. In the fifties, he was so often referred to as the most articulate of jazz musicians that the compliment became a cliché and even an embarrassment, but musicians who resented his being so singled out had to admit that he was doing a great deal of good.

Taylor was born in Greenville, North Carolina, in 1921 and graduated from Virginia State College in 1942, coming to New York that year and soon finding work on fabled Fifty-second Street, first with Ben Webster, then with Stuff Smith, later with Dizzy Gillespie. He visited Europe for the first time in 1946 as a member of Don Redman's big band, became the house pianist at Birdland, and since 1952 has led his own consistently polished trios.

He began to write and talk about jazz in the fifties, and for many years was a disc jockey, eventually becoming program director of a New York FM station. But one of his most significant activities was the development of the Jazzmobile, a summer program of free jazz performances in the streets of New York, primarily in poorer neighborhoods. Jazzmobile began in Harlem in 1965 and soon expanded to all boroughs of the city. Taylor had been a co-founder; later, he became Jazzmobile's director. To have witnessed the response of children to the music made by famous jazz players in their own backyard, more often than not the first in-the-flesh professional performance they've ever seen, is to understand the significance of Jazzmobile.

Taylor holds a Presidential appointment to the National Council on the Arts, serves on the boards of many civic and artistic organizations, teaches jazz history, and in 1976 obtained his Ph.D. from the University of Massachusetts. When he passed on leadership of Jazzmobile, it was to another musician, drummer David Bailey. Whatever Billy Taylor does he does well, and that includes playing the piano.

Though he is three years older than Taylor, Hank Jones came to New York two years later. The eldest of the most gifted trio of siblings in jazz (his

Marian McPartland

**Billy Taylor and Dizzy Gillespie at a
Jazzmobile concert in Harlem**

brothers are trumpeter, composer, and bandleader Thad and drummer Elvin; the only possible contenders are the Heath Brothers—bassist Percy, saxophonist-composer Jimmy, and drummer Albert), Hank studied piano formally in his native Pontiac, Michigan, and played with bands in the Midwest and Buffalo before arriving in New York. Since then, he has done so much that only highlights can be cited: work with Coleman Hawkins, recordings with Lester Young and Charlie Parker, tours with Jazz at the Philharmonic, a stretch as accompanist to Ella Fitzgerald, frequent stints with Benny Goodman, and many years as a musician on radio and television network staffs.

In more than thirty years of recording activity, Hank Jones has made much good music and, as a masterly accompanist and band pianist, has made many musicians and singers sound well. Ironically, he has made only one solo piano album, although he is among the few true masters of the demanding task of playing jazz alone. At his most inspired, he approaches the lofty realm uninhabited since the death of Art Tatum. But he is a gracious and modest man who never has indulged in what is so aptly called the "selling" of his talent. From time to time,

fortunately, Hank Jones can be found playing solo piano in some Manhattan boîte.

Among the big bands Hank Jones played with in his apprentice years was that of Andy Kirk, no longer in the top rank by then. Its twilight years were brightened by the presence of Howard McGhee, a trumpeter of Dizzy Gillespie's generation. Like Dizzy, he began as a disciple of Roy Eldridge, though his instrumental technique was more legitimate than Roy's. In addition to Kirk, with whom he recorded his *McGhee Special,* he worked in the bands of Charlie Barnet and Billy Eckstine. By 1944, he was deeply involved in the new jazz that soon would be known as bebop.

He went to California with Coleman Hawkins's quintet and settled there, working and recording with Charlie Parker during the period leading up to Parker's nervous breakdown and hospitalization. Some years later, after having become one of the leading bop trumpeters, McGhee suffered from the same affliction as Parker, and for some time he was in virtual obscurity. He made his comeback in the sixties and has been on an even keel since then. Some of his most effective performances in the later stage of his career have been in conjunction with

Hank Jones   **Howard McGhee**

religious services, the phenomenon of jazz in church having arisen during the late fifties and sixties. And the church, of course, loves nothing more than a reformed sinner.

McGhee, like most notables of modern jazz, would play at the Blue Note when working in Philadelphia during the fifties. The Blue Note was the city's leading jazz club, and in 1953, a twenty-two-year-old Philadelphian, Ray Bryant, became the club's house pianist. It was wonderful schooling, and it made Bryant one of the most adaptable and versatile pianists of his generation. He acquired further polish as Carmen McRae's accompanist and in Jo Jones's trio (the third member was Ray's older brother, bassist Tommy Bryant).

When Ray settled in New York in the late fifties, he was equally at home working with Sonny Rollins at the Village Vanguard, with Charlie Shavers or Coleman Hawkins at the Metropole, or with Miles Davis in a recording studio. It was almost inevitable that he should try his hand at having his own group—for a pianist, that meant a trio—and his 1960 recording of a catchy "soul" piece he had composed, *Little Susie,* became a hit. For better (in terms of money) or worse (in terms of what happens to a jazz artist who has had commercial success and gets on the treadmill of trying to follow the first hit with another), he was catapulted into the orbit of commercially viable jazz performers. But his musical integrity survived, and when the wave of popular recognition ebbed, Ray Bryant was still a fine, versatile jazz pianist, his identity intact.

The heart of any jazz group committed to the principle of swinging is the rhythm section, and the most selfless member of that section for many years was the bassist. After the advent of Jimmy Blanton, the bass began to gain recognition as a solo instrument, and the workhorse aspect of the bass player's lot was alleviated by moments in the spotlight. It reached a point where bass solos became convenient openings for conversation among listeners, but one soloist who never becomes garrulous is Major Holley.

Inspired by Slam Stewart (who, incidentally, had made the bass a solo vehicle before Blanton, albeit in a very special manner), Major bows and hums along with the note he is bowing, but he has his own sound—after two bars, you can tell it is Major, not Slam. Like Slam, Major (nicknamed "Mule") started on violin; he also specializes on tuba. He worked with Charlie Parker in his hometown, De-

Ray Bryant

Major Holley

troit; in California with Wardell Gray and Dexter Gordon; and for two years in London with the BBC. He played with Duke Ellington and Woody Herman, with Al Cohn and Zoot Sims, and for some considerable time with Coleman Hawkins and then Roy Eldridge. He brought fellow Detroiter Aretha Franklin to John Hammond's attention. A performer with great gusto and humor, he devotes his spare time to working with handicapped children. A rare moment in bass history occurred when Major Holley and Slam Stewart duetted at one of Dick Gibson's Jazz Parties—those notable ingatherings of handpicked preeminences that have produced some of the most memorable impromptu music-making of the sixties and seventies.

No matter how hard a bassist works, his efforts in the rhythm section will go for naught unless he is in step with the drummer. Poor drumming can wreck or at least seriously impede the best band, so consistently reliable drummers are always in demand. Such a drummer is Grady Tate, who was twenty-seven when he became a professional musician. Prior to that, he had been playing drums in his high-school band, in the service, and for fun, and he was teaching school in Washington, D.C., in 1959 when a saxophonist friend asked him to come along to an audition for organist Wild Bill Davis's group. On a lark, Tate sat in with the group and was stunned when Davis called the next day and asked if he wanted a job. He discovered that jazz drummers were better paid than schoolteachers and accepted.

By the mid-sixties, Tate had become one of New York's most in-demand drummers, taking part in all kinds of recordings with ensembles ranging from trios to big bands. The friendship he formed with the successful arranger, bandleader, and record producer Quincy Jones did not do him harm. Tate likes to sing, and when he was working with Peggy Lee, this aspect of his personality first came to public attention. She gave him a featured vocal spot in her act—something quite unprecedented. After that, Tate recorded several vocal albums, and any leader who hires him is well advised to offer him a singing spot or two during the night's work, but drumming is still his mainstay. Tate modestly describes himself as a "limited" drummer, and this attitude may be partly responsible for his popularity with his fellow musicians. He plays for the cause, not to display his prowess. And, of course, he swings.

Players like Tate, Holley, and Bryant play what has been called mainstream jazz, a piece of nomenclature which implies that other styles and forms may not be, so to speak, in the swing of things. The term was introduced during the latter days of bebop with the intention of making a distinction between jazz in the swing tradition (the mainstream), the newer styles (the aberrant currents), and the revivalist music (the stagnant backwater). By the early sixties, however, "mainstream" commonly was applied to everything except so-called avant-garde jazz, and in the mid-seventies, the term is as good as all-inclusive.

Thus tenor saxophonist Archie Shepp, once a stormy petrel of the jazz avant-garde, has settled into the mainstream as a professor of jazz at the University of Massachusetts, a position for which his orientation and background are well suited. Born in Florida in 1937 and raised in Philadelphia, he graduated from Goddard College with a degree in dramatic literature and took up residence in New York, working briefly as a schoolteacher but soon becoming a professional musician. He had studied piano, clarinet, and saxophone as a child and worked with a rhythm-and-blues band that also had Lee Morgan in it as a teenager.

Shepp's first significant association was with Cecil Taylor, in 1960. He co-led a quartet with trumpeter Bill Dixon, a painter manqué, who, like Shepp at this stage, talked a better game than he could play. They performed at the 1962 World Youth Festival in Helsinki, and Shepp visited Europe again the following year. John Coltrane took him under his generous wing in 1964, featuring him on records and at jazz festival appearances. During this period, Shepp became one of the most vociferous propagandists for the jazz avant-garde (later called "the new thing"), writing articles and participating in seminars and discussions and the organization of festivals and musicians' associations. His play, *The Communist,* was performed in New York in 1965.

Shepp's ideas concerning the nature, origin, and destiny of jazz, and his conviction that the music should be both a reflection of and a weapon in the black social revolution ostensibly taking place in America were closely related to those advanced by LeRoi Jones, and Shepp became the unreluctant prototype of the angry politically and culturally conscious black jazz musician of the sixties. His music was often much less radical than his words. It

At Dick Gibson's Colorado Jazz Party. Top left: Buddy Tate, Zoot Sims, Flip Phillips, Budd Johnson, Buck Clayton. Second row: Major Holley, Joe Venuti, Panama Francis, Vic Dickenson. Front: Ray Brown

Grady Tate

reflected a strong Ben Webster influence (notably on the Ellington ballads Shepp likes to play) and a touch of Sonny Rollins. By the early seventies, Shepp's working group was playing mainly a classic bebop repertoire, while his more ambitious recordings seemed aimed at the black pop music market, though there were still echoes of the radical past, such as a guest appearance by lawyer William Kunstler (not as a bebop vocalist, but as a reciter) on an album called *Attica Blues.* A later title, *There's a Trumpet in My Soul,* indicates Shepp's current orientation, but his volatile temperament and mercurial intellect will no doubt produce other surprises.

While Archie Shepp represents the "old" jazz avant-garde, with its characteristic verbal and self-consciously radical orientation, Anthony Braxton can stand for the less rhetorically inclined musical adventurers of the present. He is an articulate man, but his main vehicle of expression is the almost bewildering collection of instruments over which he presides. It includes such seldom heard and seen colossi as the contrabass saxophone and contrabass clarinet and all sorts of recorders, double-reed instruments, and exotica. His chief horn, however, is the humble, everyday alto saxophone.

Braxton was a member of Chicago's Association for the Advancement of Creative Musicians (AACM), a musicians' cooperative that has spawned much of the most interesting new music of the past decade, notably the exciting Art Ensemble of Chicago. Its spiritual leader and key organizer is the remarkable pianist and composer Richard Muhal Abrams, and it is in no small degree due to his strength of character that the AACM, unlike most other attempts at organizing jazz musicians, has been able to survive and produce. The only other viable organization is that of Sun Ra, the keyboard player-composer-bandleader, who perhaps not coincidentally also began his efforts in Chicago. But Sun Ra's Intergalactic (formerly merely Solar) Arkestra is a commune firmly ruled by its leader while the AACM is a democratic and loosely structured collective free of supernatural or any other sort of ritual.

Braxton came to international attention through his work in the group Circle, led by Chick Corea. Born in 1945, he was first inspired by Paul Desmond, later by "Ornette Coleman, Eric Dolphy, Jackie McLean, Karlheinz Stockhausen, Miles [Davis], James Brown, and the Chicago Transit

Archie Shepp

Anthony Braxton

Authority" (the original name of the jazz-rock group later known simply as Chicago). But it was John Coltrane who gave him faith in himself and his music, a music that has developed considerably since his debut album in 1968. Both in the intimate context of his small-group improvisations and in his first work for large ensemble, Braxton reveals genuine originality as well as a solid grasp of essentials. His music has humor as well as energy and is likely to be remembered for more than historical reasons.

We conclude this informal survey of keepers of the jazz flame with the youngest musician in this book. His name is Jon Faddis, he plays the trumpet, and he came to New York from San Francisco in 1971, when he was all of seventeen. Before long, he was playing lead trumpet with the Thad Jones-Mel Lewis Jazz Orchestra, and after he had toured Russia with the band in 1972, Jones declared that the youngster already was the equal of most seasoned veterans. When he had reached the age of twenty-one, Faddis was one of New York's most frequently hired free-lance jazz trumpeters. His range is astonishing, instrumentally as well as musically.

When Faddis arrived in New York, he surprised and delighted Dizzy Gillespie with his devotion to and knowledge of the musical legacy of the elder statesman of bebop. Faddis knows almost every major recorded Gillespie solo by heart, and he improvises in a style closely molded on the master's. He became Dizzy's protégé, and whenever the great man works in or near New York and Faddis has a free night, he sits in with his idol and mentor. Some day, no doubt, Jon Faddis will develop his own identity as a soloist (there are signs of this already). Physically and instrumentally, he is a player strong enough to challenge and inspire his mentor frequently, and the relationship between master and acolyte (remember King Oliver and "Little Louis"?) is living proof of the continuity and strength of the jazz tradition.

Every jazz musician has a special story to tell, for jazz is above all a music of individual expression within a collective framework. It is also, despite the advances made in recent years, an art and craft that demands much, too much, from its practitioners. Its circumstances are physically and spiritually taxing, and while it is often hailed as an art, it is still treated as a commodity.

Yet jazz prevails. It continues to cut across boundaries of race, class, culture, and language. It has been one of the lights in the tunnel of the twentieth century. Born in slavery, it has become the universal song of freedom, a celebration of the resilience and power of the human spirit. In our time, especially, that is no small achievement.

Dizzy Gillespie and Jon Faddis

RECOMMENDED JAZZ READING: A SELECTED BIBLIOGRAPHY

Albertson, Chris. *Bessie.* New York: Stein and Day, 1972. An absorbing biography of the great blues singer Bessie Smith, somewhat marred by the author's preoccupation with his subject's sex life.

Armstrong, Louis. *Satchmo: My Life in New Orleans.* New York: Prentice-Hall, 1947. The first installment of the great man's autobiography, and, alas, the only portion published to date. The unorthodox prose style has been watered down by schoolmarmish editing, but the voice of a true original prevails.

Balliett, Whitney. *New York Notes: A Journal of Jazz in the Seventies.* Boston: Houghton Mifflin, 1976. The sixth compilation of reviews and profiles by the *New Yorker*'s frequently perceptive and sometimes brilliant jazz critic. The five others are also recommended.

Bechet, Sidney. *Treat It Gentle.* 1960. Reprint. New York: Da Capo Press, 1975. The great soprano saxophonist's autobiography is one of the few indispensable jazz books and an important American document, a noble work by a proud and honest man.

Berendt, Joachim. *The Jazz Book.* New York: Lawrence Hill & Co., 1975. A useful if somewhat glib overview of the music, from New Orleans to electronic jazz, by Germany's leading jazz writer.

Blesh, Rudi, and Janis, Harriet. *They All Played Ragtime.* New York: Oak Publications, 1971. Scholarly yet eminently readable, this definitive work traces the story of ragtime from its origins through its flowering to its decline.

Chilton, John. *Billie's Blues.* New York: Stein and Day, 1975. A sober, nonsensational account of Billie Holiday's musical life.

Condon, Eddie, with narration by Thomas Sugrue. *We Called It Music.* 1947. Reprint. Westport, Conn.: Greenwood Press, 1975. Condon had a way with words, and in the late Thomas Sugrue he had an ideal collaborator. This charming autobiography ends in the early forties, but the picture it gives of the man and his music is complete.

————, and O'Neal, Hank. *The Eddie Condon Scrapbook of Jazz.* New York: St. Martin's Press, 1973. A consistently entertaining collection of snapshots, anecdotes, and reminiscences spanning Condon's long career and much besides.

Dance, Stanley. *The World of Duke Ellington.* New York: Charles Scribner's Sons, 1970. *The* source book of Ellingtonia, by a writer whose firsthand knowledge of the subject is unmatched.

————. *The World of Swing.* New York: Charles Scribner's Sons, 1974. Profiles of forty musicians, some famous, others not, who have made valuable contributions to the jazz of the golden age, adding up to an informal history of the period and beyond.

Ellington, Duke. *Music Is My Mistress.* New York: Doubleday, 1973. Composed of autobiographical fragments, impressions, opinions, and sketches of people he liked, this sprawling, deceptively casual book is not so much a memoir as a kaleidoscope through which Ellington obliquely reveals much about himself and his life's work.

Ellison, Ralph. *Shadow and Act.* New York: Random House, 1964. This collection of essays and articles by one of America's great writers contains pieces about jazz, blues, and gospel music that are among the very best of the genre, but the book as a whole is recommended to all who wish to learn more about the currents in American life and culture that helped to mold jazz music.

Feather, Leonard. *The New Edition of the Encyclopedia of Jazz.* New York: Horizon Press, 1960. The standard biographical reference work in the field, revised, updated, and enlarged from the original 1955 edition, and including a survey of jazz history and various other reference materials.

————, and Gitler, Ira. *The Encyclopedia of Jazz in the Seventies.* New York: Horizon Press, 1976. Further updating and revision of the 1960 and the out-of-print 1966 editions.

Gitler, Ira. *Jazz Masters of the Forties.* 1966. Reprint. New York: Collier Books, 1974. In effect, a history of bebop, detailed, enlightening, and readable.

Hadlock, Richard. *Jazz Masters of the Twenties.* New York: Macmillan, 1965. Original and frequently provocative assessments of the period's leading figures, including Armstrong, Beiderbecke, Henderson, Hines, and the Chicagoans.

Hodeir, André. *Jazz—Its Evolution and Essence.* 1956. Reprint. New York: Da Capo Press, 1975. One of the key works of jazz criticism. The author expects his readers to be conversant with the fundamentals of music, but even the layman can benefit from exposure to Hodeir's ideas.

Holiday, Billie, and Dufty, William. *Lady Sings the Blues.* Garden City, N.Y.: Doubleday, 1956. Some of the obvious flaws in this autobiography, notably its sensationalism and lack of objectivity, can be blamed on Dufty, others on the singer herself. But when she is being honest with herself and the reader, Billie Holiday cuts to the core.

Jones, LeRoi. *Blues People: Negro Music in White America.* New York: Morrow, 1963. The first book on jazz by a black writer, and one of the first to attempt to place the music in a social and cultural context.

Jones, Max, and Chilton, John. *Louis: The Louis Armstrong Story.* Boston: Little, Brown, 1971. An affectionate, informative, and somewhat awkwardly organized biography with fascinating contributions from the subject himself, a detailed chronology, and a filmography.

Lomax, Alan. *Mr. Jellyroll.* 1950. Reprint. Berkeley: University of California Press, 1973. This lively biography of the Benvenuto Cellini of jazz, Jelly Roll Morton, is based in the main on information provided by the subject himself during the famous recording sessions for the Library of Congress conducted by the author.

Meryman, Richard. *Louis Armstrong—A Self-Portrait.* New York: The Eakins Press, 1971. A somewhat expanded version of the famous *Life* magazine interview. Meryman's reproduction of Louis's speech is sometimes unconsciously patronizing, but he does not otherwise inject himself, and Louis had plenty to say to him—and to us.

Mezzrow, Mezz, and Wolfe, Bernard. *Really the Blues.* 1946. Reprint. New York: Doubleday Anchor Books, 1972. Mezz had quite a story to tell, and Wolfe knew how to get it on paper. To be taken *cum grano salis,* but full of authentic life nonetheless, and essential to an understanding of the interaction between black and white in a richly formative period of jazz.

Mingus, Charles. *Beneath the Underdog.* New York: Knopf, 1971. The bassist-composer's autobiography is a work of the imagination rather than an account of facts, yet it is a true self-portrait.

Murray, Albert. *The Omni-Americans: New Perspectives on Black Experience and American Culture.* New York: Outerbridge & Dienstfrey, 1970. Not a book about jazz, but with plenty of jazz in it, and reflecting the spirit of the music in the wit and vitality of its ideas and language. If you read Jones, you should also read Ellison and Murray.

Ramsey, Frederic, Jr., and Smith, Charles Edward, eds. *Jazzmen.* 1939. Reprint. New York: Harcourt, Brace, Harvest Books, 1959. The first major American book on jazz, peculiarly biased, yet often on the mark, and containing the rationale for the traditionalist revival.

Reisner, Robert G. *Bird: The Legend of Charlie Parker.* 1962. Reprint. New York: Da Capo Press, 1975. Interviews with all sorts of people who knew Parker, adding up to a composite portrait more truthful and revealing than Ross Russell's purported biography (*Bird Lives,* New York, Charterhouse Books, 1973), much of which was lifted and distorted from this source.

Schuller, Gunther. *Early Jazz: Its Roots and Musical Development.* New York: Oxford University Press, 1968. Though it demands some knowledge of musical notation and fundamentals for full appreciation, this model work of scholarship and critical insight is readily accessible to the intelligent layman.

Shapiro, Nat, and Hentoff, Nat, eds. *Hear Me Talkin' to Ya.* 1955. Reprint. New York: Dover Books, 1966. Compiled from a wide variety of sources, mostly published interviews, the book tells the story of the music, arranged chronologically, in the musicians' own words (or rather, their words as reported). One of the best jazz source books up to the mid-fifties.

Shaw, Arnold. *The Street that Never Slept.* New York: Coward, McCann, & Geoghegan, 1971. An entertaining informal history of Fifty-second Street.

Simon, George T. *The Big Bands*. New York: Macmillan, 1974. Covering "sweet" as well as "hot" bands, this breezy yet information-packed survey by the dean of American jazz writers is straightforwardly nostalgic.

Smith, Willie (The Lion), and Hoefer, George. *Music on My Mind: The Memoirs of an American Pianist*. 1964. Reprint. New York: Da Capo Press, 1975. The Lion was almost as great a talker as he was a player. The discursiveness of his lively, largely anecdotal memoir is balanced by Hoefer's sober, informative interchapters.

Southern, Eileen. *The Music of Black Americans: A History*. New York: W. W. Norton, 1971. The breadth and scope of musical expression and activity by black people in America will astonish even readers conversant with the history of jazz, with which the author understandably deals only in passing. A substantial and valuable work.

Stearns, Marshall. *The Story of Jazz*. New York: Oxford University Press, 1956. Though there has been no revision of this work since publication (the author died many years ago), it remains the best introduction to jazz history, sound, unbiased, and lucid, albeit handicapped by its age.

Stewart, Rex. *Jazz Masters of the Thirties*. New York: Macmillan, 1972. Trumpet star with Duke Ellington and Fletcher Henderson, Stewart was a gifted writer; unfortunately, his output was small. Almost all of it is collected in this book with the misleadingly dry title. It will delight the reader interested in the thinking musicians' perspective on his art, craft, and fellow creators.

Sudhalter, Richard, and Evans, Philip R. *Bix: Man and Legend*. New Rochelle, N.Y.: Arlington House, 1974. The most thoroughly researched and documented biography of a jazz musician is fortunately also well written and unsentimental. A major contribution to the understanding of an important figure in jazz history and the period in which he lived.

Wells, Dicky, as told to Stanley Dance. *The Night People*. Boston: Crescendo Publishing Co., 1971. This volume of reminiscences and opinions by the great swing trombonist is too slight and episodic to be called an autobiography, but there are some wonderful anecdotes and astute observations here.

Wilder, Alec. *American Popular Song: The Great Innovators, 1900–1950*. New York: Oxford University Press, 1972. A serious but never solemn study of a musical form with which jazz has enjoyed a long and often close relationship. Wilder, himself a talented composer, was just the man to do this much-needed book. A knowledge of musical notation is helpful but not essential to the enjoyment of reading it.

Williams, Martin. *Jazz Masters of New Orleans*. New York: Macmillan, 1967. The only non-parochial book about traditional jazz.

_____. *Where's the Melody: A Listener's Introduction to Jazz*. New York: Pantheon Books, 1967. A lucid guide to hearing the music well, designed for the novice but strongly recommended to all, including those who may not believe they need to read it.

_____. *The Jazz Tradition*. New York: Oxford University Press, 1970. A collection of mature essays by a writer whose knowledge, taste, and ability to hear the music and communicate his discoveries make him the most distinguished jazz critic America has produced.

RECOMMENDED LISTENING: A SELECTED DISCOGRAPHY

Though it focuses on artists appearing in this book, the following selected list of recordings is modestly representative of the development of jazz from the early years to the present. It should be noted that many historically significant records were made before the introduction of sophisticated recording techniques.

Since jazz is essentially a performer's art, the main listing has been arranged alphabetically by artist. A general category, Anthologies and Collections, precedes the artist listing. All recordings listed were available at the time of compilation; they are likely to remain so for some time, but the ways of record companies are whimsical, and even items of lasting significance are often deleted from active catalogues. However, such "collector's items" may be found in the stocks of specialized stores that exist in most large cities; these also carry many imported records of interest.

ANTHOLOGIES AND COLLECTIONS

The Smithsonian Collection of Classic Jazz, Smithsonian P6 11891. This six-record compilation, ranging from Scott Joplin to Cecil Taylor, is the best survey of jazz on record. Produced and annotated by Martin Williams.

The Changing Face of Harlem, Savoy JC 2208. 1944–45 recordings featuring Don Byas, Red Norvo, Hot Lips Page, Charlie Parker, Ben Webster, Teddy Wilson, and many others.

Jazz at the Santa Monica Civic, Pablo 2625-701. A 1972 Norman Granz spectacular, with the Count Basie band, Ella Fitzgerald, Harry Edison, Roy Eldridge, Al Grey, Lockjaw Davis, Stan Getz, Oscar Peterson, and others.

Jazz Giants, vol. 3, Trip TLP-5538. Classic 1944-45 recordings, with Cozy Cole, Vic Dickenson, Coleman Hawkins, Earl Hines, Red Norvo, Slam Stewart, Teddy Wilson, Trummy Young, and others.

The Greatest Jazz Concert Ever, Prestige 24024. Certainly the greatest bebop concert ever, with Dizzy Gillespie, Charlie Parker, Bud Powell, Charles Mingus, and Max Roach.

The Original Boogie Woogie Piano Giants, Columbia KC 32718. Albert Ammons, Pete Johnson, Meade Lux Lewis, Jimmy Yancey, and guests Joe Turner, Hot Lips Page, and Buster Smith.

The Original Sound of the Twenties, Columbia C3L 35. Both jazz and jazz-flavored music of the period are included in this three-record set, with samples of Armstrong, Ellington, Beiderbecke, Bessie Smith, Earl Hines, Ethel Waters, Paul Whiteman, Bing Crosby, Sophie Tucker, and others.

The Tenor Sax: Lester Young, Chu Berry, and Ben Webster, Atlantic 307. Prime and essential material, with contributions from Buck Clayton, Bill Coleman, Roy Eldridge, Hot Lips Page, Walter Page, Sid Catlett, Jo Jones, Dicky Wells, and many others.

Town Hall Concert, 1945, Atlantic 310. Timme Rosenkrantz's extravaganza, featuring Don Byas, Bill Coleman, Gene Krupa, Red Norvo, Flip Phillips, Stuff Smith, Slam Stewart, Billy Taylor, Teddy Wilson, and others.

Trumpet Kings at Montreux '75, Pablo 2310-754. Roy Eldridge, Dizzy Gillespie, and Clark Terry locking horns.

ARTIST LISTING

Allen, Henry ("Red"), see Sidney Bechet, Fletcher Henderson, James P. Johnson, Jelly Roll Morton.

Armstrong, Louis, *The Louis Armstrong Story,* vols. 1 and 2, Columbia 851, 852; *Louis Armstrong and Earl Hines, 1928,* Smithsonian R 002; *Louis Armstrong Plays W. C. Handy,* Columbia CSP JCL 591; *July 4, 1900–July 6, 1971,* RCA VPM 6044 (with Johnny and Baby Dodds and Kid Ory on the first two, Zutty Singleton and Jimmie Noone on the third, Barney Bigard and Trummy Young on the fourth, Jack Teagarden on the last, and many others); see also Ella Fitzgerald.

Ayler, Albert, *Vibrations,* Arista AL 1000 (with Don Cherry).

Bailey, Buster, see Fletcher Henderson, Billie Holiday.

Bailey, Mildred, see Red Norvo.

Baker, Chet, see Gerry Mulligan.

Basie, Count, *Basie's Best,* MCA 4050E (with Buck Clayton, Harry Edison, Benny Morton, Dicky Wells, Lester Young, Freddie Green, Jo Jones, Helen Humes, Jimmy Rushing, and others); *Fantail,* Roulette 42009 (with Lockjaw Davis, Thad Jones, Joe Newman, and others).

Bechet, Sidney, *Master Musician,* Bluebird AXM2-5516 (with Red Allen, Vic Dickenson, Sidney De Paris, Charlie Shavers, Willie ["The Lion"] Smith, and many others); *Sidney Bechet with Wild Bill Davison and Art Hodes,* vols. 1 and 2, Blue Note BST 81203, 81204.

Beiderbecke, Bix, *The Bix Beiderbecke Story,* vols. 1–3, Columbia 844–46 (with Pee Wee Russell, Frank Trumbauer, Joe Venuti, and others).

Benson, George, *Willow Weep for Me,* Columbia J-19; see also Helen Humes.

Blake, Eubie, *Live Concert,* Eubie Blake Music 5.

Blakey, Art, *At the Cafe Bohemia,* vols. 1 and 2, Blue Note 81507, 81508; *Art Blakey's Jazz Messengers with Thelonious Monk,* Atlantic S-1278.

Braff, Ruby, *Ruby Braff and George Barnes Live at the New School,* Chiaroscuro 126.

Braxton, Anthony, *Five Pieces,* Arista 4064; *Creative Orchestra Music 1976,* Arista 4080.

Brown, Clifford, and Roach, Max, *At Basin Street,* Trip 5511.

Brubeck, Dave, *All-Time Greatest Hits,* Columbia KG 32761.

Bryant, Ray, *Me and the Blues,* Prestige 24038.

Butterfield, Billy, see Lester Young.

Byas, Don, *Anthropology,* Black Lion 160.

Carter, Benny, *Further Definitions,* Impulse S-12 (with Coleman Hawkins, Phil Woods, and Jo Jones); see also Fletcher Henderson, Billie Holiday, Art Tatum.

Charles, Ray, *Ray Charles Live,* Atlantic 2-503.

Cherry, Don, *Complete Communion,* Blue Note 84226; see also Albert Ayler.

Christian, Charlie, *Charlie Christian,* Archive of Folk Music 219E (the Minton's recordings); *Solo Flight,* Columbia G 30779 (with the Benny Goodman Sextets, Count Basie, Lionel Hampton, Cootie Williams, Dave Tough, Jo Jones, and others).

Clarke, Kenny, see Dizzy Gillespie, Dexter Gordon, Fats Navarro.

Clayton, Buck, see Count Basie, Billie Holiday, Pee Wee Russell, Willie ("The Lion") Smith, Lester Young.

Cohn, Al, and Sims, Zoot, *Body and Soul,* Muse 5016; see also Stan Getz.

Coleman, Ornette, *Free Jazz,* Atlantic 1364; *The Skies of America,* Columbia KC 31562.

Coltrane, John, *Giant Steps,* Atlantic 1311; *A Love Supreme,* Impulse S-77 (with McCoy Tyner, Jimmy Garrison, and Elvin Jones); see also Miles Davis, Thelonious Monk.

Condon, Eddie, *Eddie Condon and Bud Freeman,* Atlantic 309 (with Jess Stacy, George Wettling, Pee Wee Russell, Bobby Hackett, Jack Teagarden, and others).

Corea, Chick, *Return to Forever,* ECM 1022.

Dameron, Tadd, and Evans, Gil, *The Arranger's Touch,* Prestige 24049; see also Fats Navarro.

Davern, Kenny, see Bob Wilber.

Davis, Eddie ("Lockjaw"), see Count Basie, Ella Fitzgerald, ANTHOLOGIES AND COLLECTIONS.

Davis, Miles, *The Complete Birth of the Cool,* Capitol M-11026 (with J. J. Johnson, Lee Konitz, John Lewis, Gerry Mulligan, Max Roach, and others); *Miles Davis and the Modern Jazz Giants,* Prestige 7650 (with Milt Jackson and Thelonious Monk); *Porgy and Bess,* Columbia PC 8085 (with Gil Evans); *Kind of Blue,* Columbia PC 8163 (with Cannonball Adderley, John Coltrane, and Bill Evans); *Bitches' Brew,* Columbia PG-26.

Davison, Wild Bill, see Sidney Bechet, Bud Freeman, Jack Teagarden.

Dickenson, Vic, see Sidney Bechet, Bobby Hackett, Jimmy Rushing, Lester Young.

Dolphy, Eric, *Out to Lunch,* Blue Note 84163.

Edison, Harry ("Sweets"), *Oscar Peterson and Harry Edison,* Pablo 2310-741; see also Count Basie, Art Tatum.

Eldridge, Roy, *Oscar Peterson and Roy Eldridge,* Pablo 2310-739; *The Nifty Cat,* Master Jazz Recordings MJR 8110 (with Budd Johnson and Benny Morton); see also Ella Fitzgerald, Fletcher Henderson, Earl Hines, Billie Holiday, Gene Krupa, Buddy Tate, Art Tatum, ANTHOLOGIES AND COLLECTIONS.

Ellington, Duke, *This Is Duke Ellington,* RCA VPM 6042 (with Cootie Williams, Johnny Hodges, Ben Webster, and others); *The Ellington Era,* vol. 1, Columbia C3L 27 (with Cootie Williams, Johnny Hodges, Barney

Bigard, Harry Carney, and others); *Ellington at Newport*, Columbia CS 8468 (with Paul Gonsalves, Ray Nance, and others); *Such Sweet Thunder*, Columbia CSP JCL-1033 (with Clark Terry, Paul Gonsalves, Johnny Hodges, Ray Nance, Harry Carney, and others); *Second Sacred Concert*, Prestige 24045 (with Johnny Hodges, Harry Carney, Paul Gonsalves, and others); *Blues Summit*, Verve 6S-8822 (with Johnny Hodges and others).

Evans, Bill, *The Village Vanguard Sessions*, Milestone 47002; see also Miles Davis.

Evans, Gil, *Pacific Standard Time*, Blue Note LA461-H2; *Svengali*, Atlantic 1643; see also Tadd Dameron, Miles Davis.

Faddis, Jon, *Youngblood*, Pablo 2310-765; see also Milt Hinton.

Fitzgerald, Ella, *Ella and Louis*, Verve 6S-8811; *Newport Jazz Festival, Live at Carnegie Hall*, Columbia KG 32557 (with Roy Eldridge, Lockjaw Davis, and others).

Freeman, Bud, *Midnight at Eddie Condon's*, Trip 5529 (with Wild Bill Davison, Edmond Hall, Charlie Shavers, Joe Sullivan, Dave Tough, George Wettling, and others); see also Eddie Condon.

Garner, Erroll, *Concert by the Sea*, Columbia CS 9821E; *Play It Again, Erroll*, Columbia PG 33424.

Getz, Stan, *At the Opera House*, Verve 68490 (with J. J. Johnson); *Stan Getz*, Prestige 24019 (with Al Cohn, Zoot Sims, Gerry Mulligan, Roy Haynes, and others).

Gillespie, Dizzy, *In the Beginning*, Prestige 24030 (with Charlie Parker, Sonny Stitt, Milt Jackson, Sid Catlett, Al Haig, Slam Stewart, Kenny Clarke, and others); *Oscar Peterson and Dizzy Gillespie*, Pablo 2310-740; see also ANTHOLOGIES AND COLLECTIONS.

Goodman, Benny, *Carnegie Hall Concert*, Columbia OSL-160 (with Harry James, Lionel Hampton, Gene Krupa, Jess Stacy, Teddy Wilson, and many others); see also Charlie Christian, Jack Teagarden.

Gordon, Dexter, *Our Man in Paris*, Blue Note 84146 (with Bud Powell and Kenny Clarke).

Guy, Joe, and Page, Hot Lips, *Trumpet Battle at Minton's*, Xanadu 107.

Hackett, Bobby, and Dickenson, Vic, *Live at the Roosevelt Grill*, Chiaroscuro 105; see also Eddie Condon, Jack Teagarden.

Hall, Edmond, see Bud Freeman, Art Tatum.

Hampton, Lionel, *The Original Star Dust*, MCA 198E (with Charlie Shavers and Slam Stewart); see also Charlie Christian, Benny Goodman, Art Tatum.

Hawkins, Coleman, *The Hawk in Holland*, GNP 9003; *Classic Tenors*, Flying Dutchman 10146 (with Lester Young); *The Hawk Flies*, Milestone 47015; *Today and Now*, Impulse S-34 (with Major Holley); see also Benny Carter, Fletcher Henderson.

Haynes, Roy, *Out of the Afternoon*, Impulse S-23 (with Roland Kirk); see also Stan Getz, Lester Young.

Henderson, Fletcher, *A Study in Frustration*, Columbia C4L 19 (with Red Allen, Roy Eldridge, Rex Stewart, Benny Morton, Buster Bailey, Benny Carter, Coleman Hawkins, Dicky Wells, and many others).

Herman, Woody, *The Thundering Herds*, Columbia C3L 25; *Early Autumn*, Capitol M-11034.

Hines, Earl, *Earl Hines and Roy Eldridge at the Village Vanguard*, Xanadu 106; *The Quintessential Recording Session*, Chiaroscuro 101; *Hot Sonatas*, Chiaroscuro 145 (with Joe Venuti); see also Louis Armstrong, ANTHOLOGIES AND COLLECTIONS.

Hinton, Milt, *Here Swings the Judge*, Famous Door HL 104 (with Ben Webster, Budd Johnson, and Jon Faddis); see also Buddy Tate.

Hodges, Johnny, *Hodge Podge*, Columbia CSP JEE 22001; see also Duke Ellington, Billie Holiday.

Holiday, Billie, *Lady Day*, Columbia CL 637; *The Golden Years*, vol. 1, Columbia C3L 21 (with Buck Clayton, Roy Eldridge, Benny Morton, Benny Carter, Buster Bailey, Johnny Hodges, Lester Young, Teddy Wilson, Jo Jones, and many others); *The Billie Holiday Story*, MCA 4006E.

Holley, Major, see Coleman Hawkins.

Hopkins, Lightnin', *Texas Bluesman*, Arhoolie 1034.

Humes, Helen, *The Talk of the Town*, Columbia PC 33488 (with George Benson and Buddy Tate).

Jackson, Mahalia, *Mahalia Jackson in Concert*, Columbia CS 9490.

Jackson, Milt, *Plenty, Plenty Soul*, Atlantic S-1269; see also Miles Davis, Dizzy Gillespie, Modern Jazz Quartet.

Jacquet, Illinois, *How High the Moon*, Prestige 24057; see also Buddy Tate.

Jarrett, Keith, *The Solo Concerts*, ECM 1035-36-37.

Jefferson, Blind Lemon, *Blind Lemon Jefferson*, Milestone 47022.

Jefferson, Eddie, *Body and Soul*, Prestige 7619.

Johnson, Budd, *Blues à la Mode*, Master Jazz Records MJR 8119; see also Roy Eldridge, Milt Hinton.

Johnson, Bunk, *Last Testament of a Great New Orleans Jazzman*, Columbia CSP JML 4802.

Johnson, James P., *Father of Stride Piano*, Columbia CL 1780 (with Red Allen, J. C. Higginbotham, and others).

Jones, Elvin. *Live at Town Hall*, PM 004; see also John Coltrane, Sonny Rollins.

Jones, Hank, *Have You Met Hank Jones*, Savoy 12084.

Jones, Jo, see Count Basie, Billie Holiday, Jimmy Rushing, Slam Stewart, Art Tatum, Lester Young.

Jones, Thad, and Lewis, Mel, *Consummation*, Blue Note 84346; *Suite for Pops*, Horizon 701.

Kenton, Stan, *Artistry in Jazz*, Capitol M-11027.

Konitz, Lee, *Satori*, Milestone 9060; see also Lennie Tristano.

Krupa, Gene, *Gene Krupa with Anita O'Day and Roy Eldridge*, Columbia KG 32663E; see also Benny Goodman, ANTHOLOGIES AND COLLECTIONS.

Lambert, Hendricks, and Ross, *The Best of Lambert, Hendricks & Ross*, Columbia KC 32911.

Lewis, John, see Modern Jazz Quartet, Charlie Parker.

Lewis, Mel, see Thad Jones.

Lunceford, Jimmie, *Lunceford Special*, Columbia CS 9515E.

McGhee, Brownie, *Brownie McGhee and Sonny Terry*, Folkways 2327.

McGhee, Howard, see Fats Navarro, Charlie Parker, Lester Young.

McPartland, Marian, *Ambiance*, Halcyon 103; see also Joe Venuti.

Mingus, Charles, *Better Git It in Your Soul*, Columbia CG 30628; *Tia Juana Moods*, RCA APL1-0939; *The Black Saint and the Sinner Lady*, Impulse S-35.

Modern Jazz Quartet, *The Modern Jazz Quartet*, Prestige 24005; *The Last Concert*, Atlantic 909.

Monk, Thelonious, *Genius of Modern Music*, vols. 1 and 2, Blue Note 81510, 81511 (with Art Blakey, Milt Jackson, and others); *Thelonious Monk and John Coltrane*, Milestone 47011; see also Art Blakey.

Montgomery, Wes, *While We're Young*, Milestone 47003.

Morgan, Lee, *Search for the New Land*, Blue Note 84169.

Morton, Benny, see Count Basie, Roy Eldridge, Fletcher Henderson, Billie Holiday.

Morton, Jelly Roll, *King of New Orleans Jazz*, RCA LPM 1649; *New Orleans Memories*, Atlantic 308 (with Red Allen).

Mulligan, Gerry, *Gerry Mulligan and Chet Baker*, Prestige 24016; *Jeru*, Columbia CSP JCS 8732; see also Miles Davis, Stan Getz.

Navarro, Fats, *Prime Source*, Blue Note LA507-H2 (with Tadd Dameron, Kenny Clarke, Howard McGhee, and others).

Norvo, Red, *Red Norvo's All Stars, 1933–38*, Columbia CSP JEE-22009 (with Mildred Bailey, Bunny Berigan, Chu Berry, Teddy Wilson, and many others).

O'Day, Anita, *Hey Ho Trailus Boot Whip*, Bob Thiele BBM 10595; see also Gene Krupa.

Oliver, King, *King Oliver's Jazz Band, 1923*, Smithsonian R 001.

Page, Oran ("Hot Lips"), *After Hours in Harlem*, Onyx 207; see also Joe Guy.

Parker, Charlie, *Bird: The Savoy Recordings*, Savoy JC 2201 (with Miles Davis, Dizzy Gillespie, John Lewis, Bud Powell, Max Roach, and others); *Charlie Parker on Dial*, vols. 1–6, Spotlite 101–6 (with Miles Davis, Howard McGhee, Erroll Garner, Duke Jordan, Max Roach, and others); see also Dizzy Gillespie, ANTHOLOGIES AND COLLECTIONS.

Peterson, Oscar, *Oscar Peterson and Joe Pass a Salle Pleyel*, Pablo 2625-705; see also Harry Edison, Roy Eldridge, Dizzy Gillespie, ANTHOLOGIES AND COLLECTIONS.

Phillips, Flip, *Flip Phillips Quartet*, Choice CRS 1013.

Powell, Bud, *The Amazing Bud Powell,* vols. 1 and 2, Blue Note 81503, 81504; see also Dexter Gordon, Charlie Parker, Sonny Stitt, AN-THOLOGIES AND COLLECTIONS.

Rainey, Ma, *Ma Rainey,* Milestone 47021.

Reinhardt, Django, *Django '35–'39,* GNP 9019.

Rich, Buddy, *Very Live at Buddy's Place,* Groove Merchant 3301; see also Art Tatum.

Roach, Max, *Max Roach Plus Four,* Trip 5522 (with Sonny Rollins); see also Clifford Brown, Charlie Parker, Bud Powell, Sonny Rollins, ANTHOLOGIES AND COLLECTIONS.

Rollins, Sonny, *Saxophone Colossus and More,* Prestige 24050 (with Max Roach); *More From the Village Vanguard,* Blue Note LA475-H2 (with Elvin Jones and Wilbur Ware); see also Max Roach.

Rushing, Jimmy, *The Essential Jimmy Rushing,* Vanguard 65/66 (with Vic Dickenson, Jo Jones, Buddy Tate, and others); see also Count Basie.

Russell, George, *New York, New York—Jazz in the Space Age,* MCA 4017.

Russell, Pee Wee, *The Pee Wee Russell Memorial Album,* Prestige 7672 (with Buck Clayton, Tommy Flanagan, and Osie Johnson).

Shaw, Artie, *The Complete Artie Shaw,* vol. 1, Bluebird AXM2-5517.

Shorter, Wayne, *Adam's Apple,* Blue Note 84232.

Sims, Zoot, *The Gershwin Brothers,* Pablo 2310-744; see also Al Cohn, Stan Getz.

Singleton, Zutty, see Louis Armstrong.

Smith, Bessie, *Empress of the Blues,* Columbia G 30818; *Nobody's Blues But Mine,* Columbia G 31093.

Smith, Stuff, *Black Violin,* BSAF 20650.

Smith, Willie ("The Lion"), *The Lion,* GNP 9011 (with Buck Clayton).

Stewart, Slam, *Slam Stewart,* Black and Blue 33.027U (with Jo Jones); see also Dizzy Gillespie, Lionel Hampton, Lester Young, AN-THOLOGIES AND COLLECTIONS.

Stitt, Sonny, *Bud's Blues,* Prestige 7839 (with Bud Powell); see also Dizzy Gillespie.

Sullivan, Maxine, *Close as Pages in a Book,* Monmouth-Evergreen MES 6919 (with Bob Wilber).

Tate, Buddy, *Buddy Tate and His Buddies,* Chiaroscuro 123 (with Roy Eldridge, Illinois Jacquet, Mary Lou Williams, and Milt Hinton); see also Helen Humes, Jimmy Rushing.

Tatum, Art, *God Is in the House,* Onyx 205; *Art Tatum Masterpieces,* MCA 4019 (with Edmond Hall, Joe Turner, and others); *The Art Tatum Solo Masterpieces,* Pablo 2625-703 (13 LP set); *The Art Tatum Group Masterpieces,* Pablo 2625-706 (8 LP set, with Benny Carter, Buddy DeFranco, Harry Edison, Roy Eldridge, Lionel Hampton, Jo Jones, Buddy Rich, Ben Webster, and others); see also Ben Webster.

Taylor, Cecil, *Looking Ahead!,* Contemporary 7562.

Teagarden, Jack, *The Golden Horn of Jack Teagarden,* MCA 227E (with Wild Bill Davison, Bobby Hackett, Pee Wee Russell, Benny Goodman, Joe Venuti, and others); see also Louis Armstrong, Eddie Condon.

Terry, Clark, *Clark Terry and His Jolly Green Giants,* Vanguard 79365; see also Duke Ellington.

Terry, Sonny, see Brownie McGhee.

Tristano, Lennie, *Cross-currents,* Capitol M-11060 (with Lee Konitz).

Turner, Joe, *Boss of the Blues,* Atlantic S-1234; see also Art Tatum, ANTHOLOGIES AND COLLECTIONS.

Tyner, McCoy, *Enlightenment,* Milestone 55001; see also John Coltrane.

Vaughan, Sarah, *Sarah Vaughan 1955,* Trip 5501 (with Clifford Brown); *Live in Japan,* Mainstream 401.

Venuti, Joe, *The Maestro and Friend,* Halcyon HAL-11 (with Marian McPartland); see also Earl Hines, Jack Teagarden.

Waller, Fats, *The Complete Fats Waller,* vol. 1, Bluebird AXM2-5511.

Webb, Chick, *Stompin' at the Savoy,* Columbia CSP JCL 2639.

Webster, Ben, *The Art Tatum–Ben Webster Quartet,* Pablo 2310-728; see also Duke Ellington, Milt Hinton, ANTHOLOGIES AND COLLECTIONS.

Wells, Dicky, see Count Basie, Fletcher Henderson, Lester Young, ANTHOLOGIES AND COLLECTIONS.

Wellstood, Dick, *From Ragtime On,* Chiaroscuro 109.

Wettling, George, see Eddie Condon, Bud Freeman.

Wilber, Bob, and Davern, Kenny, *Soprano Summit,* World Jazz WJLP S-5.

Williams, Cootie, see Charlie Christian, Duke Ellington.

Williams, Mary Lou, *Zoning,* Mary 103; see also Buddy Tate.

Wilson, Teddy, *Striding After Fats,* Black Lion BL 308; see also Benny Goodman, Billie Holiday, Red Norvo.

Young, Lester, *Pres: The Complete Savoy Recordings,* Savoy SJL 2202 (with Count Basie, Billy Butterfield, Dicky Wells, Roy Haynes, and others); *Classic Tenors,* Flying Dutchman FD 10146 (with Bill Coleman, Dicky Wells, Jo Jones, and others); *At His Very Best,* Trip 5509 (with Buck Clayton, Dicky Wells, Count Basie, Slam Stewart, Sid Catlett, and others); *The Aladdin Sessions,* Blue Note LA456-H2 (with Vic Dickenson, Dodo Marmarosa, Howard McGhee, Roy Haynes, and others); see also Count Basie, Billie Holiday, ANTHOLOGIES AND COLLECTIONS.

Young, Trummy, see Louis Armstrong, Jimmie Lunceford.

Index

Acknowledgments

Throughout the years I have been associated with jazz there have been many people who have honored me with their friendship and help. I thank my friend Milt Hinton for taking me around in the early days and introducing me to just about everyone in the field. With my old friend Timme Rosenkrantz I spent many pleasurable hours of music listening before I left Denmark. Later, in America, he introduced me and so many others to the varied aspects of the music. My close friends Ben Webster and Stuff Smith probably taught me more about the music than anyone else.

Directly relating to this book project, I am very grateful to Duncan Schiedt, Rudi Blesh, Hank O'Neal, Jack Bradley, and Max Jones for caring enough to preserve rare vintage photographs and for being so willing to contribute to the book. I also thank Vincent Tcholakian for the beautiful prints he made of the photographs. And finally, appreciation to Ana Borgersen for her belief in the project and for the endless hours she put into it.

Regretfully, it was not possible to photograph all jazz musicians, nor was it my intention. To the many musicians who cooperated so enthusiastically and gave me their friendship throughout the years, I dedicate these pictures.

This book could not have been realized without the help of many people. Without holding them in any way responsible for the results, I wish to thank for various favors and kindnesses Dick Allen of the Jazz Archives at Tulane University, Howard Fischer of the New York Jazz Museum, Dick Gibson, host of the annual Colorado Jazz Party, and Norman Granz of Pablo Records, as well as Stanley Dance, Art D'Lugoff, Alyss Dorese, Linda Kuehl, and Peter Levinson.

Of course, the many musicians without whose willing cooperation nothing essential could have been accomplished rate a special note of appreciation. And so do John Hochmann, for being such a patient and perceptive editor, and Joanne Greenspun, for doing the important but too often unacknowledged job of copy editing so tactfully and well.

By its very nature, a book like this could not be all-encompassing, and I trust that the musicians not singled out for inclusion or attention will understand that no slight was intended.

I am especially grateful to my wife, Ellie, not only for her active help but also for putting up with the irascibility that is an inevitable by-product of even a labor of love.

Ole Brask
Dordogne, France
May, 1976

Dan Morgenstern
New York City
May, 1976

Other DA CAPO titles of interest

Available at your bookstore

OR ORDER DIRECTLY FROM

DA CAPO PRESS, INC.

1-800-321-0050